FOOTBALLOGY

**Elements of American Football
for Non-Native Speakers of English**

Timothy Wahl

FOOTBALLOGY
Elements of American Football for Non-Native Speakers of English

Copyright © 2020 Timothy Wahl
All rights reserved. This book or any portion thereof may not be reproduced or used in any manner whatsoever without the express written permission of the publisher except for the use of brief quotations in a book review.

ISBN: 978-0-9986965-77

Printed in the United States of America

ESL Publishing
www.eslpublishing.com

ESL Publishing is dedicated to producing quality books for English-language learners

 A NOTE FOR TEACHERS

Photocopying or other reproduction of this book for handouts, worksheets, classroom or other material is not permitted. Please visit our website for specials and bulk discounts for teachers and academic institutions.

www.eslpublishing.com

Praise for Footballogy

Clueless as to what a "line of scrimmage," a "snap count," and a "tight end" are?" Want to know the football-specific meaning of "to hook up," "sudden death," "pistol," and "bench strength"? Or perhaps you're wondering about the circumstances under which a team number is retired. Look no further than *Footballogy*, a comprehensive new publication for second language learners of English by Timothy Wahl.

Described by the author as a "self-paced starter guide for America's number-one sports pastime," *Footballogy* displays not only his years of experience teaching language and culture to English learners but also his enthusiasm for the sport and its significance to American culture. The book is a fascinating read, replete with snapshots of historically important players and games as well as careful, easy-to-comprehend definitions of football terminology and fun practice tasks, such as crossword puzzles, for vocabulary reinforcement. Although largely focused on content, the book does not neglect some of the finer points of language: Wahl successfully integrates language and content with sections that focus on grammar, stylistics, and even the differences between British and American English.

The book can easily be used for self study by individual English learners. Alternatively, it can form the basis of a content-based language unit on American football in intensive English programs or adult education programs. What's more, it might even succeed in converting native speakers of English who have little knowledge of this all-American sport (such as myself) into becoming serious football fans. Check it out!

— Donna Brinton, applied linguist, author and global consultant on second language education

21st century adult education standards emphasize learners' need to engage with complex informational text, at the same time, best practices in reading instruction highlight learner choice as a key element in reading skill development. Tim Wahl's Footballogy successfully combines these two key elements of adult English instruction by providing rich text on a topic that is a favorite of many English learners (and their instructors). The use of charts, callouts and numerous illustrations helps readers navigate the text and is sure to enrich their reading experience. Even learners who are well versed in modern day football will appreciate the historical information and all learners will benefit from the exposure to a wide range of vocabulary.

— Jayme Adelson-Goldstein, ESL teacher-trainer, consultant, and author (*Oxford Picture Dictionary*, et al.)

A creative and fun way to learn both the language and the culture. Highly recommended.
— Jim Mentel, author of *Short cuts,* producer and songwriter

I never understood football but with this book, I am starting to get it
— Yamileth Andre, biology teacher (Garfield HS, Los Angeles) & former ESL learner

Dedication

This book is dedicated to the memory of Thomas J. Campiere of the New York State Department of Vocational Rehabilitation (now called VESID) in Buffalo, New York. It is not hyperbole — and certainly not a departure from the truth — that Mr. Campiere came to the rescue in my youth. He changed the course of my life. I humbly honor Mr. Campiere for what he did for me on behalf of the state of New York decades ago. Truly, a lucky guy I am.

Table of Contents

Acknowledgments		ix
Dear Reader...		xi

■ ■ ■

Chapter I	Where Does American Football Come From?	1
Chapter II	America's Favorite Pastime	13
Chapter III	"Nuts & Bolts" — The Basics	33
Chapter IV	The Team: Offense	47
Chapter V	The Team: Defense & Special Teams	73
Chapter VI	The Coaches	97
Chapter VII	The Game	107
Chapter VIII	The Officials	127
Chapter IX	America's Game Matures	153
Chapter X	The National Football League	167
Chapter XI	Passion For Data	193
Chapter XII	Policy, Rules & Decorum	213
Chapter XIII	Differences: Words & Ideas	229
Chapter XIV	Where Do Football Players Come From?	241
Chapter XV	The Draft	261
Chapter XVI	Traditions	281
Chapter XVII	Insiders	311
Chapter XVIII	Global Football	323

■ ■ ■

Useful Sources For News, Information, and Live Streaming	336
Answer Key	340
Glossary	356
References	373
About The Author	389
Other Books By ESL Publishing	390

Acknowledgments

There are many to celebrate in the fruition of *Footballogy*. First are teachers who read early drafts: Lilly Yanagita, Joan Temple, Lucinda Lai, and Dr. George Kooshian. And those who proofed: Yamileth Andre, biology teacher at Garfield High School, Los Angeles, who learned English as her second language; and Antonia Allen, adult education adviser with the Los Angeles Unified School District.

The spotlight shines on ESL authors and academics for their thoughtful notes: Bill Bliss (*Side by Side*, et al.); Jim Mantel (*Short Cuts*, et al.); Jayme Adelson-Goldstein (*Oxford Picture Dictionary*, et al.); and Donna Brinton, linguistics consultant, speaker, and author.

"The eye of a hawk" expresses the essence of Malcolm Christie, a former offensive tackle for the University of Iowa Hawkeyes. His exactness in proofing and his contributions to content were tops.

Stephanie Hsiao, NFL Marketing Director for China, gets thunderous accolades for responding to my numerous inquiries in timely fashion and gathering beta-readers in her Shanghai office.

Applause to additional beta readers and former ESL students Ellie Kitta and Yu Tang.

Big thanks to Regina Bailey, JD, MD, and former NFL cheerleader; Charles Goldstein, head coach, Gallaudet University; Chris Brown, Buffalo Bills Insider; and Gary Barta, Athletic Director, University of Iowa.

Included in the long list for proprietary permissions: Chris McLaurin, Commissioner, American Football League of China; Bonnie Jarrett, NFL intellectual property counsel; John Steffenhagen, great-grandson of NFL co-founder Leo Lyons; Allison Cantor, ESPN chief counsel; Matthew Jacobsen, editor, oldmagainarticles.com; Travis Brody, president, growthofthegame.com; Taylor Soper, managing editor, *Geekwire*; Dan Emerson, chief legal counsel, Indianapolis Colts; and Bill Heller, chief legal counsel, New York Giants.

The dream of this book would not be a reality were it not

for Jeane Slone, founder and president of ESL Publishing, who took on the challenge of something new. Who, before Jeane, had ever done a book that cultivated English in the context of American football? No one, of course. She was patient beyond compare and showed faith in the wondrous potential of this novel project. Her hard work is beyond compare.

Cris Wanzer (www.manuscriptstogo.com) earns high marks for her skill in editing and design. Both she and Jeane persevered despite uprooting wildfires in their neck of the woods in Northern California.

Finally — and above all else — thanks to my wife, Nelly, and our adult children, Alejandra and Alexander, for leading the chant, *"Sí, se puede"* ("Yes, we can"). Alexander also for his photography. Not being a native speaker of English made Nelly's comments even more meaningful.

Dear Reader...

Why this book? Why now? Who benefits?

Footballogy: Elements of American Football for Non-Native Speakers of English is a result of teaching American English and culture to people from other languages and cultures, and my lifelong love of American football. This book is a self-paced starter guide for America's number-one sports pastime, its heritage, and traditions from the view of a fan. People who will benefit include high-intermediate and above English-language learners as well as proficient speakers of English who learned English by way of study, not birth. Students, businesspeople, and travelers are part of this group.

American football is more than just a game. It is an experience that connects many Americans and *Footballogy* will connect you with this experience. Readings and light exercises in grammar and usage are intended to be useful and fun, educational and entertaining. Above all, the objectives of this book are to help us speak more skillfully and confidently about the sport and follow the action at the stadium, in print, or broadcast media. And, of course, to make friends.

To achieve its purpose, *Footballogy* recognizes the importance of "small talk." The metaphor, or symbol, for such casual discussions is the water cooler, where people meet and talk about matters not related to work. Whether the chat is in the break-room, around a coffee pot, or an actual water cooler, casual conversations join us on a personal level. Dale Carnegie, the well-regarded motivational expert, observed that the way to make friends and influence people is to show genuine interest in matters of concern to others.

"How about them Giants!"
© *Ron Leishman*
Toonaday.com

To many Americans, one of those matters is football. Since 1985, football has been America's most preferred game. It should be no surprise that the season of autumn, when the game is played, is celebrated as "football season."

How To Get the Most Out of Footballogy

Context clue to define a word or term

A hint or suggestion after a word or term set apart by a comma or the word "or" may restate the word or term. (Avoid using a dictionary or reference book until last.)

Ex: The game was **on the books**, an official 7-all tie.

We can infer or guess that "on the books" has to do with an official designation and that "7-all" means the score was equal.

A sentence that follows an unfamiliar word or words may rephrase or restate the word in the sentence that follows.

Ex: Someone on the defense was **antsy** and **jumped the gun**. Number 97, a little too eager, drew the offside penalty.

The second sentence suggests that the player was anxious or eager ("antsy") and not where he belonged.

A vocabulary list (Word Preview) precedes some of the readings. Test your word power in the activities that follow (fill-in-the-blank, true/false, multiple choice, matching, and puzzles).

Short exercises on structure provide a chance to apply *previous* knowledge of grammar and usage. (There may be brief explanations with examples.)

General Design

Learning is filling an information gap, a space between what we know at the beginning and what we learn by the end. Each unit presents elements of the game as well as exciting readings that relate to historical persons, events, and games. Most are followed by activities to test our knowledge and allow us to practice our communication skills.

"Great Moments"

These are selected features in some of the units about historic contests. Unlike other readings, assessments do not follow. However, there is an opportunity in the final chapter to put your learning on these to a test.

Answer Key

Check your answers for accuracy for all assessments.

Glossary

Contains concepts, vocabulary, and common idiomatic expressions in American football. Many words/terms are in the content of this book while some are not. These are terms we might hear in discussions about football or in broadcasts. And be prepared when they occasionally come up in conversations that are *not* about football. Some US Presidents were known for using football terminology. (A few even played the game.)

For Your Information...

Football is played at many levels, from amateur to professional, in many countries. Descriptions of rules and procedures in *Footballogy* refer to professional American football (in the United States) unless otherwise noted.

With the greatest respect to the neighbors of the United States (Canada and Mexico) where American football has also been established for many years, references to leagues and teams are limited to the United States unless noted otherwise.

Activities

 Look for this icon to indicate when a response is required.

Circle the correct response (Answer key follows)

1. Which can we infer is NOT a goal of *Footballogy*?
    a. To talk more confidently about football
    b. To play the game of football
    c. To bring people together
    d. To enable us to appreciate America's favorite sport

2. Besides a place to drink water, a "water cooler" is a symbol.
    True   False

3. Where does small talk occur?
    a. at business meetings
    b. on an airplane
    c. at the café
    d. all of these

4. Would an auto-parts salesperson on a trip to a USA car manufacturer likely benefit from *Footballogy*?
    Yes   No

Answers: 1) b   2) true   3) d   4) yes

Practice Sample Reading Passage

The following passage is an example of an assessment in *Footballogy*. This one is intended to show how we can get the meaning of a word from context. Test your skill by placing the correct word on the line.

The Chargers made the PAT, a "point-after-touchdown," that drew the team within seven points. All they need now is a touchdown and an extra point to make it a tie game.

1. According to the passage, what does PAT mean?

   _____

2. What can be inferred about the point-value of a touchdown? _____ points.

3. How much is an extra point? _____

4. Is an extra point and a PAT the same thing? (Yes or no)

   _____

5. How much do the Chargers need to even the score?

   _____

Answers: 1) point-after-touchdown   2) six   3) 1 point
4) yes   5) 7 points

Winning isn't everything, but making the effort to win is.
—Vince Lombardi

CHAPTER I

Where Does American Football Come From?

This unit takes us back to the beginnings of the sport that evolved into American football. The survey expects to answer questions about how the game came to be the popular event it is today.

Footballogy: Elements of American Football for Non-Native Speakers of English

Roots of American Football

Word Preview

These words appear in the readings. Attempt to guess their meaning in context and test your understanding in the assessments that follow.

ambiance	associated	civilized	banned
brutality	decade	distinguish	founder
lacked	old guard	punctured	revolutionized
resembled	reliance	stealing	

The origin of American football dates back 2,000 years to a sport called *harpastum* in the Roman Empire. The way it was played is not certain but it was described as "very rough and brutal" in the literature of the time. Points were awarded when a player kicked the ball across the goal line (some sources think) or by running with the ball or throwing it across the line to another player. Other accounts say a line was drawn and the goal was to prevent the other team from crossing it and stealing the ball back to the other side, which earned points. The ball was thought to be solid and hard, and about eight inches (20 centimeters) in diameter.

Roman fresco of harpastum (Wikimedia Commons)

The sport arrived in England around the twelfth century. Initially, it was viewed as a distraction from traditional English sports, which were considered "gentlemanly" or civilized. It eventually turned into two distinct sports, rugby and "association football," which came to be known as "soccer" upon its arrival in the United States in the mid-1800s.

The game of rugby had a significant part in the

development of American football. Running with the ball in rugby, for instance (a practice not allowed in soccer), became an important element of American football. Eighteen-foot goalposts with a crossbar 10 feet off the ground were the ancestors of goalposts in modern American football. Scoring a goal in rugby resembled a field goal in American football. The ball needed to pass *over the bar* from a place kick (the ball on the ground). Furthermore, American football borrowed rugby words like "touchdown," for a ball that needs to be "touched down" to the ground, a "try-at-goal," equal to modern football's extra-point-kick, and "off-your-side," for an offside penalty.

American-style football lacked excitement due to reliance on running the ball (forward passing was prohibited). But a former medical student and adviser to the Yale football team named Walter Camp had ideas that revolutionized the game.

For three decades, beginning in 1878, Camp's improvements included field measurements and markings and a system for awarding points. He is also credited with creating the quarterback position and establishing the number of players per side at 11. Most of all, Camp instituted a system of downs, which required advancing the ball for a set—or fixed—number of yards for a first down. These are among the reasons Camp is considered the Father of American Football.

Walter Camp, National Portrait Gallery, Washington, DC., Photo by Billy Hathorn, CCO

But concern over the brutality of the game led to its prohibition by some colleges where football had become popular. In 1905, US President Theodore Roosevelt expressed public worry about the high rate of injuries, which included an occasional death. That year, 18 football players are believed to have died from their gridiron injuries—a broken neck and a punctured heart among them.

Roosevelt's words inspired the formation of an association to supervise football at the college level, today known as the National Collegiate Athletic Association (NCAA). One of the first decisions of the new organization legalized the forward pass. The ball became slimmer and easier to pass and catch. Dangerous types of plays were banned. The neutral zone or the line of scrimmage, which separates the teams by the length of the ball before each play begins, was also established.

> **Line of scrimmage,** an imaginary line where the football is placed to begin a play, comes from *scrummage*, in rugby, where people *scrummed* or fought for the ball. In American football, "scrum" is an action by players who all at once go after a fumbled or loose ball.

The Beginnings of Professional Football

William "Pudge" Heffelfinger, the first professional football player, could be an answer to a trivia question. A guard on the 1888 undefeated Yale team, which shut out its opponents by a combined 698-0, Heffelfinger was the first to play football for money after college. In 1892, he earned $500 for one game—over $13,000 in today's currency.

About 100 gridiron clubs in various leagues, mostly in Ohio and Pennsylvania, started in the next three decades. The Latrobe Athletic Association in 1897 is believed to be the first team made up entirely of paid players. In 1902, the first professional league was formed. In November of that year, the first night game was played in Elmira, New York.

The first professional team: Latrobe (Pennsylvania Athletic Association). 1897. Library of Congress/Public domain

The first professional football league started in 1920 in a Hupmobile automobile dealership in the state of Ohio. The significance of this time and place was that this followed the end of World War I, said to be "the war to end all wars." Optimism was high. Music in the form of jazz blossomed, social traditions were changing, and the economy prospered, which positioned Americans to roar like a lion into the 1920s—a decade that came to be called "The Roarin' Twenties." Such energy signaled a new trend known as Art Deco—elegant geometric designs and bold colors in architecture, jewelry, fashion, and even cars. Hardly could the social ambience be more symbolic to launch a venture in professional football than the dealership of the most stylish Hupmobile.

1920 Hupmobile collage with Art Deco-style hood ornament & lettering by the author; photography source unknown (CC-BY-SA)

Among the ten original clubs in the new league (initially called the American Professional Football Association) was a team entirely of Native Americans, the Oorang Indians. It was led by Jim Thorpe, a famous Olympic star, who was appointed president of the new league (this title was changed to *commissioner* in 1941). Two years later, its name was changed to the National Football League (NFL) of clubs from Chicago in the Midwest (Illinois, Indiana, Michigan, and Ohio) to western New York state (Rochester and Buffalo). To this day, the core of the NFL, which now reaches across the continental United States, has retained "middle America" preferences, which elevate hard work, teamwork, and playing by the rules.

Canadian football, like the United States, had its origins in the late 1800s. The professional league, the Canadian Football League (CFL), launched in 1958.

There were 21 early teams and three of these still exist today. The Arizona Cardinals, which began as an athletic club called the Racine Normals in 1898, entered the league as the Chicago Cardinals. The Chicago Bears played their first two years in Decatur, Illinois, as the Staleys, named after their sponsor, a manufacturing company. George S. Halas played for and coached the team and carried equipment, wrote press releases, sold tickets, and taped ankles. For all this, and because he coached the Bears for 40 years and to six NFL titles, he earned the nickname "Papa Bear." An organizer of the NFL, Halas is remembered as the Father of the NFL. A modern championship trophy is named after him.

Game ball, 1921, between the Rochester Jeffersons and Chicago Bears (Courtesy of John Steffenhagen)

Teams that entered the NFL in the 1920s and '30s that remain to the present are referred to as "the old guard." They are the Los Angeles Rams (which originated in Cleveland), Green Bay Packers, Detroit Lions, Pittsburgh Steelers, Philadelphia Eagles, New York Giants, and the Washington Football Team, formerly known as the Redskins. The Eagles and Steelers played a season as one team, the "Steagles," in 1943 due to talented young men joining the fight of World War II. The Steelers joined the Cardinals as Card-Pitt a year later. Sportswriters joked that they were Car-Pitts (which sounds like "carpets"), suggesting that a winless 0-10 record meant that teams walked all over them.

The Decatur Staleys Football Club, 1920. NFL co-founder and team owner George Halas, front center. Public domain.

In the first years of professional football, it was not uncommon for teams to associate their name with a street. Thus, the Racine Normals (Arizona Cardinals today) were named after Normal Park on Racine Street, in Chicago, Illinois; and the Rochester Jeffersons after Rochester, New York's Jefferson Street. More common was the practice to adopt names of the baseball clubs already in town: the Brooklyn Dodgers (before the baseball team's move to LA), the New York Yankees, and New York Giants. In their first year, the Redskins were the Boston Braves, after Boston's then-baseball team, now the Atlanta Braves. Washington, DC, had a football team called the Senators—the same name as its baseball team. The Detroit Tigers—the football team—lasted just part of one season before quitting. Journalists of the day would distinguish teams by saying, "The New York *Football* Giants." The Bears were a little contrary in naming their team. Chicago had the Cubs, or Baby Bears, but football players were said to be larger and stronger than baseball players...so it was to be "the Bears."

Game ball, 1921, between the Rochester Jeffersons and Chicago Bears (Courtesy John Steffenhagen)

 I. Check your understanding of the reading by marking your answer choice.

1. *Set* or *fixed* describes something that doesn't change.

    Y____   N____

2. "Founder" and "owner" are the same.

    Y____   N____

3. *Harpastum* is an ancestor of American football.

    Y____   N____

4. The term "running with the ball" in rugby is used in American football.

    Y____   N____

5. True or False or Maybe (if not stated in the reading)

a. President Roosevelt hated football.

      T____   F____   M____

b. Walter Camp was the first pro.

      T____   F____   M____

c. Three teams merged in 1943 and '44.

      T____   F____   M____

d. The Staleys became the Cardinals.

      T____   F____   M____

e. In 1910, Ohio had a football club.

      T____   F____   M____

f. Halas coached the Chicago Bears.

      T____   F____   M____

Questions 6-8 circle your choice

6. Where are we likely to see a scrum?
    a. When money scatters on a busy sidewalk.
    b. When the public-address announcer says, "Free hot dogs to the first 50 fans."
    c. Drunks at a bar/pub who support different teams.
    d. All of the above.

7. The first individual to get paid to play football.
    a. Latrobe Athletic Club
    b. Pudge Heffelfinger
    c. George Halas
    d. The first professional football player.

Footballogy: Elements of American Football for Non-Native Speakers of English

8. "Touch-down" is to "touchdown" as "try-at-goal" is to _____.

    a. field goal   b. extra point
    c. safety   d. goalpost

II. Use the words in the word preview to complete the crossword puzzle.

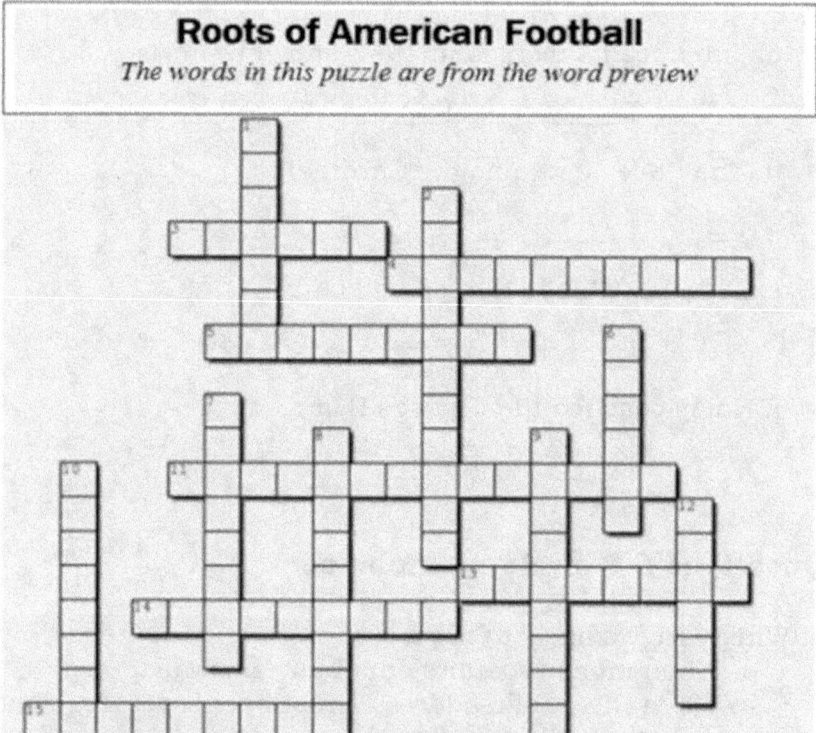

Across
3. If it's forbidden, it's _____
4. To be connected is to be _____.
5. Violence =
11. Changed quickly.
13. Another word for dependence
14. A ball suddenly deflated.
15. Early games of football ___ rugby.

All puzzles in this book are generated by www.theteacherscorner.net

Down
1. The one who starts a business
2. Effort and talent separate the best from the good.
6. Close but not close enough.
7. Taking what does not belong to you
8. Those who might oppose change (2 words)
9. Please…thank you…are examples.
10. Fall is the prefect _____ for a game.
12. 5 x 2 years

American Football's First Pro Star?

Jim Thorpe: Olympian and first administrator of the NFL. CC-BY-SA (Wikipedia)

What started the popularity of American football? Could it be the "projectile pass"? That's what the forward pass was called in the early days. It is attributed to an Olympic gold medalist named Jim Thorpe (pictured, 1909), a descendant of indigenous Americans and a member of the Carlisle Indian Industrial School football team. More than a century after Thorpe's heyday, his name is inextricably linked with professional football. This versatile athlete, who excelled in multiple sports, breathed life into the relatively new game. Thorpe became a pioneer by using the forward pass.

Back then, passes were discouraged. An incomplete pass resulted in a penalty while a pass that landed out of bounds turned the ball over to the opposing team. However, Jim Thorpe, a champion in every sport he played, championed the forward pass under legendary coach Pop Warner, which pointed American football to the future. In the pass-happy element of modern football, who can dispute Jim Thorpe and his Carlisle football club's influence on the game? That's just one of the many reasons why Thorpe's bust is in the Pro Football Hall of Fame in Canton, Ohio.

III. Select the word with similar meanings (synonyms)

1. Jim Thorpe <u>excelled</u> in multiple sports.
      a. did very well   b. shone
      c. exceeded   d. achieved

Footballogy: Elements of American Football for Non-Native Speakers of English

2. More than a century after Thorpe's <u>heyday</u>...
   a. peak   b. apex
   c. prime   d. all—a, b, c

3. Thorpe <u>championed</u> the forward pass.
   a. won   b. advocated
   c. threw   d. defeated

Items 4 & 5: choose the opposites (antonyms)

4. A <u>descendant</u> of Native Americans ...
   a. ancestor   b. relative
   c. Neither a or b   d. both a and b

5. Passes were <u>discouraged</u>.
   a. encouraged   b. confabulated
   c. confused   d. all—a, b, c

6. This is an example of a ...
   a. silhouette   b. statue
   c. sketch   d. bust

CC-BY-SA

*Some days you get the bear;
other days the bear gets you.*
— English proverb

CHAPTER II

America's Favorite Pastime

Why are people so passionate about a game that has only about 11 minutes of action? Could it be that there's more to football than just a game? In a short review of how to talk about things in the past, we'll uncover some reasons.

Passion

Word Preview

| die-hard | viral | quirky | frock | postpone |
| binds | widow | grip | scan | burst |

Without calling American football a religion, calling it a rival to church for popularity may not be far from the truth. Could Tim Christensen, a pastor in the Rocky Mountain state of Montana, be an example of this trend? Nothing could keep Reverend Christensen, a die-hard San Francisco 49ers fan, from watching the telecast of his favorite team in a 2014 playoff game. Video on YouTube of him delivering a one-minute sermon so he could go home and tune in went viral.

"Would you all like to be forgiven for your sins?" he began, pausing for just a second to listen for an answer. "Okay, that's great, you are."

The day's communion, a sacred action led by the minister to express Christian unity, was to be self-service, he noted. "Help yourselves to the bread and wine."

A quirky beginning got even quirkier. Opening his frock, the preacher revealed his true colors on the red-and-gold 49ers tee-shirt he wore. "I'm out of here," he concluded, pretending to walk away.

Rev. Tim Christensen showing his colors as a San Francisco 49ers fan. Credit: John Christenson —YouTube

The congregation was aware of their adored minister's talent for kidding. No one was surprised that he wasn't serious about abandoning his religious duties for a football game. The pastor was the perfect example of practicing what one preaches, which, in Christian teachings, promises that good things come to those who wait.

Reverend Christensen postponed (or delayed) his enjoyment of the game until after church. He was able to watch the entire game on his recording device. His cherished 49ers won.

Stories of passion for football like this one are hardly uncommon. This author can recount one of his own when a courtroom judge in Los Angeles cut short jury selection so he could get home for the college football championship. Few would disagree that all walks of life in the United States are touched by the sport. How interesting that at football's highest level, the traditional day of play is on the Sabbath, the traditional day of worship!

> **Kidding:** [Social media: "JK"— just kidding] conveys the opposite of what you mean. Americans kid to add levity (humor) to social situations. This is most effective when the listener knows the speaker is not serious. It can also be an effective tool for sarcasm but it can provoke hostility: "Hello, skinny!" (to an overweight person). Similar meanings (synonyms): joking, bluffing.

David Biderman, reporting for the *Wall Street Journal*, took up the issue of the passion for American football. Why is a game that lasts over three hours but has only about 11 minutes of action—that way since 1912—so popular? Biderman observed that other timed sports like soccer and hockey are a continuous 90 minutes of action. In contrast, he found that an average NFL play lasts four seconds with 40 seconds of inaction between plays. The ratio of inaction to action is 20:1.

To compensate for the inactivity, which includes stopping the clock for timeouts, penalties, injuries, and scores, telecasts of NFL games devote more time to replays (17 minutes) than live play. TV cameras scan the players and coaches on the sidelines, the cheerleaders and officials, and they get reaction shots of fans. A typical NFL game broadcast includes 20 commercial breaks with more than 100 ads, consuming about one hour or one-third of the total time.

Football has steadily advanced in popularity for decades. Why? First, it binds people and communities together with the common goal of wanting their team to win. It gives them a sense of belonging. And who doesn't like to belong—to feel pride when their team wins?

Football may be well-suited to modern attention spans and appetites for short bursts of action and violent collisions, says sports super-agent Leigh Steinberg. "It's symbolic [of] war without death as a consequence," he writes in a *Forbes* magazine opinion piece. "It has breaks in the action that give people a chance to discuss what has happened or take bathroom or food trips."

But the passion for football involves more than just the game. It encompasses all the things that happen during the week between games, and the activities that happen during the off-season. The NFL draft in April is a three-day televised event. The following season's schedule, a closely kept secret, generates excitement at its announcement.

Many factors contribute to the enthusiasm for American football. This book uses several sources to compile a list of reasons for this passion by Americans for American football. Not in any order of importance, the list is subjective, meaning that it is an opinion on how the sport has come to grip America.

unknown author: CC-BY-NC-ND

"Football widow" *(left)—describes a person, traditionally a woman, abandoned on weekends by her partner, who seems to speak a coded language that only he and his fellow football fanatics can understand. Recent data shows, however, that women are on board the football bandwagon.*

The female demographic, in fact, is almost half the total of the football fans in the United States. Women also comprise many football broadcast crews. ESPN's Beth Mowins (photo right) announces play-by-play. More and more, advertisers target football game ads to women.

Photo: Joe Faraoni/ESPN Images

Reasons for Football's Popularity

High Scores & Big Plays

Americans love "big" and "fast"—high-powered offenses that score a lot of points on big plays. Scores of 38-34, 75-yard passes (called "long bombs"), pick-sixes (interceptions returned for touchdowns) and length-of-the-field kick returns bring fans to their feet. Defensive struggles with final scores of 6-3, 10-7, etc., do not sell tickets.

Coming From Behind

No matter how far apart the score, a game isn't over until the gun to end the final quarter. All levels of football have tales of a team that rose from the dead in a game and stormed back to win. The NFL's Buffalo Bills were down 35-3 in the 1993 AFC championship game and won 41-38. The New England Patriots did it the 2017 Super Bowl, scoring 25 unanswered 4th quarter and overtime points to win 34-28.

A Game of Inches

This is one of the most hackneyed expressions in American football. And it can't be said enough because it's true. Inches could be the difference between a hard-earned win or a heart-breaking defeat. Fans are on the edges of their seats, all excited. Take Super Bowl XXXIV (2000), the then-St. Louis Rams and Tennessee Titans. No time left and the Titans receiver was stopped inches short of the goal line for a Rams victory. "Life is a game of inches where the margin of error is so small," says Al Pacino in the football-themed movie *Any Given Sunday*.

Any Given Sunday

Another hackneyed phrase, this represents one of the most reverent ideas in American lore—the underdog. A team with low expectations rises and beats a much stronger team. This can happen anytime, anywhere. It doesn't happen often, but for eternally optimistic Americans, that it *can* happen is what matters.

Worst-to-First

Hard work, dedication, and a no-quit attitude make the impossible possible. That's the American way. A team finishes in the cellar (last place) one year but first the next. The 1999 Indianapolis Colts did it with a 13-3 season record after going 3-13 the year before. In 15 of the 16 NFL seasons, 2002-2018, a team went from last place to first. The Chicago Bears did it in 2018, winning the NFC Central title.

Rags-to-Riches (The Horatio Alger story)

Horatio Alger, a 19th-century writer of young adult fiction, wrote about persons from low origins who overcame troubled lives to reach a high level of success. This kind of story is said to represent the American Dream, which became real for Kurt Warner, a grocery store clerk in Iowa who the St. Louis Rams (now in Los Angeles) auditioned (tried out) as a quarterback. He was to lead the team to a Super Bowl victory and be named the MVP (Most Valuable Player).

Another instance was Vince Papale, a low-wage bartender who answered a public call for a tryout with the Philadelphia Eagles. Against big odds, his hard work and determination earned him a roster spot. His story is told in the feature film *Invincible*. (Notice the play on words: *Vince* in the title that means *unbeatable*.)

> A Cinderella Story: Any team that rises beyond expectations after being a bad team is called a "Cinderella," after the children's story about a poor girl who became a princess.

A Game For All Seasons

What do football games and postal deliveries have in common? Rain or shine, hail, sleet, ice or snow, cold or hot, clear sky or fog, on goes the show. In most sports, extreme weather forces cancellation of the game. Not football!

Philadelphia-Chicago playoff, 1988). Fog severely restricted the ability to see. Photo: Public domain courtesy of NFL.com by way of the National Weather Service.

A game in a snowstorm. Karen Eckberg, Flickr (CC-BY-NC-ND 2.0)

Tailgating

This Great American social event, tailgating, can begin hours before kickoff. Fans celebrate with food and beverages. The event is a place for total strangers to meet and develop friendships. The stadium parking lot is a colorful spectacle of team colors, aromas, and talk of the game.

Mind Game

Football is like chess. The 40-second gap between plays is a chance to match wits with the coaches. What should they do in a certain circumstance? Where should they position players? There are many choices for plays in a game, all of which depend on player matchups, field position (where the ball is ready for play), time remaining, and so on.

Statistics

Americans love statistics. Record-keeping and comparing are embedded in the American way of life. In football, there is so much to keep track of. Stats are kept for everything from the most points in a game, season, in a game played on artificial turf and natural grass; how many times a quarterback was sacked, hurried, and intercepted at night, in cold weather, at home and away, etc. Stats provide a sense of how the upcoming foes match up as a team at each position on the home field. They deliver expectations. (But see "Any Given Sunday.")

Fewer Games

Major League Baseball has 162 games per season. Basketball and hockey number in the 80s. A losing streak of three games or so isn't so significant. The NFL has just 16 games, colleges 10-11, so each game matters. Between games comes the hype. Tension has a week to build up like steam in a teapot. Additionally, the playoffs have a one-and-done formula unlike a series of games in other sports.

Quality of Time, Not Quantity

Soccer has 90 minutes of continuous action. A lot of the time is dribbling or kicking the ball back and forth. (Defensive players can "relax" when the ball isn't on their side of the field.) All that for one or two scores a game? But the football action is packed into just 11 minutes. When the play is on, it matters. Everyone pays attention.

Tradition!

Rivalries: An annual event, a rivalry pits two teams with a long history of antagonism toward each other. These games are tense and fights are known to break out among participants and spectators. The instant the new season's schedule comes out in the spring, the date of "the big game" is circled.

Homecoming: An important tradition in about every university. Alumni return for a weekend of merriment, special ceremonies, and a parade.

Autumn (casually referred to as "fall" in the United States): Hardly anything is more brilliant in the great outdoors than fall, notably the swatch of colors from leaves in the northern climate zone. An ideal fall day is sweater weather—cool, crisp, and dry, under clear skies.

Thanksgiving: If baseball and the Fourth of July (American Independence Day) go together, then the fourth Thursday in November goes with football. Thanksgiving remembers the settlers of America and the Native Americans who celebrated a meal with them. In modern times, it's a day for families to get together and do things, which includes eating lots of turkey, potatoes, squash, and all the things the early Americans did. On TV is the Macy's Thanksgiving Day parade. And then it's football. The Detroit Lions started the tradition in 1951 and have been playing every year since. College rivalries include the annual University of Texas-Texas A&M rivalry.

Thanksgiving postcard circa 1900—public domain (via Wiki)

The Super Bowl

Once the professional season concludes, the month-long road to the Super Bowl begins. The 12-teams that qualify (six from each conference) get one chance each week to win a playoff game (compared with other sports that play a best-of-seven series). The two remaining teams square off the first Sunday in February at the Super Bowl, an event unlike any other in America. "Super Sunday," as it's called, is like a holiday. Absenteeism from work the next day is attributed to a Super Bowl hangover (an after-effect associated with heavy drinking), which explains why there is a high rate of workers calling in "sick" the next day.

 I. Check your understanding

1. Which letter has a similar meaning (synonym) as "reverend?"
    a. minister   b. preacher
    c. pastor   d. all—A-B-C

2. Fourteen pass completions in 20 attempts is an example of...
    a. mind game   b. statistics
    c. tradition   d. rivalry

Footballogy: Elements of American Football for Non-Native Speakers of English

3. Horatio Alger wrote about the underdog.
   True   False

4. Guess the meaning from the context clue: In 1919, this Pro Football team benefitted from corporate sponsorship by the Indian Packing Company, which gave $500 for equipment and uniforms.
   a. Bears   b. Staleys
   c. Cardinals   d. Packers

5. What day is an undeclared national holiday?
   a. Thanksgiving   b. Homecoming
   c. Super Sunday   d. the day after the Super Bowl

6. Only a _____ fan would attend a football game in the freezing rain.
   a. die-hard   b. unhappy
   c. kidding   d. stay-at-home

Questions 7-9 (Use the correct form of the word provided in each item 7-9 to complete)

Verb = word of action
Noun = person, place, thing, abstract idea
Adverb = modified verb, adjective or another adverb
Adjective = describes a noun
Gerund = verb + "ing" (functions like a noun)

7. Tradition (noun); / traditional (adjective) / traditionally (adverb)

The Cowboys *traditionally* host a football game every Thanksgiving, a _____ day set aside for giving thanks. The _____ includes eating many _____ foods introduced by the First Americans. A modern _____ is to watch the Macy's parade and football. The Detroit Lions has been the _____ host of one game since 1951. Van Patrick, _____ announcer for the

Lions, used to say the Lions _____ feast on (eat) the opposition on this day.

8. *Rivalry* (abstract noun—idea)/ *rival* (concrete noun—person or thing) *rival* (verb)

Princeton is a _____ of Harvard. Their _____ dates to 1875. Another long _____ is Cornell and Dartmouth. In modern times, these games may not _____ games like Ohio State and Michigan.

9. *Score* (noun or verb); *scoring* (gerund)

The Chiefs lead the NFL in _____. They _____ an average of 32.3 points a game. They were the league's highest _____ offense last year, too. Whenever the team needed a _____, their offense seemed to always find a way to _____. I expect them to _____ a lot of points next season. After all, _____ is the Chiefs' middle name.

10. Mashed potatoes and gravy, homecoming, Macy's parade, Detroit Lions...
    a. holidays   b. traditions
    c. festivals   d. Thanksgiving

11. Reverend Christenson didn't _____ his duties as a pastor.
    a. abandon   b. abandoned
    c. neglected   d. keep

12. To admire something is to _____ it.
    a. adore   b. eat
    c. defer   d. hate

13. What term does not characterize that anything is possible?
   - a. rags-to-riches
   - b. "Any given Sunday"
   - c. a Cinderella story
   - d. game of inches

Matching
Word opposites (antonyms) from words used in the reading.

Column A
1. ___foe
2. ___days gone by
3. ___hackneyed
4. ___shrouded
5. ___heralded
6. ___divergent
7. ___grit
8. ___foliage
9. ___bounty
10. ___vanquished
11. ___(to) rival

Column B
a. victors
b. present time
c. leafless
d. friend
e. scarce
f. imaginative
g. to equal
h. same
i. unpublicized
j. weak
k. uncovered

May-might-could are modal verbs used to express a degree of possibility.

— They are used with a verb stem.
— Similar meaning to "will probably," and "perhaps/maybe he/she will"

Example: He **will probably play.** (Perhaps he will play = He might play.)

II. Change these sentences using one of the above modals

1. After the game, they will probably celebrate with their friends.

   _____

2. Since the game is 400 miles away, he will probably fly.

   _____

3. However, perhaps he will take a train.

   _____

4. Maybe he will find a good airfare online.

   _____

5. It's a big game, so the hotels are likely to be booked up (full).

   _____

> **Reporting verbs:** said, noted, observed, stated, asked

Direct Speech
Observe the punctuation, capitalization, and placement of quotation marks ["..."] in the following examples:

- *He said, "We should play hard and be competitive." (Quote after reporting the verb and after the period.)*

- "We should play hard," he said, "and be competitive." (Divided quotation.)

- "We should play hard and be competitive," he said. (Quotation before the reporting verb.)

- "Aren't you afraid?" he asked. (Question including question mark inside the quotation.)

III. Rewrite the following sentences using the correct punctuation.

1. Tryouts will be held next Monday at 10 AM the coach said so don't be late.

___

2. Will you come to my Super Bowl party she asked.

___

3. My feeling is that the Rams should win this game he stated

___

4. The poster stated under no circumstances can alcohol be brought with you to the game

___

5. The guard appeared to be holding the announcer insisted but the officials missed it

___

The Greatest Game Ever Played

The game that started the passion ...

The final score of the 1958 NFL Championship game.
Logos used with permission: Indianapolis Colts; New York Giants

Where the Passion Began...

Professional football was on the rise in the 1950s. This was a time when the United States was captivated by a generation known as "the beatniks"—young men who wore sideburns and greased hair and girls who wore poodle skirts, bobby sox, and saddle shoes. The country rocked and rolled to the beat of Elvis Presley, Fats Domino, and many others. At the end of the Art Deco era, cars had stylish fender skirts, tailfins, and hood ornaments. (See the collage at the end of this unit.)

Late in 1958 came something that rocked the world: the NFL Championship game. After this game on December 21 between the New York Giants and the Baltimore Colts at Yankee Stadium in New York City, life would not be the same. This first-ever national telecast of a professional football game came to be called "the Greatest Game Ever Played." As a result, pro football—not as well-known then as college football—skyrocketed in popularity. By the mid-1960s, it became the nation's favorite sport to watch and has remained on top ever since.

The drama was high as the NFL's title game moved into its final minutes of regulation, or 60 minutes (four

Footballogy: Elements of American Football for Non-Native Speakers of English

quarters). But something unthinkable happened. While the crowd watched, the television audience lost contact. Someone accidentally pulled a cable, which put NBC, the television network, off the air for several minutes. Up to then, the game was seesawing, the Colts and the Giants exchanging leads. The power outage only added to the suspense. When it was restored, fans were in for a treat.

Johnny Unitas, recognized not just by his number 19 jersey but also for his black high-top cleats, led the Colts offense onto the field with under two minutes left in the game. The Colts, trailing by a field goal 17-14, began from their 14-yard line. After two passes fell incomplete, Unitas connected with halfback Lenny Moore for 11 yards, which got the offense moving.

After Unitas missed on a long pass to L.G. "Long Gone" Dupre, he turned to his favorite target, Raymond Berry. They hooked up for a 25-yard gain to the midfield. Two more quick strikes to Berry put the Colts in business at the Giants' 13-yard-line with just seven seconds to play in regulation. In those days, regular-season games could end in a tie after four quarters.

But this was the NFL Championship, so the Colts booted a 20-yard field goal to tie the score 17-all. This sent the game into the first-ever "sudden death"—overtime where the first team to score by any means would win.

The Giants won the coin toss but failing to move the ball, they were forced to punt—in other words, to kick the ball to the opposition. Baltimore wasted no time moving the ball methodically for 80 yards in 13 plays. Finally, history was made when fullback Alan Ameche punched through the line on a one-yard, game-winning touchdown. Eight minutes and 15 seconds into overtime and the Colts had a 23-17 win and the NFL title. America's passion for professional football was born.

> Despite this game's dignified place in pro-football history, historians note that the game had its share of messy plays—six lost fumbles, missed field goals, interceptions, and conservative play-calling.

Footballogy: Elements of American Football for Non-Native Speakers of English

 I. Comprehension—circle your answer choice

1. What marked the beginning of professional football's popularity?
    a. The early part of the 1950s
    b. The fall of Rome
    c. The title game between the New York Giants and Baltimore Colts
    d. Johnny Unitas

2. Baltimore's offense "methodically moved the ball" probably means...
    a. The team moved a few yards at a time and used time from the clock.
    b. The passing attack was clicking (working well).
    c. The Colts got big chunks of yardage at a time.
    d. The Colts used safe passes and didn't fumble.

3. "Sudden Death" means...
    a. the result of an argument
    b. to die without saying goodbye
    c. to lose the championship game
    d. overtime until someone wins

4. For the most part, "The Greatest Game Ever Played" was
    a. played well from start to finish
    b. mostly boring and played with a lot of mistakes
    c. played with Johnny Unitas as quarterback for the Giants
    d. won by a field goal

5. Alan Ameche "plunges to pay dirt" means:
    a. He hit the ground hard.
    b. He was tackled for a loss.
    c. He ran a yard or two for a touchdown.
    d. He evaded a tackle.

6. According to the passage, the drama of the game began
   a. in overtime
   b. in the final two minutes of regulation
   c. after a long pass incompletion
   d. at the coin toss

7. Who was Johnny Unitas' favorite target (receiver)?
   a. Raymond Berry
   b. Lenny Moore
   c. "Long Gone" Dupre
   d. Alan Ameche

8. L.G. "Long Gone" Dupre probably got his nickname because
   a. he was a terrific halfback
   b. defenders couldn't catch him once the ball was in his hands
   c. his teammates gave it to him
   d. passes flew over his head

9. In football, what is "to hook up"?
   a. a completed pass
   b. a first down
   c. a date
   d. a certain place to meet on the field

10. What sent the game into overtime?
    a. The raucous crowd wanted more.
    b. The TV cable got unplugged.
    c. A field goal kick at the end of regulation tied the game.
    d. A late touchdown in regulation evened the score.

II. Synonyms (words with same or similar meanings). Match column A with column B

Column A

1. _b_ booted
2. ___ skyrocketed
3. ___ christened
4. ___ regulation
5. ___ cleats
6. ___ strikes
7. ___ title
8. ___ punched
9. ___ exploded
10. ___ accidentally

Column B

a. sneakers/athletic shoes
b. kicked
c. named
d. rose sharply
e. not intended
f. burst
g. limit
h. hits
i. championship
j. hit

Iconic 1950s Americana (L-R top): Poodle skirt, neon & juke box, dance called the swing (also "jitterbug"), Elvis Presley, automobiles with stylish grilles & tailfins and Marilyn Monroe (collage derived from Visual Hunt CC-BY-SA)

Oh, the places you'll go! There is fun to be done!
— Dr. Seuss

CHAPTER III

"Nuts & Bolts"—The Basics

Have you ever played "find someone who"? It's never too late to find someone who wants to learn what we know. A place to start is to teach them the sights at the game. We'll start with a little about the origin of what started it all—the ball itself.

The Accidental Ball

Instructions: Read the following passage, look for the underlined words and be ready to tackle the assessment that follows.

American football uses the foot just 5% of the time, so it may be puzzling that it's called "football." Another <u>contradiction</u> is the casual label of the ball as a "pigskin." The modern football is made of cowhide (leather).

Though the origins of the sport of football go back beyond Ancient Rome, the event that <u>originated</u> the ball for American football came in 1869. Princeton and Rutgers, two of the oldest universities in the United States, played a game that resembled soccer. Yet, it *wasn't* soccer.

Reported Henry Duffield, an eyewitness at the game: "The ball was not oval but was supposed to be completely round. It was too hard to blow up right." Duffield explained that each member from each team took turns blowing up the ball at various times during the game. In the end, they "got tired and put the ball back in play somewhat <u>lopsided</u>."

This <u>unintended</u> shape, partially <u>deflated</u> and uneven, was to become ideal for the ball used in modern American football. It bounces <u>erratically</u>, unpredictably, all over the field and it can fly in a <u>tight spiral</u>, spinning evenly. The oval shape makes the ball adapt to multiple purposes such as running, catching, throwing, and, yes, using the foot for kicking. As new rules and types of plays in the game developed so did changes with the football. The ball became longer and slimmer in the 1930s to adjust to a game that had discovered the forward pass.

Since 1941, the Wilson Sporting Goods Company in Ada, Ohio, has been the official manufacturer of footballs for the professional league in the United States, the National Football League (NFL). Each ball is inscribed "The Duke," a tribute to Wellington Mara, the late owner of the New York Giants. As a child assistant who brought water to players (a "water boy") for the professional team he would one day own, players joked he was "The Duke," after the

Duke of Wellington of England.

Footballs for high schools and universities have a solid white stripe at both ends which aid in seeing the ball in flight. By contrast, the NFL uses a solid color for a bigger challenge to catch.

The football over the years 1894-present — courtesy of the Smithsonian

 I. Vocabulary check. Select the letter that represents the closest in meaning.

1. erratic
    a. inflated
    b. regular
    c. lopsided
    d. unpredictable

2. The best description of the shape of an American football is
    a. deflated
    b. oval
    c. round
    d. unintended

3. Look at the title of this unit. "Nuts and Bolts." This means...
    a. essential information
    b. parts for a machine
    c. basic things
    d. both A and C

4. The main component of the modern American football.
    a. pigskin
    b. rubber
    c. leather
    d. plastic

Footballogy: Elements of American Football for Non-Native Speakers of English

5. When was the first game of football played?
   a. in Ada, Ohio   b. Between Rutgers and Princeton
   c. in 1869   d. by Henry Duffield

6. If something is uneven, it is
   a. lopsided   b. easier to see
   c. easier to kick   d. also lighter

7. When we have good words for someone, we give that person a ...
   a. tribute   b. tight spiral
   c. contradiction   d. contribution

8. "Accidental football" suggests that the shape of the ball was
   a. inflated   b. deflated
   c. underinflated   d. unintended

9. Who does "The Duke" in NFL football refer to?
   a. Winchester Cathedral   b. John "the Duke" Wayne
   c. Wellington Mara   d. Duke of Wellington

II. Parts of speech. Decide if the underlined word is an adjective (describes a noun), a noun (person, place, thing, or idea), or a verb (word of action). Write your answer on the line.

1. It is <u>inaccurate</u> to describe the game as football. _____

2. There are <u>inaccuracies</u> in the name. _____

3. The <u>original</u> ball was almost deflated. _____

4. Many think the <u>origin</u> of football was in Ancient Greece. _____

5. Did the game really <u>originate</u> in Greece? _____

6. The first known <u>football</u> game was played in 1869. _____

7. The NFL <u>football</u> is a solid color. _____

8. The main <u>manufacturer</u> of the ball is in Ohio. _____

9. Are footballs <u>manufactured</u> in Ohio? _____

10. There have been many <u>changes</u> in the game. _____

Sights at the Game

Word Preview

end zone	sideline	goal line	goalposts
hash marks	yard line	artificial turf	gridiron
uprights	crossbar	scouts	

The Football Field

In much of the English-speaking world, outdoor sports are played on a pitch, a grassy surface that in the USA is called a *field*. In football, it's a *gridiron,* a 700-year-old word for a metal grid for cooking over a fire. In the early days of American football until the 1920s, the markings on the field resembled a checkerboard or a grid for cooking waffles.

Gridiron, Archbold Stadium, Syracuse University 1910
Source: Syracuse University Archives

The surface of the modern field can be natural grass or artificial turf (synthetic fibers that look like natural grass). The field can be outdoors or housed in "domes"—indoor stadiums with a roof. Since outdoor games are played in a variety of climates, grounds crews maintain the turf to meet weather challenges.

In the United States, the football playing field is measured using the Imperial system of measurement. The length of the field is 100 yards (about 91 meters); the width 53 yards (48.5 meters). By contrast, the playing surface of Canadian football is 110 yards long and 65 yards wide. The perimeter or boundary of the playing field (called the sideline) is marked by a six-foot (1.67 meter) solid line.

At the end of each length-side of the playing field is the *end zone*. It is often decorated with the name and colors of the home team. A solid white line from one side of the field to the other at the front of the end zone marks the *goal line (in the back of the end zone is the end line)* where a player in possession of the ball scores.

The four corners of the end zone are marked by brightly colored markers called *pylons* (picture, right), which can be significant in determining whether a player scores.

Pylon: partyworksinteractive.com

The *goalposts* are in the back of the end zone in the middle. These are two vertical poles called uprights that extend from a single pole to a height of 35 feet (10.67 meters) and are 8.5 feet apart (about six meters). A 10-foot-high (9.1 meter) *crossbar* connects the two. (These measurements differ between professional and non-professional leagues.) The goalposts are critical to determining the success of kicks, which is one of the ways to score in American football (discussed in the section on scoring). There are flags on top of each goalpost and a net is raised to stop kicks from sailing into the spectator section.

Yard lines: Solid white lines spread across the width of the field every five yards. Numerals appear at 10-yard intervals on each side of the 50-yard line, called the *midfield*. Canadian football uses two 50-yard lines, 10 yards apart, which accounts for a 110-yard-long field.

Football field with hash marks and yard lines. The bolder line (bottom) marks the goal line. Source: Wiki Commons

Hash marks: A set of lines that look like dashes indicate each yard. The referee spots the ball on or between the *hash marks* at the end of each play, closest to where the ball carrier was stopped, went out of bounds (sideline), or was tackled (stopped). Punted balls that land out of bounds are marked for the next play at the closest hash mark. NFL hash marks are about 23 ½ yards (21 meters) from the sideline. Colleges and high schools are 20 yards (18 meters).

Yards-metric conversion table (Rounded off)

Yards	1	2	3	4	5	10	100
Meters	.9	1.8	2.7	3.7	4.5	9.2	91.4

Online: www.metric-conversions.org

Consider this: *You can lead a horse to water but you can't make it drink.*

Since 1866, attempts have been made to change the system of measurement in the United States. The U.S. Congress passed the Metric Conversion Act (1975) but it was not popular and was not taught in schools. Except in scientific settings, measurement in the USA today remains in the Imperial system—miles, pounds, ounces, inches, feet, and yards. American football is often hailed as "a game of inches." Somehow, "a game of centimeters" doesn't have the same ring.

Sidelines: Seating consisting of benches off the playing field, on the sidelines, are more than an area for players to rest and for those not in the game at the moment to watch. The head coach can be seen with headsets. He communicates with the coaches not nearby but above the field in the press box, where it's better to observe the action. This makes it easier for them to convey strategies to the head coach on the field. In the NFL, as well as other levels of football, *Microsoft Surface* provides technology support for coaches and players to analyze previous plays and strategize how to defend or attack the opposition.

Microsoft Surface™ is a modern tool coaches use to discuss strategy with players
With permission: Taylor Soper/Geekwire

Tents erected on the sidelines allow medical staff and trainers to examine injured players in privacy. Players with minor injuries may be cleared to return to the game. Those not cleared will be seen, without their helmet, being helped back through a tunnel to the locker room for additional medical examination.

The Tunnel

Kickoff minutes away, all eyes turn to the end zone. Starting lineups, one-by-one, emerge from a tunnel (passage) for introductions. "No words can describe this sensation," remarks Leo Carroll, a businessman in Alhambra, California, who played defensive end for Vince Lombardi. "The adrenalin is sky high." Fans, too, get a charge of adrenalin as the rest of the team blazes in a spectacle of pyrotechnics onto the field.

The Press Box

High on one side of the stadium is an area that seats news writers, broadcasters, and others connected to the game. In pro games, an area is set aside for the team owners as well as very important people (VIPs). This is a place for scouts from other teams to take notes on one or both teams on the field if they are on that team's schedule. The NFL places ATC (Athletic Trainer Certified) observers here. They constantly survey the field for a player demonstrating symptoms of a concussion (a serious head injury), which is a major concern at all levels of football.

In the news reporters' area of the press box, demonstrations of favoritism or biases like cheering for "good" plays or jeering for "bad" ones are not permitted. Journalism in the United States is held to a high standard and ideally, is free from impartiality or prejudice. So, in the press box at least, journalists are expected to behave as reporters of facts. Besides, such expressions of bias can be emotional and turn a pleasant atmosphere hostile.

The Stands

In contrast to its name, the stands (also called the grandstands) is where people sit. NFL stadiums can seat between about 65,000 to 83,000 people. Some stadiums have removable seating, referred to as "bleachers," and can add more seating if a popular team comes to town. College games can range from stadiums with a capacity of a few thousand to over 100,000.

Ticket prices are usually cheaper in the bleachers and in

the section described as the "nosebleed section." This is a joke, of course, for a high elevation where the air is so thin due to low barometric pressure that it can cause nasal bleeding. Such a reference is an example of the quiet humor in American culture to be able to laugh at oneself.

Almost anywhere in the stands, high or low, near the field or far, binoculars are handy for close-ups of the players and action. A good use of binoculars is to single out a player and watch his actions from start to finish. Tickets cost more at or near ground level and near the 50-yard line. Prices can depend on the visiting team (a top-tier team, a weak team, or a rival).

> A player who celebrates after a score or a big play is said to *grandstand* or *be grandstanding* (also to *showboat* or *be showboating*). Celebration can result in a team penalty. If this is done after a scoring play in college football, it can cost the team the score.

Scoreboard Clock

The game clock makes following the action easier. It displays the score, the quarter, and the time left in the quarter. Pros and colleges have 15 minutes to a quarter; high school 12 minutes. If a game goes to overtime, the pros award 10 game minutes to break the tie. If the tie isn't broken in that time, the game ends in a tie. Colleges and high schools use a different overtime system where teams play until the tie is broken.

The clock also lists which team has possession of the ball and the team's location on the field, the down, and the distance to a first down. Most will have a play clock, which counts down the time between plays. In the NFL, that's 40 seconds, or 25 seconds after a timeout when the referee signals the ball ready for play.

College and high school rules are basically the same with slight variations. For instance, in college football, the clock stops on each first down until the ball is spotted and is ready for play. (The CFL allows just 20 seconds to initiate a play.) The play clock begins on the referee's signal.

The game clock stops on timeouts, incomplete passes, penalties, and injuries, and doesn't start until the next play begins or when the referee signals that the ball is ready for play.

The scoreboard also indicates how many timeouts are left in a half (each team has three per half) and the scores of other games.

A Jumbotron is an ultra-large scoreboard seen at some venues. This entertains fans with video replays of the action and things like animations and short, catchy phrases to entertain the audience between plays. Audio blasts unique chants. In Los Angeles, a baritone booms, "Whose house is it?" Excited fans chant back, "Rams' house!" At the other end of the country, in New York state, the Buffalo Bills' rendition of the Isley Brothers' 1980's song "Shout!" unites generations.

Good public-address announcers do more than recite the action. During the many seconds between plays, they turn a routine incident into something dramatic. Not just what the announcers say but how they say it is vital to fan engagement during the many seconds between plays.

I. Multiple choice.
Circle "T" for true and "F" for false.

1. A medical tent is at the side of the field.
   T   F

2. "Get loud" and "make some noise" might appear on a Jumbotron.
   T   F

3. All coaches are on the sidelines.
   T   F

4. A football field can have artificial turf or real grass.
   T   F

5. We call a football field either a pitch or gridiron.
   T   F

6. Reporters in the press box can cheer for their favorite team.
   T   F

7. The <u>play clock</u> *does not* list scores of other games.
   T   F

8. Americans prefer the metric system.
   T   F

9. Down and distance are shown on the scoreboard clock.
   T   F

10. A crossbar is part of the goalposts.
    T   F

Footballogy: Elements of American Football for Non-Native Speakers of English

Sightings and Doings at the Stadium

ACROSS
4. The line where scoring happens: The _____ line.
6. Two vertical posts (goalposts)
10. Not natural grass but artificial...
11. Short dashes, or a hash _____.
13. ATC looks for players with _____.
16. A song everyone likes is...
17. The nose_____ section
19. Reports for a newspaper
20. 50-yard line

DOWN
1. He spies on the competition
2. Rest of the world = metric; the USA = _____.
3. Gridder plays on a _____.
5. Where injured players are taken
7. Look to this to see the score and time left
8. to showboat
12. Seating section high up
14. Extends between the uprights
15. Where players not in the game stand
18. USA name for "pitch"

Alone we can do so little; together we can do so much.
—Helen Keller

CHAPTER IV

The Team: The Offense

In the drawing below, to what unit do these players belong? Offense or defense? What are they talking about? What player is leading the discussion? Who else are members of a team? What do they do and how do they do it? Let's find out.

Drawing credit: author unknown ui-ex.com

Word Preview

suit up	home games	on the road	teamwork
(to) line up	starters	bench strength	reserves
backups	depth chart	inactive(s)	practice squad

The number of players on a team roster varies from 53 in the NFL to nearly unlimited in high school and college. Colleges may dress up to 100 and more players for home games. Road games carry a maximum of 70 players. Obviously, with rosters so large, not all players get game action.

In all levels of football, the number of players on the field at a time is 11 per side. One unit, the offense (or offensive team), is described as *on offense*—they try to score. The other, the defense (or defensive team) is *on defense*—their job is to stop the offense. All players on each unit, or team, work together like parts of a machine. This is called *teamwork*, which is said to build players into good people for life outside of sports.

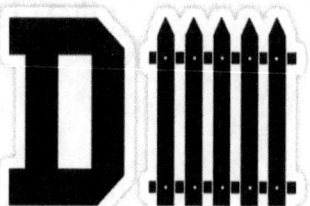

Signs that can't be missed at football games. Which unit does this encourage? "D" + "fence"= DEFENSE (credit: Redbubble Stickers)

Having separate players for offense and defense was not always the case. In football's early years, players lined up on both offense and defense. In high school football, this still happens but since around 1960, players in colleges and the NFL play either on the offense or on the defense, not both. (The last player to play both was Chuck Bednarik of the Philadelphia Eagles [1949-62], who lined up as a center on offense and a linebacker on defense.)

> A common question at a job interview is: "Are you a team player?" Of course, the only correct answer is "yes."

The 11 players on offense and the 11 on defense who start a game are called "starters" or (informally) the "first string." Except for specialists—players with one unique role—the remaining players make up the reserves, also called the "second string" or "backups." But they train and prepare like starters. A player might play if a starter is injured, needs a rest, or when the coaches call a special play that uses that reserve's unique skills or physical abilities. Teams with talented reserves are claimed to have "good bench strength."

> A reserve should not be referred to as "second-stringer" or "benchwarmer"—terms you'll hear casually spoken. Players work hard to achieve a high level of success. Besides, the higher the level, the difference in talent and ability is razor-thin.

A depth chart lists the starters and reserves at each position. Although an NFL roster has 53 players, only 46 are active or eligible to play on game day. The remaining seven are listed as inactive. This could be because a player is injured or is based on team needs for that day. An NFL team may have up to 10 additional members on a practice squad comprised of inexperienced players who practice with the team but don't suit up for the game unless added to the active roster. Such a promotion usually happens when an active player is injured, traded, or cut from the team.

> The pre-practice squad days, namely the 1950s and '60s, had a "taxi squad," a term used by legendary Cleveland Browns' head coach Paul Brown. The team owner, Mickey McBride, put extra players on the payroll of his taxi company, although they did not actually drive taxi cabs.

Positions on Offense

A football team operates like cogs in a machine. All the 11 parts that work in unity are said to be "well-oiled." The task of the offensive unit is to move the ball by a variety of methods with the ultimate prize being to score.

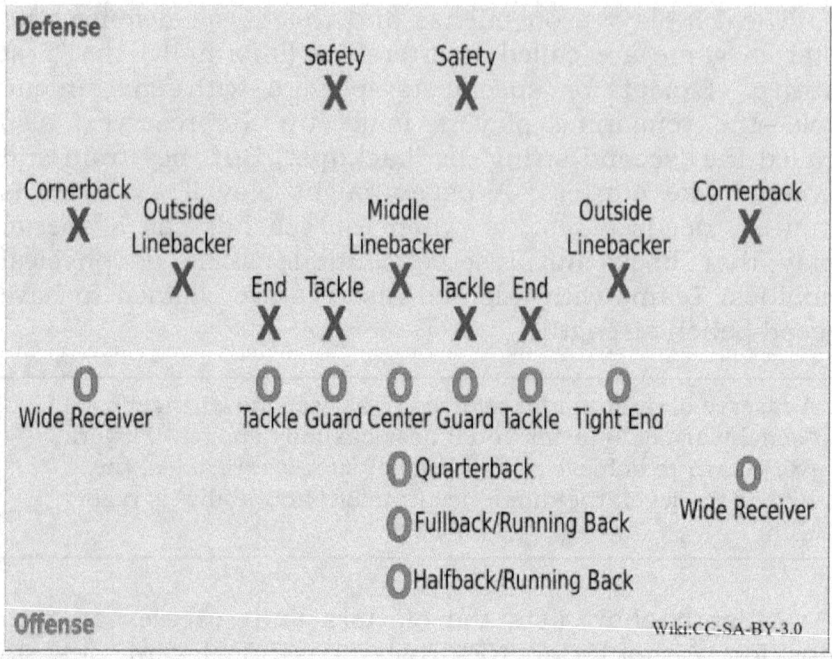

The Huddle

Before a play is run, the offensive players meet in a circle 10 yards behind where the official spots, or places, the ball for play. This is called a "huddle." The leader in the huddle is the quarterback, who either kneels or stands with his fellow players, who pay attention to what he says. He calls the next play with codes, not words, that his teammates learned in practice. The codes tell them their assignments, the formation, blocking assignments, and pass patterns. Very important is the snap count—the number on which the center, in the middle of the offensive line, is supposed to hike (also called "snap") or pass the ball backward between his legs to the quarterback to begin the play.

Position Roles and Player Characteristics

Illustration by Unknown author CC-BY-SA

The interior line: The linemen are the unsung heroes of the offense. They cover "the trenches," where the biggest men on a team—300 pounds and more—line up. Their main job is to block on running plays and protect the quarterback on pass plays. Not many notice their work unless one makes a mistake. "Toughness," Brian Ferentz, offensive line coach at the University of Iowa told *Footballogy*, is what "separates the great linemen from the good ones."

C—Center: The center starts the play by hiking the ball to the quarterback, either right behind him or a few yards back, depending on the formation. He communicates the blocking scheme with fellow linemen who, like him, block forward on a run or drop back in pass protection.

LG and RG—left guard and right guard: The left and right guards flank both sides of the center and must be very strong to push away defensive linemen and linebackers to provide running room for the ball carrier. In addition to size and strength, this position requires quickness and agility when a guard "leads interference" or pulls away from the line to lead the charge on a run play.

LT and RT—left tackle and right tackle: These are the outer two members of the offensive line and the giants of the offense, bigger and taller than their fellow linemen. They also block on run plays and protect the passer on pass plays. The left tackle's special duty lies in protecting the "blind side" (backside) of a right-handed quarterback while that duty is the right tackle's for a left-handed quarterback. Blind-side hits are when fumbles or injuries to the quarterback frequently occur.

The Receiving Corps

TE—tight end: The tight end is trim and fast like a receiver but with the size and strength of a lineman. He lines up close, or tight, to either tackle on the line. That side is called the *strong side*. A good tight end has "sure hands"—he's good at catching—and possesses a lineman's skill to block defenders.

WR—wide receiver: Offensive ends in the pre-Super Bowl era are known by many names today such as *flanker, split end, wide out,* and *slot receiver*. The wide receiver lines up on the line of scrimmage, far to one side, opposite the side of the tight end. Since there is normally more than one wide receiver in the game at a time, the second receiver must be lined up slightly behind the line, in "the slot," to be an eligible receiver. The main duty of each is to run pass patterns down the field, long or just a few steps from where the play began, and catch the football. (Since they do their jobs in the open field, they take a lot of punishment from hard-charging linebackers and defensive backs.) Generally, there are two physical types: tall and long-limbed (long arms and legs), who can go over defenders and pull in a pass; and those who have a slight build and are spry, usually under six feet tall, who move with speed and quickness.

Listen for announcers to say a receiver has "soft hands." That describes one who catches the ball as if he has a pillow. He still must grab it firmly with both hands. One-handed catches are rare but spectacular when they do happen. Receivers have different uses. Some are called "possession receivers," who the quarterback can rely on for short and medium passes to keep the football moving forward at a steady pace. Then there are deep-threat receivers, also called "game-breakers," who have speed and can get deep for long passes. When this happens, the stands come alive and people are on their feet.

The Backfield

Center, quarterback, running back. Credit: Keith Allison (Visual Hunt) CC-BY-SA

QB—quarterback: Occasionally called "the field general," the quarterback is the one who directs the offense on the field by running with the ball, handing it off to a player who runs with it, or passing it to a receiver.

He calls the plays in the huddle—either his own or those sent in from the bench. In addition to talent to release the ball like a dart to a close-by receiver tightly covered by a defense, or to launch it long downfield, he needs to be adept at "reading" or interpreting defenses in a fraction of a second. He also needs to be able to improvise, especially if the play breaks down (doesn't go as planned). Quarterbacks come in all sizes but taller ones (6 foot 2 inches and more) have an advantage over shorter ones in that they can see the field over tall, charging defensive linemen. Eddie Le Baron, whose career spanned the 1950s and '60s for Washington and Dallas, was the smallest quarterback in the history of the league at 5'7" and 168 pounds.

Unknown author (CC-BY-SA)

Off the field, a quarterback is looked to for his leadership ability. A team without a quarterback with this intangible quality seldom has consistent success. It's important for teammates to rally around him and look up to him. He's the one everyone looks to perform well in "the clutch." When the game is on the line, a defeat or a victory is in his hands.

RB—running back: The running back takes the ball and runs with it. He needs to be versatile, able to take the ball handed off to him or "pitched" (tossed) to him from a few yards away by the quarterback or to run out for a pass. He is often called on to block for another running back or to protect the quarterback on a pass play. When a running back gets his hands on the ball, it is referred to as "a touch," a term used by radio and TV announcers. The running back uses his strong legs and instincts to gain as many yards as possible. He must secure the ball tightly since hits are hard and can cause fumbles (loose balls) and defenders will try to pull it free. Running backs called by any other name—*tailbacks, halfbacks, wingbacks, scat backs*—are still running backs. The versatility of the running back is further tested when he must throw the ball, and when he's lined up in a wildcat formation, takes the direct snap, and must make the decision to run or throw.

John Riggins, a durable back of the 20th century — Schulte Sports Marketing and PR--CC-BY-SA 4.0

FB—fullback: The fullback has had a change of roles in the modern era of the Super Bowl. In the past, he was the featured runner. Cleveland Browns fullback Jim Brown, fast and durable, set many rushing records. The present "stocky build" of a fullback (under six foot and broad shoulders) makes him ideal for short-yardage situations. His principal role in modern times is to block.

> Trivia: In 1999, fullback Sam Gash of the Buffalo Bills was named to the NFL's All-Pro team for the best player at that position without any touches.

Uniforms

The football uniform is designed for safety but it also serves to identify the team. People recognize a team by its colors and style, such as the typeface (font) of the numerals and stripes on the sleeve of the jersey. The numerals on the front and back help fans, coaches, officials, and sportswriters identify each player. Pro leagues require the player's name on the back of the jersey but this is optional in high school and college. Typically, the visiting ("away") team wears a white jersey while the home team wears colors.

Leagues maintain a dress code, meaning that players are expected to keep their shirttails inside their pants. If a shirt is untucked as a result of a play, that player is expected to tuck it inside his pants. The NFL can fine a player who does not comply. Football players are not allowed to display personal or commercial messages or emblems other than their team's on their uniforms.

Under the jersey is one apparatus that separates football from other sports—shoulder pads. Besides making a football player look larger and perhaps more ferocious, their practical purpose is to protect the shoulder and rib areas from injury. (All padding, of course, is designed to protect a player's muscles, bones, and internal organs.)

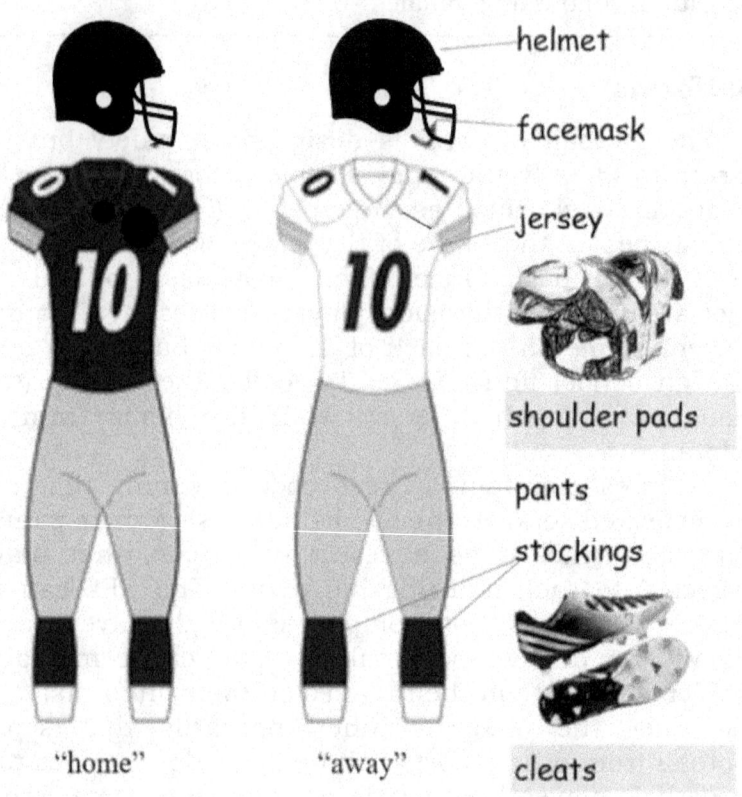

Images: CC-BY-SA (Wiki); diagram: author

To keep things interesting, the NFL occasionally allows member teams to use "color rush"—very bright colors that make the team appear to radiate cosmic energy. While some college teams are traditional and maintain the white-away/color-at-home formula, others whimsically toy with the colors and style of the uniform, including the helmet, so often that it can make team identification difficult whether at home or on the road. Some schools are even known to depart from the traditional appearance and have uniforms that resemble those from roller derby, an indoor contact sport on roller skates.

Once a season, college and professional teams wear "throwback" uniforms, which show the team's look at a designated time in the club's history. Teams may also adapt their uniforms to reflect an occasion, such as pink accessories (shoes, socks, etc.) for breast cancer awareness month and olive green for armed forces Veteran's Day in November.

The original days of football were played without head protection. However, there was a clear need in this rough game to protect players from head injuries. Early helmets were made of leather. Those in use today are made of polycarbonate (a hard, unbreakable plastic) with padding on the inside to cushion the head. It wasn't until the 1950s that face masks were introduced and today they are standard in all levels of football. Linemen are most apt to have many grids (latticed bars) guarding their faces whereas the quarterback, receivers, and kickers prefer fewer such obstacles to their ability to see the ball in flight. Chin straps hold the helmet on. Mouthpieces are additional protection.

A football player's pants are made of strong material that can be stretched, which allows players to move freely. Under the pants is padding that protects the knees, thighs, and hips. The pants come to just below the knee where they meet the stockings (another word for socks). Rules state that they must extend up to the bottom of the pants. While many pants can be traditional with stripes on the sides, modern designs, which include entire uniforms, may look like graphics from *Star Wars*.

Players have choices for footwear, called cleats. On grass fields under normal conditions, they may wear cleats that dig into the ground, but they may choose cleats with longer spikes to enable better traction on wet surfaces. Rubber soles are the main choice for gripping artificial surfaces.

The collage on the next page depicts how the uniform has developed over the years, from the introduction of football in North America to the mid-1960s.

Footballogy: Elements of American Football for Non-Native Speakers of English

Clockwise from top left: John Heisman (1891), player/coach and namesake for the Heisman Trophy, college football's most prestigious award; the first armor—the nose guard (1892); the first powerhouse college football team, Yale University (1882); Nile Kinnick (1936), Iowa halfback and Heisman Trophy winner; Duke Slater, NFL's Rock Island Independents (1925); Bobby Layne (1955), the last NFL player to go without a facemask; Johnny Unitas (1966), quarterback, Baltimore (Indianapolis) Colts. (Nile Kinnick image courtesy of Jon Baldwin, FineArtAmerica.com; remainder CC-BY-SA and/or public domain.)

Footballogy: Elements of American Football for Non-Native Speakers of English

Offensive Formations

After offenses break a huddle, they approach the line of scrimmage, where they will present a "look" or formation. There are many formations but we will discuss just a few. Most other formations are based on these. Essentially, formations are either for running or passing situations for short yardage. The side the tight end is on is the strong side due to the unbalanced offensive line.

> *Footballogy* presents just a few of the multiple formations we'll see at a football game. The important thing to remember is that after the team huddles, it approaches the line of scrimmage where the ball will be put in play (hiked) by the center. Knowing formations can give us a clue as to what kind of play is about to occur. That's why football has been called a "chess match." The defense must adjust to the play it anticipates based on the formation. Will it be a pass play? If so, long, medium, or short? A running play? If so, what kind? There are many to choose from in the playbook.

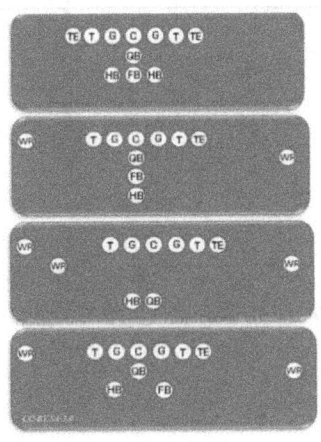

Source: Wiki CC-SA-BY-3.0

"T" formation (top photo)
Dating back to 1892 and invented by Walter Camp, this is the standard formation on which all other formations are based. It consists of three running backs lined up abreast about five yards behind the quarterback, forming the shape of a T. At the ends of the offensive line are a wide receiver and a tight end. If two tight ends are used, it's called the "Power T," which means a short-yardage situation and a rush (run) from one of the backs lined up behind the quarterback, who is "under center."

Another variation is the "Split T," where the linemen put more space between each other, which forces the defense to adjust and can create gaps or holes at the line of scrimmage for the backs.

"I" formation (second-from-top graphic)
The "I" consists of two backs—the powerfully built fullback and the quick-footed halfback (also called *tailback*, *setback*, or *I back*)—lined up vertically behind the quarterback. A variation has the fullback set slightly to the weak side or the strong side, depending on which side the tight end lines up. The "Power I," for short-yardage running plays, consists of two fullbacks and two tight ends for additional blocking.

Shotgun (second-from-bottom graphic)
The quarterback lines up about five yards behind the center. This gives the quarterback a better view of the defense and the field, and more time to get the pass off (to throw the ball). Expect this to be a passing situation although the team may, on occasion, surprise with a run.

Pro-set (bottom graphic)
This is like the "I" formations except the two backs are split behind the quarterback. This creation, which may use a third wide receiver instead of a tight end, is favored by "pass-happy offenses"—those that like to pass a lot. It was popularized in the 1980s by the San Diego Chargers and the San Francisco 49ers, whose fabled West Coast Offense challenged defenses.

Other Important Formations

Empty backfield
No backs behind the quarterback can signify desperation for the offense to obtain a quick score or at least long yardage to make a first down. (An obvious passing situation, the defense, accordingly, will adjust its defensive alignment and strategy.)

Goal line
In addition to the strong interior offensive linemen, bigger skills players like extra tight ends or a fullback are in to block for a short-yardage situation (about one yard), or for one of them to carry the ball.

Pistol
A variation of the shotgun except the quarterback moves closer to the center. He has a better option for passing the ball, handing it off, or running with it himself.

Punt
The line-up has a concave appearance with an extra set of blockers between the line and punter to prevent defensive players from blocking the punt.

Spread
Almost strictly a pass formation popular in the so-called "run-and-shoot" offenses, it utilizes four wide receivers and no tight ends.

Victory/kneel-down formation
The "feel good" for the team that's winning. At the end of the game, the team with the lead needs to run time off the clock, and since the opponent is out of timeouts, the ball is hiked to the quarterback, who kneels while the clock keeps running. All players are bunched close together to prevent a defensive player from getting across and knocking the ball loose.

Wildcat
The ball is hiked directly to a running back or receiver lined up in the backfield. He may choose to run with it or pass it. It is not uncommon for him to pass it to a quarterback who had lined up as a receiver.

Wishbone
Not as common as it once was, it can still be seen in high school and college on a run-pass option play. This is used when the quarterback is more of an athlete who can run as well as or better than he can pass. Three running backs line up in a wedge (looks like the letter "V" behind the quarterback).

Types of Plays by the Offense

A play begins once the ball, whistled ready by the official, is either hiked or free-kicked (a kickoff). The play does not stop until the official blows his whistle indicating that the play is dead (finished). That occurs when the player in possession of the ball is down. In the NFL and CFL, this is when the ballplayer's knee touches the ground after he is touched by a defender. However, in college, he is considered down—and the ball dead—when the ball carrier's knee hits the ground whether or not he was touched by a defender. This also happens when the carrier steps across the sidelines, out of bounds. A third way for the play to be over is when the pass does not connect with a receiver and it falls to the ground. In all instances, the officials blow their whistles and set the ball on the ground where the next play will begin.

Rush

A rushing play is another name for running with the ball. Most of this is done by a running back but sometimes the quarterback will keep the ball and run, or a receiver takes the ball. Listen for announcers to state these plays during a game. When you're at a game, with or without your binoculars, see if you can identify these plays and predict what will happen once the ball is snapped.

Bootleg
The quarterback fakes a handoff and keeps it himself, running in the opposite direction from the running back. A variation is the *naked bootleg*. If the defense buys the fake, the QB is on his own, running horizontally, without blockers, before turning upfield.

Counter
The runner and his linemen start to go one way, then the runner heads, or counters, the other way. This play, variously called *misdirection*, gets defenders to go in the direction it appears the play is headed.

Draw
The offensive line drops into pass-block position but the quarterback slips (hands) the ball to the running back.

End-around
A wide receiver heads toward the backfield the moment the ball is snapped and gets the ball from the quarterback. He usually runs with it. If he spots an uncovered (open) receiver, he may throw it.

Off Tackle
The running back hits the line between a guard and tackle. Variation: A *quick-hitter* occurs after a short quarterback count and the snap of the ball.

Pitch out (toss)
A running back takes the ball tossed a few yards to him from the quarterback.

> **Over the top**—Look for this on short-yardage touchdown attempts. Inches from the end zone, "fourth and goal" or whatever the down count is, the runner leaps over the blockers and defenders and lands on the pile for the score—or maybe not!

Quarterback sneak
In a very short distance situation (4th and a yard or less), the quarterback calls his own number and relies on the push of the offensive line to enable him to achieve the distance needed.

Reverse
This can be an exciting play due to the element of surprise. It looks like a running play at first but before hitting the line of scrimmage in one direction, the running back hands off to a wide receiver running across the backfield in the other direction. The defense was turning toward the side the running back was running toward, and now must adjust the other way. When successful, such a play can result in a big gain of yardage.

RPO (Run-Pass Option)
The quarterback can decide to give the ball to a running back, pass it, or keep it himself.

Sweep
Keep an eye on the offensive line, which pulls back from the line of scrimmage and runs horizontally before turning downfield to lead the interference (blocking). This play was made famous by the Green Bay Packers in the 1960s.

Trap
The ball carrier runs between the guard and the tackle.

Up the middle ("up the gut")
A basic run, the quarterback hands off to the running back, who goes up the middle between the center and a guard. Most often used in short-yardage or goal-line circumstances.

Pass

There are many kinds of pass plays in a game. In the huddle, the quarterback signals the kind of routes or patterns his receivers will run. This can be for running backs too, who may be the design of a pass play.

Flag
Also called a "corner route," this is like the deep post except that where the receiver angles in toward the center of the field, he angles slightly *out* toward the sideline.

Flea-flicker
Most teams have gadget or trick plays in the playbook. The flea-flicker is the most common. The quarterback hands off to a running back, who then tosses it back to the quarterback who then launches (usually) a long pass.

Go
Also called a "fly pattern," it sends usually the fastest receiver (called a "deep threat") to go as far as he can.

Ideally, he is so fast and the quarterback has a strong and accurate arm so he alone is waiting for the ball.

Hail Mary
A play named after a Catholic prayer to suggest that only a miracle can save the team from defeat (last play of the game, team trailing, all receivers to the goal line to receive a last desperation pass, etc.). This instance in the end zone is called "jump ball," where receivers try to bring the ball in for a completion while defenders try to knock it away.

Hook
Also called a "hitch," a receiver runs down the field a fixed number of yards, stops, and turns back to face the quarterback. The tactic is that the defender cannot react to such an abrupt change.

In
This is essentially the mirror opposite of "out route." It can be a useful strategy by taking low-risk pass plays to control the clock and maintain possession in a game where the opponent features an explosive offense (the best defense is a good offense that keeps them off the field).

Lateral
The pass, in a trajectory that is not forward, is the only instance where a passer doesn't need to be behind the line of scrimmage. There are two dangers, however: If the officials claim the movement of the ball was forward, there is a penalty. Biggest of all, unlike an incomplete pass where the ball is dead when it hits the ground, a lateral not completed is a live ball, and like a fumble, it can be recovered and advanced by the opposition (as well as by the team on offense).

Out
An "out route" or a "possession route" is where a receiver darts just a few yards downfield and makes a 90-degree turn toward the sideline. For this to work correctly, the passer must make the same read on the defense as the

receiver. (When players do things in unison like this, it's called being "on the same page.")

Play action
This can be a very exciting play. After the quarterback takes the snap, he fakes a handoff but drops, hoping to fool the defense to commit to defending the run. While the running back pretends to take a handoff, the quarterback, trying to hide the ball from the defense, eyes an open receiver. The running back continues to move upfield as if he has the ball. Even the offensive line pretends to run a block before shifting into pass protection. This play works well for teams that have established a good running attack. Otherwise, no one on the defense is fooled.

Post
There are two kinds of post routes. First, a wide receiver heads down the field about 10-15 yards before he angles toward the center of the field. The second, a deep post, can be up to 40 yards beyond the line of scrimmage.

Screen pass
This pass is thrown to a receiver, normally a running back, who is still behind the line of scrimmage. The linemen have dropped back into pass coverage and the running back may pretend to be a blocker, but he isn't. The ball needs to travel just a few yards to him. A "bubble screen" is when three receivers are close together on one side of the line after the play has begun. The ball is quickly thrown to one while the two in front of him become blockers.

Shovel pass
Typically, a very short forward pass thrown underhand or sidearm.

Slant
A receiver takes a couple of steps beyond the line of scrimmage and cuts across the field behind the linebackers and in front of the safeties. Receivers sustain some of the hardest hits in a football game on this type of play.

Swing
Also known as the "flat route" because a designated area of the field a few yards beyond the line of scrimmage and between the hash marks is known as "the flats." When it is vacated due to the movement of other players on offense and defense, running backs make ideal targets for these short passes. They begin the play by running toward the sidelines, then turn downfield and look for the pass.

 I. True/false

1. ___ Reserves are not backups.
2. ___ A depth chart lists the players at each position.
3. ___ The depth chart contains secret plays.
4. ___ Inactives are on the practice squad.
5. ___ As a rule, teams do better at home games.
6. ___ Individual effort is more important than teamwork.
7. ___ Bench strength is a measure of the quality of the reserves.
8. ___ Players suit up in the locker room.
9. ___ A win away from home is said to be "on the road."
10. ___ A team has 11 starters on the field at a time.

II. Choose the correct answer

1. NOT a reserve
   a. second-stringer
   b. backup
   c. starter
   d. benchwarmer

2. Number of players on each team on the field
   a. 22
   b. 11
   c. 9
   d. 6

3. 4-3 scheme uses ___ linebackers
   a. 4
   b. 3
   c. 2
   d. 0

4. Where players discuss the next play
   - a. huddle
   - b. sideline
   - c. locker room
   - d. line of scrimmage

5. Unsung heroes
   - a. offensive line
   - b. seldom touch the ball
   - c. rarely score points
   - d. all are correct

6. Good for short passes to keep drives alive (making first downs)
   - a. soft hands
   - b. possession receivers
   - c. tight ends
   - d. swing pass

7. He calls out signals to the offense
   - a. head coach
   - b. center
   - c. quarterback
   - d. offensive coordinator

8. A formation that is most typical
   - a. shotgun
   - b. "I"
   - c. "T"
   - d. wildcat

9. Quarterback runs the ball up the middle in short-yardage situation
   - a. sneak
   - b. over the top
   - c. RPO
   - d. flea-flicker

10. Circle the rushing plays in the following list:

draw	bootleg	flea-flicker
"go"	end-around	Hail Mary
trap	screen	play action
post	off-tackle	lateral
hook	reverse	out

Legend of the Game
Iron Man — "Double O for Zero Misses in 15 Years"

Word Preview

durability	undersized	calling	mystique
fit (right) in	remarkably	nagged	tough

*Jim OTTO—
CCO Public Domain*

"If someone came from another planet and wanted to know what a football player looked like, I'd show him Jim Otto," said John Madden, a retired NFL coach (whose name is on Madden Football, a popular electronic football game).

There's a reason Jim Otto left a legacy of "Iron Man." It's a rough game, after all, so whatever its meaning, it must include durability. That was Jim Otto, Number 00, who never missed a game for the Oakland Raiders in 15 seasons, from 1960-1974. The undersized center, not drafted by an NFL team, was to find his calling in the American Football League in Oakland, California. Still, about 10 years before the AFL and NFL merger, this team (which named itself the Raiders) was to earn its reputation, the *Raider Mystique,* by taking in players deemed misfits and outcasts much like the notorious motorcycle gang Hell's Angels, who called Oakland home. Jim Otto, not wanted by the NFL, fit right in.

Double Zero was to make the Oakland Raiders his one-and-only team for his 15-year career in which he was named an all-star 15 times. Remarkably, "Double O" played in 308 consecutive games despite enduring numerous injuries and surgeries that have nagged him to this day. It's no small wonder that John Madden, one of his coaches, said in the foreword to the book *Jim Otto: The Pain of Glory* (Sports Publishing, 2012) that Mr. Otto was the best center who ever played the game. "If you think of what a football player should be—tough, dedicated, an iron man—that would be Jim Otto," Mr. Madden said.

 I. Choose the correct word from the word preview list.

1. A product that can stand years of abuse has _____.

2. The three-year-old child surprises everyone. _____, he can write his name.

3. Only a person who is _____ and durable can play football for a long time.

4. There are opportunities for small or _____ people to play.

5. He earned lots of money as a businessperson but found his _____ as a teacher.

6. She learned English in her country so she _____ when she came to the USA.

7. The teacher _____ the pupils to do their homework on time.

8. There's a _____ about the ancient Mayans, Aztecs, and Incas that attracts me.

"The Pick"

Like any playoff game, one team goes on and the other has a long winter to think about "what if" and "next year." On this zero-degree day, January 4, 1981, it was the Oakland Raiders who moved ahead to the AFC championship at the expense of the Cleveland Browns.

With 44 ticks left on the clock, the Browns controlled their destiny. Thirteen yards separated them from the Oakland end zone. Quarterback Brian Sipe had engineered a faultless drive that nearly spanned the distance of the field after a Raider turnover-on-downs at the Browns' 15. Trailing 14-12, the Browns didn't need a touchdown. Just a field goal would do. But on this day, considering that the Browns had already missed two field goals and an extra point thanks to the swirling wind off Lake Erie, why take a chance? A miss would cost them the game.

The Browns, on second down, called a play coded "Red Right 88." As is often the case, when a play works, it's labeled genius but when it blows up, it can bring dishonor. Which was this? Believing his primary target to be covered, Sipe saw future Hall of Fame tight end Ozzie Newsome streaking across the end zone. What he didn't see—or who—was a highly capable, sure-handed safety by the name of Mike Davis. As he tumbled to the frozen, bone-jarring turf, Davis made the game-saving pick that defined his career. And it propelled the Raiders, whose playoff life continued on to win Super Bowl XV.

If you see a defense with dirt and mud on their backs, they've had a bad day.
— John Madden, NFL coach & media analyst

CHAPTER V

The Team: The Defense & Special Teams

The silhouette [sil-oo-et] below is a football player on defense. What gives us this idea? What position might he play?

Illustration by Unknown author (CA-BY-SA)

Newton's Law says that for every action there's an equal and opposite reaction. Was Newton talking about football? Hardly. But think of how uninteresting a game this would be if a team could score every time with ease! A game without conflict—like life without obstacles to goals—would bore audiences. Now let's look at the men who make the offense earn their points.

Note that the positions listed are general. The exact names may differ from team to team depending on the defensive scheme and the plan or team preferences, where the terminology changes (although the duties remain similar).

Defensive Schemes

The two basic designs are **3-4** and **4-3**, used primarily on first and second downs, but they can change with various circumstances. A **4-3 defense**, the traditional package, consists of four down-linemen and three linebackers (plus the other positions in the defensive backfield up to 11 personnel on the field). The second basic defensive alignment is the **3-4 defense**, three down-linemen and four linebackers. A down-lineman is defined as anyone who begins play with one or both hands on the ground. When it's one hand, we will often hear it called a "three-point stance." Defensive linemen are normally the tallest and biggest players.

The Front

DT—defensive tackle

In a 4-3 defense, this is two players who line up on the inside of the defensive line. Their job is to stop the running back, to apply pressure to the quarterback or to disrupt the offensive line for the linebackers to stop the play. Generally, their jobs are to overcome offensive blocking and to meet in the backfield, where they combine to tackle the quarterback or ball carrier.

NT—nose tackle
Also known as the "nose guard" (NG), in the 3-4 scheme, he forms the middle of the defensive line, directly opposite the center on offense (hence, "nose").

DE—defensive end
Also called the "edge rusher," he lines up on the outside of the defensive line (on the edge), whether 3-4 or 4-3. Size and quickness make him ideally suited to get off at the snap of the ball and not let the ball carrier get outside. His height and reach (long arms) give him an advantage in obstructing the quarterback's view and knocking down passes, even occasionally intercepting one.

LB—linebacker
These players carry a reputation as the meanest, most terrorizing group on the team. In other words, they take no prisoners. Normally a bit smaller than the defensive linemen they are lined up behind (hence, "backers"), they are strong, fast, and versatile to stop the run, get after the quarterback or drop into pass coverage, break up passes, and make tackles.

    4-3: Two outside linebackers (OLB) and a middle linebacker (MLB). Teams may designate the one lined up opposite the tight end as the "strong-side linebacker," whereas the one not opposing the tight end is the "weak-side linebacker."

    3-4: Two inside linebackers (ILB) and two outside linebackers.

The Defensive Backfield

Also called the *secondary*, four team members most often comprise this unit. Generically, each player is called a defensive back (DB).

S—safety
The players who line up the deepest in the secondary — the last line of defense. There are free safeties and strong

safeties, and they must defend the deep pass and the run. The **free safety** defends the middle of the field and seldom has man-to-man duties. The **strong safety** lines up on the same side as the opposing team's tight end. Typically, a strong-side safety is more physical than the free safety and is used against the run or on a safety blitz, where they charge the quarterback to sack him, which means he is tackled behind the line of scrimmage, or to force him into a mistake like hurrying a throw that is incomplete or intercepted. Aside from kickers, these positions at the pro level are known to have players who weigh less than 200 pounds.

CB—cornerback
Among the lightest and fastest players on the field, *corners*, as they are also called, line up on the outer parts of the playing field generally opposite the offensive receivers. Besides speed, this position demands special talent such as the agility to be able to backpedal, or run backward, and keep pace with the wide receiver; or to cover an area of the field in a beat—fast as lightning—if it's zone coverage.

Special Teams

Specialists
These are players with one specific duty—they enter the game in special circumstances for one play, such as an extra point, field goal attempt, a kickoff, or punts.

Author unknown CC BY-NC-ND

Punter
On the fourth down and too far for a field goal attempt, the punter lines up 15 yards from the line of scrimmage. He grabs the hiked ball with both hands, takes a step, and impacts the ball with his foot, sending it, ideally on an end-over-end trajectory to the opposite end of the field, forcing the other team to start their drive close to its own goal. On fourth down and too long for a field goal attempt, the offense

kicks the football to the other team to take possession. The punter lines up about 15 yards behind the line of scrimmage. After the ball is hiked to him, he takes a couple of steps with the ball in hand and plants his foot into the ball.

Long snapper (LS)
His role is to hike (snap) the ball, keeping it barely above the ground for an eight-yard journey to a holder, who places the ball down for a field goal attempt. On punts, he snaps the ball in a 15-yard arc to the punter (sometimes less if the team is backed up close to its own end zone). Any error can mean disaster.

Holder (H)
The holder places the ball upright, laces out (away from the kicker) for field goals and PAT attempts. He puts the football on the ground in the pros and college but on a kicking tee in high school. This person is often a backup quarterback or the punter.

Placekicker (PK)
The placekicker kicks the ball after it has been set down by the holder. It can be a PAT (extra point) or a field-goal attempt. Most kickers kick "soccer style," meaning they approach the ball from an angle, not straight.

Punt returner (PR)
This is often a backup wide receiver whose speed and agility give him the ability to change directions and elude tacklers.

Kick returner (KR)
The kick returner has similar assets to the punt returner, only normally he is taller and longer-legged, like track runners who can turn on the speed when needed.

Complete Chart of Player Positions

OFFENSE		DEFENSE		SPECIAL TEAMS	
QB	quarterback	DE	defensive end	K	kicker
RB	running back	DT	defensive tackle	PK	placekicker
HB	halfback	DL	defensive lineman	P	punter
FB	fullback	NT	nose tackle	KR	kick returner
WR	wide receiver	LB	linebacker	PR	punt returner
TE	tight end	ILB	inside linebacker	H	holder
OL	offensive lineman	MLB	middle linebacker	P/H	punter/holder
RT	right tackle	OLB	outside linebacker	LS	long snapper
RG	right guard	DB	defensive back		
C	center	SS	strong safety		
LG	left guard	FS	free safety		
LT	left tackle	S	safety		
G	guard	CB	corner back		
T	Tackle				

> When announcers hail someone as a *"journeyman"* (a term borrowed from the world of work, meaning an experienced worker who shows up every day and works hard) they mean a veteran of the game, not a star.

Positions on a Team

Use the clues for positions on a team for the following Crossword

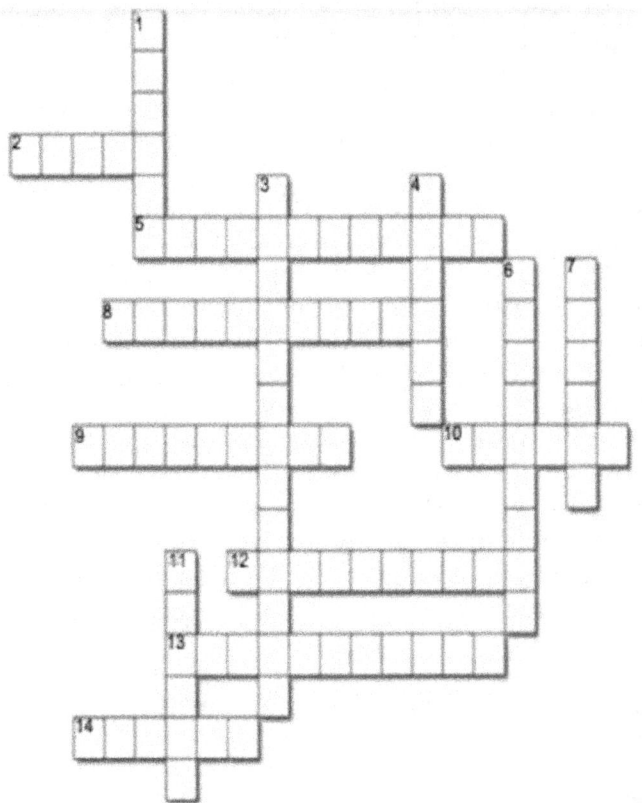

ACROSS
2. on the offensive line
5. rushes/runs with ball (2 words)
8. "field general"; calls the plays
9. big for blocking; good hands for receiving
10. on 4th down, kicks the ball away
12. mean, on defense; in back of line
13. in 3-4 defense, in middle of line
14. on defense, nor a corner but a ___

DOWN
1. places the ball for extra points
3. quick, runs fast, good hands for catching long or short passes
4. big guy, stands outside on offensive interior line
6. another name for defensive backfield
7. uses foot for extra points & field goals
11. in the middle of it all, over the ball

Defensive Styles & Coverages

Rush describes "pass rush" or "rush the passer" by putting pressure on the quarterback to either tackle him for a loss (a statistical category called a "sack"), make him hurry his throw for an incompletion, or better yet, an interception. Big linemen try to get their hands in the air to prevent the quarterback from seeing the field or his receivers. Occasionally, one will knock down a pass, or as announcers say, *he batted (or swatted) away a pass.*

Stunts are part of a tactic to confuse offensive linemen and get them to focus on the stunt rather than their blocking assignment, which may leave another defensive player unguarded. Stunts take many forms but watch for movement of the defensive linemen and linebackers before the snap. For instance, a linebacker who positioned himself on the line as if to blitz (below) gets the offense to change the play call, then suddenly drops off into pass coverage.

A **blitz** occurs when the defense sends nondefensive-line personnel (linebackers or defensive backs) to rush the quarterback. When safeties do it, it's a safety blitz but there is a danger: receivers can be uncovered for an easy reception.

Coverages have to do with defending passes.

Packages

This is language used for defensive schemes that depend on the circumstance and time left in the game. We will hear announces describe the coverage they see on the field.

Dime
Uses six defensive backs when the opponent faces a very long-yardage passing situation.

Goal line
Use of the big guys to stuff the line in a short-yardage situation at the goal line.

Man-to-man
Each defensive back has the responsibility of one offensive player. Teams with superior defensive backs have more confidence to use this coverage.

Nickel
Five defensive backs (in place of a linebacker) used in anticipated passing situations.

Prevent
Late in the game, a team with a lead gives the offense a cushion where they yield and keep the player inbounds so that he cannot stop the clock. The idea of the defense is to keep the play in front to not allow ("prevent") a long touchdown.

Tampa 2 (and Tampa 3)
Developed by THE Tampa Bay Buccaneers, it requires speed, even by the big linemen, to focus on getting to the ball and hitting hard to cause turnovers.

Zone defense
Linebackers and backfield are assigned an area to cover. A defensive player can observe the quarterback and anticipate the target of the pass. (A reason that Patrick Mahones, Kansas City Chiefs' quarterback, was so successful in his 50-touchdown pass season in 2018 was that he looked in the opposite direction of where the throw went.) Zone coverages are physically demanding as this is when tremendous collisions—and injuries—are likely.

A System of Numbers

When we attend an NFL game, chances are we'll purchase a copy of *Gameday*. In addition to interesting articles, the magazine lists the players in the game and each player's height, weight, age, birthplace, and college attended. An abbreviation for the position he plays is used. One thing to consider is that while starters perform one position, reserves will often see action on special teams. A wide receiver (WR) might see duty as a punt returner, or PR, for instance. Thus, *Gameday* lists him as WR/PR. The punter (P) could be the holder (H) on place kicks, and thus be designated P/H. Teams may use different designations such as "OL" to note a player on the offensive line, but "RG" to note a player at right guard, or just "G" for guard, which can mean he's flexible enough to play either the left or the right side.

On defense, teams use different schemes—3-4 or 4-3, as noted—which determine the names of positions. In a 3-4, "NT" means nose tackle for the man lined up opposite the center, but another team might designate "NG" for nose guard (similar duties) instead of defensive tackle. (A rose by any other name still smells the same.) Part of the fun with *Gameday* is discovering what college produced the player, his position, height, weight, and game statistics.

Footballogy: Elements of American Football for Non-Native Speakers of English

Positions and Duties

Partial roster

#	NAME	POS.	HT.	WT.	AGE	EXP.	COLLEGE
11	Austin, Tavon	WR	5-8	179	27	5	West Virginia
26	Barron, Mark	LB	6-2	225	28	6	Alabama
98	Barwin, Connor	OLB	6-4	255	31	9	Cincinnati
66	Blythe, Austin	C	6-3	300	25	2	Iowa
90	Brockers, Michael	DT	6-5	302	27	6	LSU
68	Brown, Jamon	G	6-4	330	24	3	Louisville
34	Brown, Malcolm	RB	5-11	227	24	2	Texas
86	Carrier, Derek	TE	6-4	244	27	5	Beloit
41	Christian, Marqui	DB	5-11	200	23	2	Midwestern State
10	Cooper, Pharoh	WR	5-11	207	22	2	South Carolina
24	Countess, Blake	DB	5-10	185	24	2	Auburn
33	Davis, Justin	RB	6-1	198	22	R	Southern California
99	Donald, Aaron	DT	6-1	280	26	4	Pittsburgh
25	Dunbar, Lance	RB	5-8	187	27	6	North Texas
50	Ebukam, Samson	LB	6-3	240	22	R	Eastern Washington
59	Edebali, Kasim	LB	6-2	253	28	4	Boston College
81	Everett, Gerald	TE	6-3	245	23	R	South Alabama
5	Ficken, Sam	K	6-1	191	25	0	Penn State
97	Fox, Morgan	DE	6-3	275	23	2	Colorado State-Pueblo
16	Goff, Jared	QB	6-4	223	23	2	California
30	Gurley II, Todd	RB	6-1	227	23	3	Georgia
54	Hager, Bryce	LB	6-1	237	25	3	Baylor
79	Havenstein, Rob	T	6-8	328	25	3	Wisconsin
6	Hekker, Johnny	P	6-5	241	27	6	Oregon State
89	Higbee, Tyler	TE	6-6	257	24	2	Western Kentucky
32	Hill, Troy	CB	5-11	184	26	3	Oregon
43	Johnson III, John	S	6-1	204	22	R	Boston College

Permission: footballdb.com

Footballogy: Elements of American Football for Non-Native Speakers of English

 Interpreting the Program. Circle the best answer

1. Which player is <u>not</u> a running back?
   a. Tyler Higbee   b. Lance Dunbar
   c. Justin Davis   d. Malcolm Brown

2. Excluding the quarterback, how many eligible receivers are on this roster?
   a. 2   b. 3   c. 4   d. 9

3. Which player is a product of the University of Iowa?
   a. Jared Goff   b. Todd Gurley II
   c. Austin Blythe   d. Troy Hill

4. The signal caller?
   a. QB   b. Johnny Hekker
   c. Jared Goff   d. Sam Ficken

5. It's 4th down and long. A field goal is out of reach. Which position comes into the game?
   a. P   b. PK
   c. S   d. QB

6. Who on the roster would attempt a field goal?
   a. Davis   b. Ficken
   c. Brown   d. Hekker

7. How tall is the tallest player?
   a. Rob Havenstein   b. 330 lbs
   c. 6' 8"   d. 25

8. Which player is the lightest?
   a. 179 lbs.   b. Tavon Austin
   c. 328 lbs   d. Jamon Brown

9. Which veteran has the most experience?
   a. Michael Brokers   b. Morgan Fox
   c. Conner Barwin   d. Bryce Hager

10. Does the roster include any rookies?
    a. Yes—2   b. no
    c. Yes—3   d. Yes—4

A Game of Numbers

Every National Football League team conforms to a standard system of numerals for their uniforms. The time of Red Grange, a halfback who wore number 77 for the early Chicago Bears (1920s), is in the distant past when, for instance, quarterback Bobby Layne (Detroit Lions) had number 22 and Charlie Conerly (New York Giants) had number 42. Each would have to wear a number from 1-19 in the modern numbering system, begun in 1973, which requires that a player wear a number unique to his position.

A benefit is that this makes it easy for game officials, spectators, sportswriters, game announcers, and coaches to spot (or identify) a player's position by the number on his jersey. Another benefit is that some players, such as offensive linemen, are usually not eligible receivers. Officials keep an eye on this (more on this in the section on rules). Offensive linemen cannot go beyond the line of scrimmage on pass plays until after the ball is released. Rules for numbers do not apply to high schools or colleges. There can be so many people on a college roster that some numbers need to be duplicated.

Numbers provide a hint of a position. Can you guess what position this player might be? (Photo by Unknown Author, CC-BY-SA)

Retired Numbers

Some players have made special accomplishments, which includes off the field to society as well as to their team. Such players will be in the Pro Football Hall of Fame. A few of these will have their numbers retired by the team for which they made their biggest impact. Retirement means, of course, that the number will never be worn by another player.

Retiring a number is not a decision taken lightly, and the NFL discourages the practice for fear of the team running out of numbers. Some teams have very few retired numbers. Washington and Tampa Bay have one each and Oakland none. San Francisco, the New York Giants, and the Chicago Bears lead the league with retired numbers—9, 11, and 13 apiece respectively. A number can be brought out of retirement. The Denver Broncos brought Number 18 out of retirement so that Payton Manning, the stand-out quarterback traded by the Colts to the Broncos in 2012, could wear it.

Position	number
Quarterback, kicker, punter	1-19
Interior Linemen (center, guard, tackle)	50-79
Wide receiver	10-19, 80-89
Running back	20-49
Tight end	40-49, 80-89
Long snapper	40-99
Defensive linemen	50-99
Linebackers	50-59, 90-99
Defensive secondary (safeties & corners)	20-49

The numbers for long snappers have leeway (flexibility) because a long snapper can be a backup tight end or an interior lineman.

The Numbers

Complete the crossword below. Answers are found in the chart and the reading.

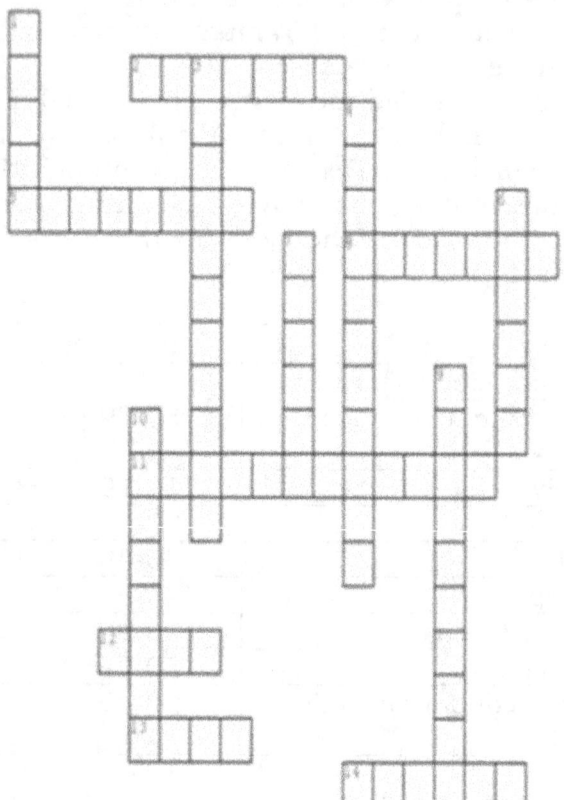

ACROSS
2. Who wears 50-79
5. Manning's number
8. A jersey number no longer used
11. hikes balls on punts
12. The Raiders' number of retired jerseys
13. With binoculars, she ___ players' numbers better.
14. Position on defense number 20-49

DOWN
1. Hall of Fame member who wore 22
3. highest jersey number (hyphenated)
4. On offense, wears 1-19
6. Long snappers don't have ___ for mistakes
7. Another name for jerseys
9. If he is not eligible to receive passes, then he is _____
10. US state of Number 77.

Legend of the Game
Dick "Night Train" Lane

holy terror	instilled	ferocity	intimidation
roamed	dumpster	sandlot	football
cringed	runaway	overshadow	squared off

In the days before the current number system, there was a defensive back—number 81—who instilled fear in wide receivers and running backs. Meet Richard "Night Train" Lane, who roamed the gridiron from 1952 to 1965. To opponents, Night Train was a holy terror. His style of play was one of ferocity, intimidation, and raw power. Known for his open-field tackling and cat-like reflexes, Lane's style included "ripping" a receiver down by his neck, a style responsible for the clothesline and facemask penalties of today.

Lane's journey to the football field began on April 16, 1928, in Austin, Texas. Born to a mother who was a prostitute and a father who was a pimp, he was found at about three months of age—left for dead in a dumpster—by Ella Lane, a widow with two children, who adopted him. While growing up, Lane took an interest in playing sandlot football with the neighborhood boys but his mother worried about his rough hobby and encouraged him to take up other interests. Eventually enlisting in the US Army, Lane served in the Korean Conflict.

After his service, in civilian life he found himself stuck in a dead-end, menial job. So, Lane sought other work. By

Dick "Night Train" Lane—a "gambler," they said, never afraid to take a risk on the field. (Public domain)

happenstance, he got a tryout with the Los Angeles Rams.

Initially, the Rams tried him as a wide receiver but soon realized his potential as a defensive back. In Lane's rookie season in 1952, he set a record, which still stands, for the most interceptions in a single season (14). That accomplishment is even more remarkable considering that the NFL played only a 12-game regular season, not the present-day 16. Lane also ranks 3rd all-time for career interceptions with 68, which is attributed to his gambling style of play. But it was Lane's ferocious tackling that is most memorable.

Receivers in the '50s and '60s could be forgiven if they cringed at the thought of facing the Night Train, whose nickname came from an R&B recording by the same name. The name stuck for good after a performance against Washington Redskins' running back Charles Justice, nicknamed "Choo Choo" (a casual term for a locomotive). Justice was said to run like a runaway train. But not that day: *"Night Train Derails Choo Choo,"* announced the news headlines.

The increased attention to Lane's rough style of play did not overshadow his ability to dominate games through skill and athletic agility. Legendary coach Vince Lombardi, whose Green Bay Packers squared off against Lane on many occasions, claimed him to be the best defensive back he'd ever seen. Dick "Night Train" Lane was inducted into the Pro Football Hall of Fame in 1974.

Teams Night Train Lane played for:

Los Angeles Rams 1952-53
Chicago Cardinals 1954-59
Detroit Lions 1960-65

Footballogy: Elements of American Football for Non-Native Speakers of English

 I. Vocabulary. Match the words from the reading in column A with column B.

A
1. ___instilled
2. ___roamed
3. ___a holy terror
4. ___ferocious
5. ___intimidation

6. ___dumpster
7. ___sandlot football
8. ___cringe
9. ___announced
10. ___runaway
11. ___squared off
12. ___overshadow

B
a. wander
b. place for garbage
c. one who makes trouble
d. played against
e. to dominate; be more important
f. "shrink" with fear
g. pressure; bullying
h. stated
i. out of control
j. vicious, mean
k. inspired; produced
l. informal game

II. Comprehension Circle your answer choice

1. Dick Lane played the most years for the Rams.
    T   F

2. "Holy terror" probably means Lane was feared.
    T   F

3. A player with "a gambling style" like Lane.
    a. doesn't take chances   b. has a bad habit
    c. visits Las Vegas   d. takes risks

4. What was the source of Dick Lane's nickname?
    a. an R & B tune b. Charles Justice
    d. a newspaper   e. Vince Lombardi

5. Charles Justice said Night Train was the best defensive back he'd ever seen.
    T   F

6. Which team did Lane play for the least?
   a. the Rams   b. the Lions
   c. the Cardinals   d. the Chicago Bears

7. Where does the illegal & dangerous clothesline tackle occur?
   a. the neck   b. the shoulder
   c. the knee   d. the head

8. "Night Train" is
   a. Choo Choo   b. an R & B song
   c. a locomotive d. a type of tackle

9. In Lane's career, he did not intercept many passes.
    T   F

10. Green Bay played Lane's teams more than once.
    T   F

III. Each sentence has one error (underlined) Correct it by writing the correction above the passage. The first one is done. (A clue follows each line; 6-10, however, you're on your own to decide.)

1. Dick "Night Train" Lane is <u>consider</u> *considered* to be one of the best all-time defensive backs. (passive)

2. Vince Lombardi proclaimed him to be the <u>more</u> ferocious back he'd ever seen. (superlative)

3. Lane <u>has played</u> for the Lions from 1960 to 1965. (Present perfect or past?)

4. <u>Lane's</u> ripping style of play was feared by opponents. (Is this plural or possessive?)

5. Choo Choo Justice, <u>who</u> team was the Redskins, played running back. (possessive)

6. <u>To facing</u> "Night Train" Lane made opponents fearful.

7. Players cringe at the thought of <u>play</u> against a ferocious running back.

8. Each and every Sunday, everyone should <u>playing</u> hard.

9. Gridders are football <u>player</u> playing plays played on a gridiron.

10. A team that <u>play</u> hard ought to win.

Injuries: Hard Realities of a Football Life

Beyond bumps and bruises, injuries are a way of life in the brutal world of American football. Lesser injuries might take a short period to heal, but greater ones can cause a player to miss several games or even the rest of the season. Sadly, injuries have even been known to be catastrophic. Darryl Stingley, a receiver with the Patriots, in 1978, became a quadriplegic (loss of control of arms and legs) after a vicious hit.

Though rare, high school and college players are reported to die each year as a result of their activities on the gridiron. Some parents hesitate to let their children participate in such fierce competition where concussions, or hits to the head, are a particular worry and can affect still-developing brains. But regardless of the level of play, head injuries can lead to loss of mental function and dementia. As a result, football in the USA and Canada has developed improved protective equipment, from padding to helmets, and changes to the rules to protect players from all types of injuries, especially to the spine, neck, and head.

All levels have implemented concussion protocols for how to deal with head trauma and to determine whether a player can return to action. The NFL uses two independent certified athletic trainers (ATC spotters) at every game, whose job is to spot possible injuries to the head and neck. They can stop the game and order an immediate evaluation in a medical tent along each sideline. In the days and weeks that follow, a player may not be activated until cleared by an independent medical professional, not the team itself.

Common Injuries

Concussions can result from a direct blow to the head or when a blow to the body makes the head move rapidly back and forth. Concussions, as noted, are serious and each is a threat to brain health. They are hard to diagnose, but a few common symptoms include:

- Amnesia
- Confusion
- Depression
- Dizziness
- Fatigue
- Headache
- Slurred speech

> **For Your Information**: We hear people in the sports world speak of CTE, which stands for chronic traumatic encephalopathy, a degenerative, or worsening, neurological disease caused by repeated head injuries. As a result, American football leagues, high school to the pros, have a concussion protocol, a system of strict oversight before a player injured by concussion can return to the playing field. He could miss a game or

Feet and ankles are flexible and stretch within limits during regular use. When the ligaments are stretched too far during an aggressive twist, roll, or turn of the foot, a sprain occurs. Rest, ice, compression, and elevation along with anti-inflammatory medications are usually all that is needed to treat a sprained ankle. Players should rest until the pain and swelling have resolved because playing on an ankle that has not completely healed can increase the likelihood of re-injury and chronic sprains.

Herniated discs have happened to some of the biggest names in the game. Spinal discs, situated down the spinal vertebrae, act as mini shock absorbers, or cushions, for the bones surrounding them. Repetitive motion or trauma can cause the disc to rupture, or herniate, which results in pain, numbness, or weakness in an extremity (arms or legs). Rest and ice along with muscle relaxers, anti-inflammatory medications, and steroid injections are commonly used to reduce the symptoms and promote healing. Surgery, in severe cases, has a good success rate in treating the problem.

Knees, which have a lot of moving parts, are commonly injured, particularly the anterior cruciate ligament (ACL).

This type of injury—a "torn ACL"—is a dreaded diagnosis, as it often ends the injured player's season.

Neck injuries can cause "burners" and "stingers"—unpleasant nerve sensations in the upper arm that spread from the shoulder to the hand.

Shoulder injuries especially hamper a quarterback's ability to throw the ball. However, all players can experience a shoulder injury, such as a joint sprain or dislocation, due to direct contact with another player or with the ground (like a receiver landing hard on his shoulder after making a catch).

Spinal cord contusions are like concussions of the spine. Such an injury can result in neurological problems from pain and weakness to paralysis. Clearly, players must stop playing for a good while so the injury can heal. In some cases, these injuries are career-ending.

Upper leg injuries, notably a hamstring injury, are among the most common muscle injuries—strains, pulls or tears. The hamstring, a group of three muscles, is used to bend the knee and extend the hip. It is especially prone to injury if a player is not warmed-up properly. Other common upper-leg injuries affect the quadriceps, in the front of the thigh. Depending on the severity, an upper-leg injury can take six to eight weeks to heal, causing a player to miss up to half of an NFL season.

> Idiom: "Hamstring" (irregular verb): to make ineffective; to cripple, disable, incapacitate. *The sturdy defense of the Crimson Tide* **hamstrung** *the Buckeyes.*

It's not about what you're capable of; it's about what you're willing to do.
— Mike Tomlin, Pittsburgh Steelers' head coach

CHAPTER VI

The Coaches

What would the football team be like without another kind of team? That's the coaches, whose roles include motivating and helping athletes reach their potential and plotting a winning game strategy. This chapter explores a few of the titles and duties of this important part of a team, whose performance is said to reflect the coaching.

The iconic image of coaching American football is synonymous with a chalkboard covered in X's and O's with various arrow lines showing routes for players to run. In truth, coaching is far more than that. Depending on the level—youth, high school, college or pro—coaches perform many roles and responsibilities that encourage the development of the players.

All levels of football have a head coach and assistant coaches. High school coaches do more fundamental teaching—blocking techniques, mechanics in passing and receiving—and deal with parents. On the other hand, college and pro coaches, led by a head coach, are more specialized, which means programs have a larger staff. Twenty or more coaches may comprise a coaching staff at the professional level. The head coach works long hours viewing video of opponents, holding meetings with players and assistants, and running practices. Pro head coaches get involved in personnel decisions as well. For example, they decide which players to select during the college draft and which free agents to sign. In addition, they decide what players make the final roster and which ones to trade.

The head coach is responsible for the performance of the other coaches, which means if a unit on his team is underperforming, the head coach has the unpleasant task of firing that coach. (Personal relationships are irrelevant to the business of producing a winning product on the field.) In a game, the head coach is the final authority on the play selection; however, he may designate play-calling to an assistant, namely a coordinator, the top assistant on either the offense or defense. As many as 20 or more coaches may comprise a team at the professional level.

Head Coach

The head coach works long hours viewing video of opponents, holding meetings with players and assistants, and supervising practices. Pro head coaches get involved in personnel decisions as well. For example, they help decide which players to select during the college draft (discussed in Chapter XV) and which free agents to sign. In addition, they decide what players make the final roster and which ones to trade.

The head coach is responsible for the performance of the other coaches, which means if a unit on his team is underperforming, the head coach has the unpleasant task of firing that coach. (Personal relationships are irrelevant to the business of producing a winning product on the field.) In a game, the head coach is the final authority on the play selection; however, he may designate play-calling to an assistant, namely a coordinator, the top assistant on either the offense or defense. In either case, the head coach gets most of the credit for winning and the blame for losing.

Offensive Coordinator

Like a symphony conductor, he brings together all components of the offense from the running to passing attacks. He may also design the plays to run, even for experienced quarterbacks. During the week between games, he works with the head coach to develop a game plan based on what his own team does best and the perceived strengths and weaknesses of the upcoming opposition. An offensive coordinator may be on the sidelines during the game or up high in the press box area, where he can get a broad picture of the action and player positioning on the field. He communicates his findings to the sidelines, where it gets to the players on the field.

Defensive Coordinator

This coach "conducts" the defense. He decides what schemes to run based on his team's strengths and the other's weaknesses. A major challenge is to develop schemes (plans) that will keep his team's weaknesses from being discovered or exploited by the opposition. Like an offensive coordinator, he looks to maximize the potential of the talent of his players. At game time, he too may be in the coaches' box above the stadium or on the sidelines.

Special Teams Coach

He oversees the players who come into the game under special circumstances—the kicker, punter, and players, mostly non-starters, involved in kickoffs, punts, field goals, and extra points. Whenever there is a kickoff or punt return for a touchdown, or a blocked punt or kick, the cameras turn to him on the sidelines, smiling—or the opposite, frowning, upset that the play went against his unit.

The following, called "position coaches," align their efforts with the respective coordinators. As the title suggests, each works with players at maximizing their skill at their positions. (Being a position coach is a path to becoming a coordinator.)

- Quarterbacks
- Offensive line
- Defensive line
- Secondary
- Linebackers
- Tight ends
- Running backs
- Strength & Conditioning

> **Quality control coach**: This is the way many coaches start out in the pros in Canada and the USA. Like a scientist in a laboratory, these members of the coaching staff spend hours analyzing future opponents' game films and dissect statistics and chart tendencies, which they share at team meetings.

Connectors

Sometimes "connectors" with different meanings can be used. This depends on what you, the writer, want to communicate. For example, "Some teams have just a few coaches; however, some have many." The connector "however" shows contrast. Compare: "Some teams have just a few coaches; otherwise, some have many. "Otherwise" shows a choice or an option.

A Partial list of sentence transition words/connectors—"subjunctive adverbs"

There are two methods for connecting two sentences (also called independent clauses) together: 1) Connect two clauses that show a relationship (the first clause is punctuated with a semicolon, followed by the second clause with its first word not capitalized) and 2) Two complete sentences, the capital letter to begin and punctuation (usually a period) at the end of each.

in addition also furthermore	A	**Addition/sequence** • We studied the game film; **in addition**, we practiced hard. • Some people are born with talent. **Also**, some skills cannot be taught.
therefore thus as a result Consequently	B	**Cause/effect (consequence of an action)** • The Lions needed to run time off the clock; **therefore**, the coach decided to keep the ball on the ground. • They planned well. **Thus**, they came away with a victory.
however by contrast on the other hand nevertheless on the contrary,	C	**Contrast** • Linemen are big and heavy; **by contrast**, some running backs weigh less than 200 pounds. • The Anteaters faced a team with a poor defense against the pass. **However**, they chose to run the ball.
otherwise	D	**Choice or warning** • We need to practice; **otherwise**, we might lose. • Exercise is important. **Otherwise**, our bodies get soft.
for example, for instance,	E	• Thomas runs fast; **for example**, he did 100 meters in 9.58 seconds. • The coach is blamed for the team's failure. **For instance**, Smith was fired after posting a 2-win season. .

Sentence/clause transitions: 1. Place the letter of the clause group (A, B, C, D, E) in the blanks. 2. Circle C or NC (C for capital on transition word or NC for no capital).

Ex: The head coach had a bad record; ____B____ team fired him.

        C   (NC)

1. A team has many coaches; ____only one can be the head coach.

        C   NC

2. A team can have just a few coaches. _____, one can have many.

        C   NC

3. Coaches shouldn't publicly criticize the officials. _____, those who do can be fined.

        C   NC

4. I need to do weight training; _____, I need to see the strength and conditioning coach.

        C   NC

5. A positions coach specializes in positions. _____, a quarterback coach works with quarterbacks.

        C   NC

6. A quality-control coach analyzes film. _____, he is concerned with statistics.

        C   NC

7. High school coaches work with younger athletes; _____, their role is a teacher.

        C   NC

8. Professional team coaching staffs are larger. _____, they are paid more.

               C   NC

9. A red flag is to challenge an official's call; _____, any coach can throw it.

               C   NC

10. The offensive coordinator wanted a passing play; _____, the head coach had other plans.

               C   NC

Extra Points

How a world-famous car got its name.
(Hint: A football coach did it!)

An urban legend is a story or anecdote enhanced with unconfirmed details and widely circulated as true. Does the story of how the Ford Mustang got its name fall into the category of an urban legend? You decide.

On September 28, 1963, Southern Methodist University, nicknamed the Mustangs, played the University of Michigan in Ann Arbor, Michigan. The hometown Wolverines were expected to win by a wide margin over the visitor from Dallas, Texas. Proximity to the Ford Motor Corporation in Detroit made it convenient for Ford employees, including executives, to attend the game. One important figure in attendance was Ford's Chairman of the Board, Lee Iacocca.

The Wolverines defeated the Mustangs but something about the Mustangs motivated Mr. Iacocca to visit the SMU locker room after the game. He told coach Hayden Fry that he admired the "pluckiness," or fighting spirit, of the Mustangs. It was here that he asked Coach Fry for his opinion about a new car named after the Mustangs. "It will be compact, quick, and agile, like your team," Iacocca said.

Although Ford's ad agency was believed to have already prepared Mustang-branded material before that game, the fact that Mr. Iacocca visited the SMU post-game locker room is uncontested. The conversation said to have taken place offers a feel-good, heartwarming story of how the Mustang got its name. It's the stuff of urban legends.

Great moments

"The Routs"

When a team wins by a lot of points, it's called a "rout" [răh´ōt]. Such lopsided scores normally reflect how one team dominates the other. What may not be obvious are the morals to be learned. The two tales that follow show how important it is to respect our enemies.

The first lesson involves the 1940 NFL Championship, the first national radio broadcast of an NFL title game. The Chicago Bears blew out the Washington Redskins 73-0. The margin of victory and the team touchdowns in a game (11), regular or post season, remain NFL records.

Here's the backstory: Just a few weeks before, the Bears had hosted the Redskins. Chicago lost a close one, 7-3, but Redskins' owner George Preston Marshall said something after the contest that angered the Bears. (It's not nice to make Bears angry!) He told reporters that the Bears were "quitters" and "cry babies." The 7-3 score turned into 73, all on the Bears' side, for the rematch. Things got so bad that in the second half, officials pleaded with George Halas (the Bears' owner and head coach) not to kick extra points.

Fifty-two football seasons later, the Dallas Cowboys took to the field in Super Bowl XXVII against the Buffalo Bills. The Cowboys' 52-17 triumph over the Buffalo Bills could have been worse if it hadn't been for an action that showed disrespect for the downtrodden opponent, whose massive turnovers led to five Cowboys touchdowns. Cowboys defensive end Leon Lett was about to return a turnover for a 64-yard score that would have given his team a 42-point lead. Indeed, scoring is a rarity for a defensive lineman and on pro football's biggest stage this was an opportunity of a lifetime. But instead of securing the ball and crossing the goal line, he began to showboat at about the 10-yard line. The Bills' Don Beebe caught up with the celebrating Lett and swatted away the football. This resulted in a touchback. It was the Bills' ball at the 20.

Individual commitment to a group effort—that is what makes a team work, a company work, a society work, a civilization work.
                —Vince Lombardi, Hall of Fame coach

CHAPTER VII

The Game

Americans like it when teams score a lot or "light up the board." This doesn't mean that once in a while Americans dislike a low-scoring game if it's because of good plays by the defense not because of the poor play of an offense. When a low-score win is recorded, it can be said to "win ugly" for the victor. For the loser, all losses are ugly. In this section, we will learn about scoring, who does it and how.

Game Capsule

The American football game, 60 minutes long, is divided into four quarters, each 15 minutes in length. There is a 10- to 15-minute intermission called "halftime" at the end of the second quarter. The actual game will occupy about three hours due to game clock stops (for example, when a player with the ball goes out of bounds or when there are injuries, timeouts, and incomplete pass plays).

Moments before the game, team captains meet with the chief official (the referee) at midfield. A coin toss determines who gets the ball first. One of the visiting team captains calls "heads" or "tails." If the team that wins the toss decides to receive the ball to open the game, the second half will begin with his team "kicking off."

The team kicking off (called the "kicking team") boots the ball to the opponent, called the "receiving team." Where the ball is spotted (placed) for kickoff depends on the level of competition. It's the 35-yard line of the kicking team's side of the field for the pros and colleges in the United States and Canada but the 40 for U.S. high school.

Kickoff. CC-BY-SA (Wikipedia)

After the team receives the kickoff, it goes on offense. Its objective, of course, is to score. The offensive team, which is comprised of 11 men, has an offensive line comprised of five of the biggest men on the team. The one in the middle, the center, passes (or "snaps") the ball backward through his legs to the quarterback (the team leader) who hands the ball off to a running back, passes it to an eligible receiver, or runs with it himself. The offensive line protects the quarterback on pass plays and blocks opposing players on running plays.

The offense gets four chances, called "downs," to move the ball forward at least 10 yards. For example, if on first down they move the ball five yards, it becomes the second down and five (yards to go). If the play on second down gets two yards, then it's third and three. Each time the ball is advanced at least 10 yards within its four downs, another first down is earned. The team gets four more chances to get at least 10 yards for another first down. Of course, a team may not need all its downs to get a first down. On any play, it might gain 12 or 36 yards—or the entire length of the field to the end zone for a score.

Each time the offense has the ball is called a "series." An offensive series can be short—just a few plays and little time off the game clock—or it can be several minutes long as well as in between. A three-and-out series means one series of four plays. The offense got the ball, couldn't advance 10 yards, so on its fourth down, they were forced to punt. Other times, a series will consist of 10, 12 or more plays and cover many yards, and perhaps will result in a score.

Some series take a lot of time off the clock, such as when a team runs for a few yards at a time (called the "ground game"). Sometimes a series, whether just one or two plays or several, ends abruptly when the defense intercepts a pass or picks up a loose ball or a fumble.

Teams have many ways to score, which can come by way of the defense or by kicking or receiving teams, as well as the offense.

Scoring Point Values

Touchdown -	6 points
Extra point conversion -	1 point
Two-point conversion -	2 points
Field goal -	3 points
Safety -	2 points

Hand signal for safety is different than pictured.

> ***To draw first blood***—The team that scores first is said to "draw first blood."
>
> ***Pay dirt***—An alternate word for a touchdown (often used with "hit"). "It took the Broncos just 50 seconds to hit *pay dirt*."

Touchdown

A TD, short for a touchdown, is worth six points. This is when a player in possession of the ball crosses the opposition's goal line by running with the ball or by obtaining possession in the end zone by catching a pass or recovery of a loose ball.

Extra Point Conversions

After a touchdown, teams have a chance to "tack on" or add one or two extra points. This is known as a PAT (point-after-touchdown), which can make the touchdown-scoring play worth either seven or eight points, or leave it at six if the conversion is not successful. There is only one PAT opportunity and no time is run off the clock. Decisions to try for one or two points depend on the score and game time remaining.

Although rules differ among leagues, the NFL spots the ball at the two-yard line for two-point attempts. Colleges and high schools put it at the three and the Canadian Football League puts it at the five-yard line.

Since the two points carry a higher risk—a 50% success rate in the NFL—the kick is more reliable. NFL statistics say that PAT kicks are made 90% of the time.

For the placekick (worth one point), the ball is spotted at the 15-yard line in the NFL. High schools and colleges use the two for kicks but it's way back to the 32 for the CFL. The ball

Place kicker (rear) and holder preparing for the place kick. Broken Spheres/Wikimedia Commons

is hiked to a holder, normally the second-string quarterback or the punter, who kneels eight yards behind the line of scrimmage. He places the ball vertically, laces out, on the ground for the placekicker, who frequently kicks "soccer style." A couple of steps and he plants his foot into the ball, which must travel between the uprights and over the crossbar, 10 yards deep into the end zone. That's a total distance of 33 yards in the NFL, about the same as a "chip shot" (easy) field goal.

Extra points carry risks beyond not being successful. If a team's extra point is blocked, a defender who catches it before it hits the ground can return it the other way for a two-point score for his team. On a two-point try, an interception or fumble returned the distance the other way carries the same results.

> Other than statistics for the kicker, this is the only facet of the game where statistics are not recorded. An interception or incomplete pass, for instance, does not factor into the quarterback's game statistics nor would an interception on a conversion award a stat to the defender.

Field Goal

If they fail to make a first down, an offense might try a field goal, which is worth three points. This follows the same procedure as a PAT kick. Thus, on fourth down, coaches face a decision. Wind direction and speed, time remaining in the game, and the score influence a coach's decision whether "to go for it" on the fourth down and try to make first down or to take a chance with a kick. The leg strength and coaches' confidence in the kicker are important considerations. Kicks of more than 50 yards are typically out of reach at the high school level but for colleges and the pros, such a range is realistic. Sixty-yard attempts are rare and, of course, are rarely successful. The NFL record is 64 yards (54 yards playing field + 10 yards end zone).

If the kick attempt was from *outside* the 25-yard line, the football is turned over to the opponent at the spot where the ball was kicked. If the field-goal try was *inside* the 25, the ball is spotted for play by the other team at the 25-yard line. Often a kick is not an exciting part of the game unless the kick is very long or it occurs in the final seconds of the game and will decide the outcome. Occasionally, the ball bounces off one of the uprights and out of play. And sometimes it bounces through for three points. Either way, that's dramatic and exciting! Entertainment is the name of the game.

> **Ice the kicker** describes a tactic used by the defense to freeze, or ice, the kicker. A frozen—or a nervous—kicker is likely to miss the attempt, right? **On ice** is another term in sports to describe a team that is comfortably ahead. Think champagne—on ice and ready for the celebration.
>
> When is the game *"on ice"?* When a team has a comfortable lead with reasonable assurance that the other team will not come back and win. But in the NFL, there's a good reason for "on any given Sunday," where anything is possible

Safety (two points)

A team picks up two points by tackling an opponent possessing the ball in his own end zone. A safety can also occur when the quarterback, under pressure in his own end zone, throws the ball away to avoid a sack or when an offensive player is called for holding in the end zone (see the section on rules). The team that gives up the safety will either kick off or punt the ball from its 20-yard line to the scoring team.

Ways to Score a Touchdown

Offense

Rushing: A person with the ball, normally a running back, crosses the goal line, ball in hand courtesy of the quarterback or a direct snap from the center. The score can be from just a few inches away or the entire length of the field.

Passing: Normally, it's the quarterback who passes the ball to any eligible receiver who catches it and runs the rest of the distance into the end zone, or the receiver is already in the end zone waiting for the quarterback's throw.

Fumble recovery: This is an infrequent instance where an offensive player recovers his own or a teammate's fumble in the end zone.

Defense

Interception: This is called a "pick 6" for the six points it produces.

Fumble: A ball recovered in the offense's end zone or recovered ("scooped up") and returned the distance to the end zone.

Special Teams

Kickoff or punt return: The ball is returned all the way from one side of the field to the other.

Blocked kick or punt recovered: The ball is in the opponent's end zone or scooped up in the field of play and returned all the way.

Fumble recovery: The ball is in the opponent's end zone or recovered in the field of play and returned.

Muffed kick: When a player tries to catch the kick but cannot control the ball, which comes loose. In high school, the kicking team can recover and advance the ball for a touchdown; however, pro and college declare the ball is down at the spot the kicking team recovers it. Thus, no TD unless the recovery was in the end zone.

> The element of surprise: Watch for a fake punt or field goal in which one of the special teams' players in the backfield "has something up his sleeve"—a trick—and passes or runs with the ball. A TD is rare but it does happen! And so does the play being stopped.

Elements of the Game

Game clock: On the scoreboard, this indicates the time left in the quarter. Although the total time at a football game can be more than three hours, the actual football game time is 60 minutes long, 15 minutes per quarter.

Coin toss: As mentioned previously, the coin toss occurs at midfield to determine which team kicks off and which receives. This is a moment for both teams to be cordial with a handshake—a reminder that it's a game, not a fight-to-the-death duel.

Down: A team gets four downs, or plays, to advance the ball and get a first down. If it fails, the team usually punts the ball to the opponent or tries a field goal. Some teams might "go for it" on the fourth down. This can occur late in the game if the team is behind with little time left on the clock. Or it can happen if the coach has tremendous confidence in his offense or doesn't respect the other team's defense—or both. If the team fails to get a first down, the opponent takes over the ball at the spot of the stop.

> **"Down by contact":** The NFL indicates the ball is down where the ball carrier's knee touches the ground *after* contact with a defensive player. By contrast, in college, the ball is down where the ball carrier's knee hits the ground by contact or not.

End zone: A ten-yard-long area (9.4 meters) at both ends of the field where a player in possession of the ball scores a touchdown or where the defense scores a safety.

Fair catch: A receiver of a punted ball signals with an arm extended upward his intention not to run with the ball.

Flags: (two colors):
YELLOW — Thrown by an official for a penalty.
RED — Thrown onto the field by a head coach to challenge an official's ruling of a play.

NFL: Coaches are allowed two challenges per game. If a challenge is not successful (the officials' ruling is upheld), that team is charged a timeout. Thus, if a team has three timeouts, the "charged" timeout results in it having two remaining. On the other hand, if the two challenges are successful (the officials' decision is overturned), that team will be awarded a third challenge if it becomes necessary. Inside of two minutes, coaches cannot challenge but a league official monitoring the game in New York can order a review of a close play.

College: Coaches are allowed one challenge per half. However, officials may initiate a review on their own if they are in doubt.

Fumble: The act of losing possession of the ball while running with it. A hard tackle can cause the ball to come loose. Any member of the offense or defense can recover a fumble. If the defense recovers the fumble, the fumble is called a "turnover."

Hash marks: The lines on the center of the field that signify each yard on the field. Before every play, the ball is spotted between the hash marks or on the hash marks, depending on where the ball carrier was tackled on the preceding play.

Interception: A pass that's caught by a defensive player, ending the offense's possession of the ball. *Pick 6* is an interception returned for a touchdown.

Kickoff: A free-kick that the receiving team can't attempt to block that puts the ball into play. A kickoff is used at the start of the first and third periods and after every touchdown.

Line of Scrimmage: An imaginary line from one side of the field to the other. The ball is placed on this line at the end of each play.

Punt: On fourth down and too far away from the opponent's end zone to attempt a field goal, a player lines up 15 yards behind the line of scrimmage. After the snap, the punter kicks the ball as far as he can to the opponent.

Punt return: One of the most exciting plays in football is the action of taking a kickoff or punt return all the way "to the house"—to the opponent's end zone. These plays and ones of long returns without TDs always make highlights on sports TV shows.

Game strategy: The distance could be too far for a field goal yet a punt could result in a touchback, giving the receiving team the ball at the 20-yard line. So the punter may try a "coffin corner," where he angles the ball to go out of bounds as close to the receiving team's goal line as possible. The offense then starts backed up to their own end zone. This is a strategy of "field position." A score may not happen on every series (or drive) but a good strategy is to keep the opposition backed up close to their end zone. This limits its play selections, which creates an advantage for the defense.

Sack: When a defensive player tackles—or "dumps"—the quarterback holding the ball behind the line of scrimmage for a loss of yardage.

Snap (or hike): The action that starts the play in which the ball is pitched backward by the center between his legs, usually to the quarterback but also to the holder on field-goal tries or to the punter.

Touchback: Usually, a play in which the ball bounces out of the end zone on a kick, punt or fumble. No points are scored and the ball is put in play by the receiving team at its own 25-yard line if it happens on a kickoff, or 20 on a punt.

> If the team on offense fumbles the ball out of the opponent's end zone, it's a touchback and the ball is turned over to the other team at the 20. However, if the offense fumbles it out of its own end zone, it's a safety.

Turnover: The ball is awarded to the opposition when an offense fails to make a first down on a fourth-down play. This is called a "turnover-on-downs." Normally, a turnover occurs on a fumble or interception. Teams with fewer turnovers, statistics usually show, are winners.

On the books but rarely used:

Fair catch kick—*What it is*: A free field goal attempt. *How it works*: A kick returner fair-catches a kickoff near the end of a half. This gives his team a chance to kick a field goal from the spot of the catch (or where the ball is downed) without challenge—only him and the ball. Last attempted in 2013; the last successful kick was 1976.

Dropkick *What it is*: It's a marriage of a punt and a placekick. (It looks like a punt but can score like a place kick.) *How it works*: Remember the oblong shape of the ball? It bounces erratically, right? (That's the reason this peculiar play is seldom used.) The ball is hiked to the person who will attempt the kick. He drops it once to the ground. On its first bounce, he kicks it. If successful, it's a field goal. The last person to successfully execute a dropkick was Doug Flutie in 2006. Before that, the year was 1941.

Comprehension (Circle the best answer.)

1. The Patriots kicked off to start the game. In the second half, they will _____.
   a. receive the kickoff
   b. kick off
   c. snap the ball
   d. kick a field goal

2. The QB is dumped behind the line of scrimmage. He _____.
   a. throws a fit
   b. is penalized
   c. blames the offensive line
   d. is sacked

3. How much is a safety worth?
   a. $3-5 million a year
   b. two points
   c. one point
   d. six points plus a two-point PAT

4. The ball on punt bounces beyond the end zone. The play is _____.
   a. downed
   b. a touchback
   c. placed on the 25-yard line, first and ten
   d. kickback

5. When the offense fumbles the ball through the other team's end zone it is called _____.
   a. a safety
   b. a quarterback
   c. a turnover
   d. both a and c

6. The center _____ the ball.
   a. hikes   b. snaps
   c. neither A nor B   d. both A and B

7. Which is not true?
   a. A touchdown is worth 7 points.
   b. A field goal is kicked by the special teams unit.
   c. A touchback is not the same as a touchdown.
   d. A team that scores a safety gets the ball on a kickoff.

8. A successful field goal from the 47-yard line is _____.
   a. a chip shot
   b. 47 yards
   c. 57 yards
   d. wide right

9. The head coach doesn't agree with the referee. He can_____.
   a. do a dance
   b. throw a yellow flag
   c. throw a fit
   d. throw a red flag

10. Whose job is it to hike the ball on field goal tries or punts?
    a. center
    b. quarterback
    c. long snapper
    d. holder

11. Stephone Anthony recovered a blocked extra point for the Saints and returned it to the opposite end zone for a _____.
    a. safety
    b. touchback
    c. fair catch
    d. two-point conversion

12. A field goal is not successful from the 37-yard line. What happens?
    a. The ball is turned over.
    b. They get another chance.

c. It becomes a touchback.
d. They cut the kicker from the team.

13. A team makes a fair catch on its own 40-yard line with seconds to go in the first half. What seldom-used play can be done in this circumstance?
    a. a Hail Mary pass to the end zone
    b. a dropkick
    c. an unopposed field goal attempt
    d. a flea-flicker

14. The Dolphins made a pick 6. What did they do?
    a. intercepted a pass for a touchdown
    b. got a touchback
    c. got a sixth-round draft choice
    d. blocked a punt and returned it for pay dirt

Verbs Often Confused: "to do" vs. "to make" ("to do" is to perform a task; "to make" is to create)

DO/did/has done/is doing	Make/made/has made/is making
Work, job, tasks ...your exercises, a good job, homework	Product material or origin ...of gold, in China, by me, from grapes
Food & Drink, meals ... coffee, cocktails, dinner	A reaction (with object pronoun); force ... me laugh, him smile, them cry, me work
Activities (non-specific) ...something, nothing, everything, anything	Plans, decisions ...arrangements, a choice, a strategy
When verb is known or obvious ...our hair, do the laundry, dishes, test	Speaking and sounds ...noise, comment, suggestion

I. Fill in the correct form of "do."

1. He has ____ his exercises.

2. He _____ 40 reps (repetitions) this morning.

3. Are you _____ your homework?

4. I have guests visiting tonight so I should start _____ the housework now.

5. I wouldn't like to ____ that job.

6. I've got lots of things to _____!

7. Don't stand around— ____ something!

8. What can I _____ to help?

9. She hasn't _____ her hair yet.

10. Thanks for helping with the dishes. I'll ____ the drying since you've already _____ the washing.

(Of course, "do" is an auxiliary verb for present tense: *Do you like football?* or past: *Did you like the game?*)

II. Fill in the correct form of "make."

1. If they _____ a touchdown, they'll take the lead.

2. Every morning, he _____ a cup of coffee before heading to work.

3. He hopes to _____ a 48-yard field goal.

4. Footballs are _____ in Ada, Ohio.

5. High-scoring games _____ everyone excited.

6. The coaches _____ a great game plan for last week's game.

7. He appears to have _____ a decision to keep the ball and run with it.

8. Men in the trenches—those linemen—_____ all kinds of noises.

9. Before the team took to the field, the head coach _____ a short speech.

10. New league rules will _____ every player take a drug test.

III. Let's do "do" and "make" by making circles around your choices:

1. The team **made/did** its warm-ups.

2. The coach is **making/doing** the team **make/do** and extra practice session.

3. Shen Li and Xuan Lu will **make/do** the trip to the first-ever game in Beijing.

4. Tyrod **makes/does** his mother proud because he **made/did** the team.

5. Coach has **made/done** a strong impression on his team to **make/do** their work.

6. The defensive back **made/did** an open-field tackle of the wide receiver.

7. A halfback can **make/do** 40 yards in less time than a guard.

8. A blocked punt **makes/does** the game more interesting.

9. Eleven persons **make/do** a football team.

10. Which team **made/did** history by **making/doing** four straight Super Bowl appearances?

11. Teams may **make/do** their best but the one that makes/does the best effort usually wins.

Ad Libs: Your task is to select from the words in the text box to complete the first paragraph that follows. Use the parts of speech clues by each blank to make your choice. The second paragraph, you are on you own to complete.

and	field	team	are
score	defense	on	stop
fourth	eleven	football	punt
first	has	long	yards

Noun—name of person, place, thing, abstract idea

Adjective—describes a noun or pronoun (examples: color, size, quantity)

Adverb—describes an adjective, verb or another adverb

Verb—action word or links subject with another noun or adjective.

Conjunction—connects words or clauses

Preposition—shows direction, location, or time, or introduces an object (noun, pronoun)

Cardinal number—one (1), two (2), three (3) . . .

Footballogy: Elements of American Football for Non-Native Speakers of English

Ordinal number—first (1st), second (2nd), third (3rd) . . .

The game of American [noun]_____ is played on a [noun] _____100 yards [adverb] _____and 45 [plural noun] _____wide. There [linking verb] _____[number] _____players [preposition] _____each side. The objective of the offense is to [verb] _____points. The job of the [noun] _____is to [verb] _____the offense, which [verb] _____ four opportunities, called downs, to make a [ordinal number] _____down and keep the ball. Sometimes a team's drive stalls (stopped by the defense), [conjunction]_____ a [ordinal number] _____down forces it to [verb] _____the ball to the other [noun] _____.

> **On Your Own:** Use clues in the brackets to fill in your own answer. Compare your answer to those in the answer key.

The [color] _____zone is when a team moves the [noun] _____inside the [number] _____-yard line. If it doesn't score a [noun]_____, worth [number] _____ points, it can try a [noun as adjective]_____ goal for [number] _____

124

points. After a [initials] _____, a team can try [article] _____ [adjective] _____ point. A way for the defense to score is a [noun] _____, which counts for two [plural noun] _____. [article] _____ game is [number] _____ minutes, [conjunction] _____ can go into an extra period called [noun] _____ if both teams are even, or [adjective] _____ at the end of regulation. A game that [linking verb] _____ tied at the end of OT is recorded as a [noun] _____.

Don't waste time second-guessing yourself—there will be millions who will do it for you.

— Norm Schachter, NFL referee

CHAPTER VIII

The Officials

They are called "zebras" for fun because of their striped black-and-white uniforms but to call them all referees is wrong. There is only one referee. He's in the white cap. He's the boss of the other officials, who wear black caps. This unit explores officials' roles, how they control the game, and the significance of their hand signals.

Word Preview

litigious	prejudice	pressure-wise
blink of an eye	depiction	infraction

The United States is a litigious society, which means that it places great value on the rule of law over the biases of "men." It has a system to resolve disputes that maintains order. In this regard, football game officials, acting as police, judge, and jury, are held to a high standard without personal malice or prejudice. At all levels, from amateur to professional leagues, they have unique duties to keep the game moving in an organized and orderly way. They blow whistles and throw yellow towels called "flags" for penalties. They must be physically fit to race back and forth on the gridiron and mentally sharp to maintain current knowledge of the rules, which change from year to year.

The NFL employs 121 officials, about 20% of them full-time. Ed Hochuli, a retired official and trial attorney, compared his practice of law with being an NFL official. There's considerable stress being an official.

"A trial is nothing, pressure-wise, compared to the NFL," he says, adding that in the NFL, snap (instant) decisions are made on the field before millions who can second-guess them by watching video replays. This was an issue in the 2019 NFC Championship game between the Los Angeles Rams and the New Orleans Saints. Video showed the Rams were guilty of pass interference late in the game deep in Saints' territory. A reversal of the call would have allowed the Saints to keep possession of the ball and a new first down. Odds are they would have scored and won the game.

Imagine how uncomfortable it must be for officials to have to live with missed calls on plays that happen in the blink of an eye and become a factor in the outcome of an important game. Yet evidence provided by the NFL supports that officials get the call right 95-97% of the time.

Hand signals, which began in 1926 as a response to

fans who didn't know what a call was, and the roles of the officials and common infractions (violations), are listed below. In addition to the depiction of hand signals, it describes methods of the enforcement of penalties. Differences exist between the professional leagues in the United States and Canada as well as between the amateur leagues (high school and college). The NFL and CFL use seven officials, whereas Division I college football uses eight and lower divisions use six. Five are used in high school football. The infractions discussed are NFL unless otherwise noted.

Officials wear their "job titles" on their uniforms: "R" = referee; "U" = umpire; "DJ" = down judge (formerly called the head linesman); "SJ" = side judge; "FJ" = field judge; "LJ" = line judge; "BJ" = back judge. In college football, single initials are worn.

> "Refs," short for "referees," is a term used casually for all the officials.

The graphic on the next page shows the officials and their respective positions prior to the snap of the football. This is followed by a list of the many responsibilities of the officials. The referee (the white cap) is the official who conveys hand signals and announces proceedings on the field—anything from timeouts to the down and distance to a penalty.

Footballogy: Elements of American Football for Non-Native Speakers of English

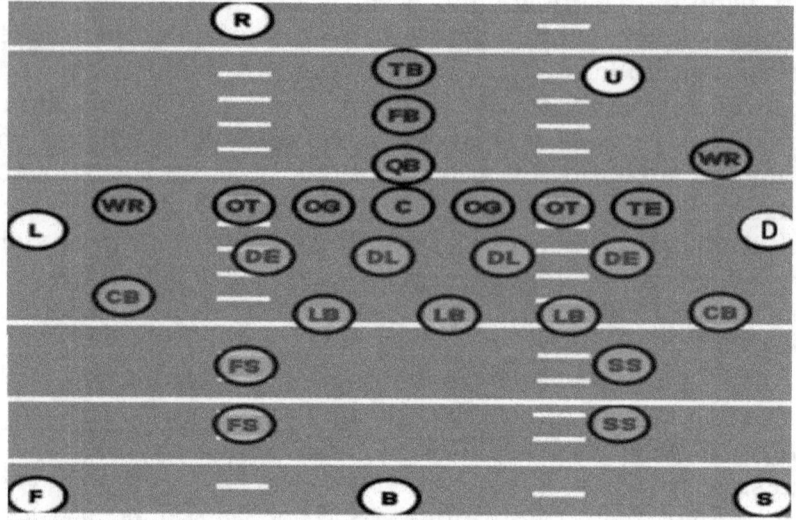

Graphic: Wikipedia
L=Line Judge; R=Referee; U=Umpire; D=Down Judge; S=Side Judge; B=Back Judge; F=Field Judge. Derivative work from Wikipedia--unknown original author. CC-BY-SA

Officials' Positions

Duties of the Officials

Referee (R) (white hat)

- Leader of the officiating crew.
- Has the final say in all rulings.
- Pre-game, conducts the coin flip with team captains at the center of the field.
- Signals and announces which team kicks off and which receives.
- On scrimmage plays, the referee is positioned on the offensive side of the ball, 10-12 yards behind the line of scrimmage on the throwing side of the quarterback.
- Watches the quarterback and observes kicker/punter and offensive tackles.

- Uses hand signals and makes announcements to explain penalties or disputed plays.
- Signals scoring plays (this role is shared by all the officials).
- Reviews all scoring plays, turnovers, and close (controversial) plays on Microsoft Surface.

Referee reviewing a play on Microsoft Surface™.
Photo with permission: Eddie Radosevich

Down Judge (DJ or D) (former title "head linesman" or HL)

- Stands at one end of the line of scrimmage.
- Looks for line-of-scrimmage violations and other pre-snap fouls.
- Marks the spot of forward progress or where a player goes out of bounds.
- Signals whether a pass is complete or incomplete.
- Supervises the measurement of the chain crew for a first down.
- Counts offensive players on the field.

Line Judge (LJ or L)

- Looks for pre-snap line of scrimmage violations.
- After a play has begun, looks for illegal use of the hands and holding.
- Monitors the sidelines to determine where a player is out of bounds.
- Counts offensive players.
- Keeps track of the ball to determine whether the pass is lateral or forward.
- Notes line of scrimmage in the rare event the quarterback crosses before releasing the ball.

Field Judge (F or FJ)

- Stationed 20 yards behind the defensive secondary (same side as the tight end).
- Watches the actions of running backs, receivers, and defenders.
- Evaluates pass success, complete/incomplete or pass interference penalties.
- Counts the number of defensive players.
- Spots forward progress or where a player steps out of bounds.
- Standing in the end zone, he signals if extra points/field goals are good or not good.

Side Judge (S or SJ)

- Operates behind the defensive secondary, same sideline as the down judge.
- Monitors running backs, receivers, and defenders.
- Looks for penalties: pass interference, illegal linemen downfield, and illegal blocks.
- Counts defensive players.
- Monitors kickoffs.
- Serves as the primary timekeeper.

Umpire (U)

- Keeps an eye on the blocks of offensive linemen.

- Monitors defenders trying to avoid those blocks.
- Looks for the movement of offensive linemen.
- Maintains awareness of the relationship between the quarterback and line of scrimmage.
- Protects the quarterback by blowing his whistle to end the play if he determines the QB is in the grasp of a defender (unable to escape).
- Marks off (measures) penalty yardage.

Back judge (B or BJ)

- Lines up behind the defensive secondary on the tight-end side.
- Watches running backs, receivers (especially the tight end) and defenders.
- Monitors the blocking downfield.
- Observes kickoffs and determines their legality.
- Keeps track of the play clock and calls "delay of game" infractions.
- With the field judge, signals whether field goals and extra points are successful.

(You can find complete information about NFL officials and their roles at https://operations.nfl.com)

Officials confer (Note: Head Linesman's (HL) present designation is "D" (Down Judge) Photo credit: Ed Yourdan, (CC-BY-SA) Fotor.com

Footballogy: Elements of American Football for Non-Native Speakers of English

Tools of the officials' trade:
1) A **yellow flag** is used to signal a penalty. It's weighted so that it lands on the turf. Rare: if an official recognizes two separate penalties on the same play, he may use 2) his **cap** as the second "flag." 3) A **blue bean bag** is used to mark the spot of a fumble or the spot where possession was gained on a punt. Other situations include when a penalty is enforced from the spot of the fumble or the spot where possession was gained on punts. 4) A **whistle** is used to blow a play dead (finished) or to indicate that the ball is ready for play.

Officials' Hand Signals

Below the diagrams of the officials' hand signals, you will find a description of on-the-field activities (game procedures and penalties). A complete list with diagrams can be found at www.NFL.com

Illustrations: permission NFL.com.

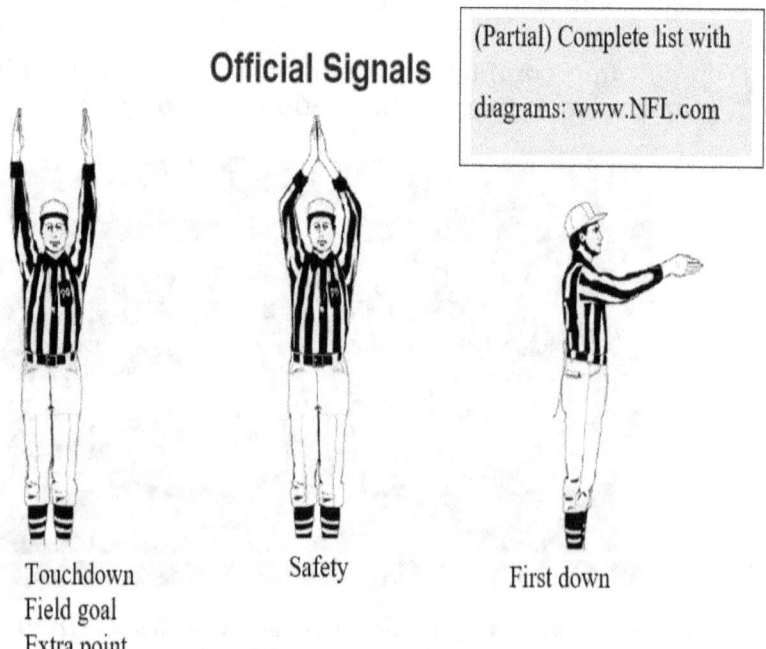

Official Signals

(Partial) Complete list with diagrams: www.NFL.com

Touchdown
Field goal
Extra point

Safety

First down

Footballogy: Elements of American Football for Non-Native Speakers of English

No time out
Start clock on whistle

Delay of game
(arms folded)

Illegal procedure, motion or false start (hands rotate)

Time out (hands crisscross —go back and forth—above head)

Personal foul (example: grabbing facemask; roughing the passer (arm moves forward); roughing the kicker (swings leg)

Holding—grabs wrist with one hand.

Incomplete pass (hands motion in front, like scissors); penalty refused; attempt for field goal or extra point no good.

Offsides penalty; neutral zone infraction (hands rest on hips)

Unsportsmanlike conduct

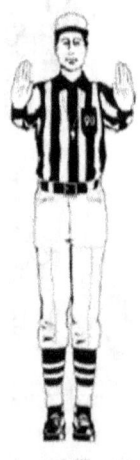

Intentional grounding of pass (waves arms in diagonal motion across body)

Pass interference (pushes hands forward from body outward)

Invalid "fair catch" signal

Footballogy: Elements of American Football for Non-Native Speakers of English

> The best way to become familiar with the penalties is to watch games and listen to announcers explain them during slow-motion replays. You can also get comprehensive guidance on penalties and their significance, along with videos, at NFL.com. Another good way is to attend a game. Most people would not mind being asked to explain something regarding a subject they are passionate about. Remember the wisdom of Dale Carnegie — *Get a person to talk about his interests and you have a new friend!*

Penalties in American football come in groups, or clusters: pre-snap, procedural, unsportsmanlike, and personal foul. Depending on the infraction, the offending team loses yardage—5, 10 or 15 yards or a spot foul, when the ball is placed where the penalty occurred. Occasionally, the penalty is yardage plus an automatic first down.

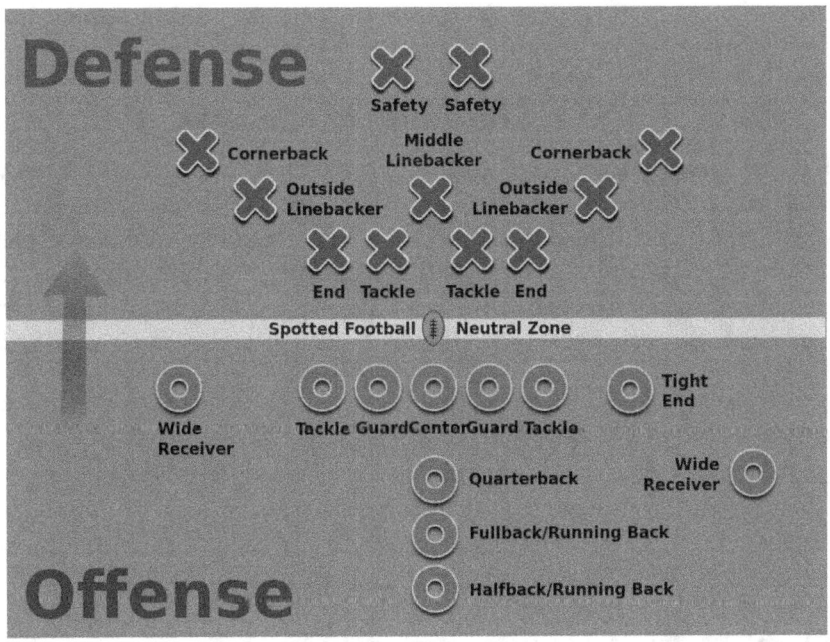

Pre-snap ("dead-ball") positions with neutral zone: No player except the center, who snaps the ball, can be in this imaginary line (the length of the spotted, or place football) prior to the start of play. CC-BY-3.0

Pre-snap (five yards)

Delay of game: When the offense does not snap the ball in its allotted time (25 or 40 seconds) after the referee marks the ball ready for play. Though rare, this can also be called against a defense that interferes with the offense to put the ball in play or start the action.

Encroachment: A defensive player crosses the neutral zone and contacts an offensive player before the snap.

False start: Before the snap, an offensive player, set in position, moves in a way that simulates the start of play.

Neutral zone infraction: A defender moves toward the neutral zone, which causes an offensive player to react.

Offsides: A player (usually defense) who lines up across the line of scrimmage. On kickoffs, a player who crosses the restraining (kickoff) line before the kick.

Illegal Procedure (five yards)

Illegal formation: 1) Eligible receivers are not at the very ends of the line of scrimmage; 2) there are less than seven players on the line of scrimmage (NFL, high school); 3) more than four players are in the backfield (college); 4) five ineligible players are not on the line of scrimmage. On kickoffs, five players must be lined up on either side of the kicker.

Illegal motion: Before the start of action, a running back or eligible receiver may be in motion either laterally or backward. However, he must not turn toward the line of scrimmage unless he his set, which means his movement stops for one second prior to the snap of the pigskin.

Illegal Shift: A player not in motion is not set before the snap.

Illegal substitution ("Twelve men on the field"): An extra player fails to make it off the playing surface prior to the snap or an extra man is in the huddle.

Kickoffs out of bounds: A ball not reaching the opposing end zone crosses the sidelines. The ball is spotted at the receiving team's 40-yard line

A player (tight end-#81) in motion. This is permitted as long as it's parallel to the line of scrimmage. Wikipedia CC-BY-SA 3.0

Other (five yards)

Defensive holding: Using the hands to grab, pull, or push an opponent. In addition to five yards, there is an automatic first down for the offense.

Illegal contact: Called against the defense. A player contacts a receiver who is more than five yards past the line of scrimmage.

Illegal touching: Numbers 50-79 on the offense (interior linemen) are ineligible receivers and cannot touch or receive a passed ball unless a) it is tipped by a defender or b) he announces his intention to the referee prior to the play and lines up as an eligible receiver. An eligible receiver or returner of a punt or kickoff who steps out of bounds and returns to the field of play is also ineligible to receive the ball.

Ineligible man downfield: On pass plays, interior linemen cannot advance beyond the line of scrimmage before the passer releases the ball. (For college, up to three yards are allowed beyond the line of scrimmage. In the NFL, just one yard.)

Running into the kicker: A defensive player makes incidental (minor) contact with the kicker after the ball has left his foot.

Personal Foul
(most are 15 yards, except where noted)

Unsportsmanlike conduct (also called "dead-ball fouls" since they occur after the play): This infraction results from losing control of emotions, which changes the game by killing drives (if against an offense) or sustaining them (if against a defense). The penalty results in loss of yardage and, if against the defense, awards the other team a first down.

Taunting: Teasing or mocking an opponent to make him mad.

Untoward behavior at an official: Using profanity or touching him.

Voluntary removal of helmet: A player intentionally removes his helmet on the playing field.

Unnecessary Roughness
(all are 15 yards and automatic first downs)

Roughing the passer: A defender tackles a quarterback after he has released the ball. Circumstances determine whether the participant is disqualified (removed from the game).

> In high school, only roughing the passer and roughing the kicker carry automatic first downs; otherwise, the penalty is 15 yards.

Roughing the kicker (see "running into the kicker"): The defender contacts the plant leg of the kicker (the non-kicking leg "planted" on the ground) while his kicking leg is still in the air, or slides into the kicker when both of the kicker's feet are on the ground.

Spearing: The defender makes a tackle into the offensive player leading with the crown of his helmet.

Helmet-to-helmet contact (NCAA: "Targeting"): Using the head to initiate contact with the opponent's helmet.

Late hit: Hitting any downed ball carrier or one out of bounds at a point when play is reasonably expected to be over.

Piling on: Jumping onto a downed player after the whistle has blown and the play is dead.

Horse collar tackle: Pulling a player down from behind by the inside of his shoulder pads or jersey.

Fair catch interference: The punt returner, who signals a fair catch, is run into by a defender or is not given enough room to make the catch.

Illegal use of the hands/Facemask: Grabbing, twisting, or turning a player's facemask.

Clipping: Blocking an opponent from behind below the waist.

10-yard Penalties

Block in the back: A player may only block a defender who is facing him.

Holding (offensive): When blocking, players cannot use their hands to grab, push, or pull an opponent.

Intentional grounding (penalty includes loss of down): A quarterback, under pressure and still in the pocket (an imaginary area between the tackles behind the line of scrimmage), throws the ball away, not near an eligible receiver. If this occurs in his team's end zone, the other team is awarded a safety.

Offensive pass interference: A receiver who physically hinders a defender from an opportunity to defend a pass play, which includes his ability to intercept.

Tripping: Sticking out one's legs attempting (or succeeding) to make an opponent fall.

Spot Fouls

Illegal forward pass: The passer throws the ball forward while he is beyond the line of scrimmage. (Five yards from spot of foul plus loss of down).

Illegal kickoff: On a kickoff, the ball goes out of bounds before it crosses into the end zone. Penalty: The receiving team can take the ball at the spot where it went out of bounds or 25 yards from the spot of the kickoff (their own 40-yard line).

Pass interference: (Defensive) The ball is placed at the location of the foul (NFL). If it occurs in the opponent's end zone, the ball is spotted at the one-yard line. College football is a 15-yard penalty. (Offensive) College and pros: 15-yard penalty.

Special Circumstances

Offsetting penalties: When a player or players on each team are flagged on a play, the penalties are said to be "offsetting" and the down is replayed.

Ten-second runoff: In the last two minutes of a game or half, if the team on offense has no timeout remaining and commits a penalty—or a timeout is necessary for an injured player on offense—ten seconds are ticked off the clock. Clearly if ten or fewer seconds remain, the game is over.

Spiking: In the last two minutes of game or half, the quarterback may slam (throw) or spike the ball to the ground as soon as it is hiked by the center and not be called for intentional grounding. Since this maneuver stops the clock, it gives a team a way to save precious time while attempting to score in the final seconds of the game.

Half the distance: A penalty that would place the ball at more than half the distance to the offending team's goal. The yardage is marked as "half the distance." Thus, a 15-yard penalty occurring at the 20 would not be at the five-yard line but the 10. The ball for a 10-yard penalty at the 16 would be placed at the eight, not the five.

 I. Circle the correct response (multiple choice or True or False)

1. A defender moves across the line and touches a member of the offense before the snap.
    a. offsides b. illegal shift
    c. encroachment d. neutral zone infraction

2. A 15-yard penalty occurs at the offending team's 14-yard line. On what yard line is the ball placed?
    a. three b. nine
    c. one d. seven

3. Roughing the passer, a late hit, clipping, and pass interference are examples of unsportsmanlike conduct.
    T F

4. Both arms of the official are extended straight up indicates _____.
   a. offsides
   b. first down
   c. touchdown
   d. safety

5. Which of the following does not describe a referee?
   a. observes the tight end
   b. wears a white hat
   c. reviews plays
   d. is the boss

6. The quarterback releases the ball, then is hit.
   a. pass interference
   b. roughing the passer
   c. intentional grounding
   d. illegal forward pass

7. Time expires on the play clock before the ball is snapped.
   a. offsides
   b. pass interference
   c. delay of game
   d. encroachment

8. On an RPO—a run-pass option—a quarterback decides to heave a forward pass just before he reaches the line of scrimmage. What is a possible concern?
   a. illegal forward pass
   b. illegal touching
   c intentional grounding
   d. ineligible receiver downfield

II. Match the actual penalty with its cluster

P – Procedure	S – Spot foul
PF – Personal foul	T – Ten yard
PS – Pre-snap	UR- Unnecessary roughness
UC – Unsportsmanlike conduct	

1. _____ Offside
2. _____ Illegal shift
3. _____ fighting
4. _____ roughing the kicker
5. _____ spearing

6. _____ defensive pass interference
7. _____ making the other guy angry
8. _____ letting the play clock expire
9. _____ kickoff goes out of bounds
10. _____ clipping
11. _____ encroachment
12. _____ intentional grounding
13. _____ grabbing the facemask
14. _____ calling the official a bad name
15. _____ 12 men on the field

III. Use the following words to fill in the blanks

offside	false start	intentional grounding
holding	pass interference	unsportsmanlike conduct
roughing the kicker	illegal formation	half-the-distance

The game started out as a flag-fest—so much yellow for all those penalty flags. On our first drive, 12-men were in the huddle, so our team got flagged with an (1) _____. Then one of our offensive linemen moved before the snap and got us moved back five more yards for a (2)_____. We got these yards back on the very next play, plus a first down when a defensive lineman was guilty of (3) _____. You can say that our offense started out that day a little like Limburger cheese—it stunk. It was three-and-out—three plays that ended up with a fourth down—and we had to punt. A defender got through and although he didn't block the punt, he knocked the punter off his feet. The umpire threw a flag for (5) _____, which got us 15 yards and a new set of downs.

Our quarterback immediately went to work and heaved a long pass. It wasn't caught but a safety, who bumped into the receiver, was flagged for (6) _____ at the eight-yard line. On the next play, an anxious defender jumped (7) _____, so (8) _____ to the goal gave us the ball at the four. The defense tightened, however, and pressured our quarterback, who panicked and threw the ball away. Many on our side thought he shouldn't have been flagged for (9)_____, since there appeared to be an eligible receiver nearby. But the worst was yet to come. After an official spotted the ball at the 14, someone kicked the ball in anger. The (10)_____ penalty not only moved us back an additional 15 yards, but the player was ejected.

IV. Use words from the word preview to complete these sentences.

1. In a _____, he was gone.
2. A cartoonist made a good _____ of the angry crowd.
3. A jury in a court of law is supposed to act without _____.
4. I have a nice job without any _____.

5. The policeman gave me a ticket for a(n) _____.
6. Opinions are less important than facts in a _____ society.

Norm Schachter: Renaissance Man

Word Preview

legendary	moonlighting	logging
call	earmuffs	light-hearted
outstanding	rise	vast

Schoolteacher, author, and NFL referee Norm Schachter. Courtesy Alfred University

Legendary NFL referee Norm Schachter earned a doctorate from Alfred University in New York state. After service in the United States Marine Corps, he served as a teacher and administrator 2,500 miles away at Los Angeles, California high schools where he also coached basketball, winning two city championships. And he refereed football. He also authored books on football and a dozen textbooks on English and vocabulary, including *English the Easy Way*, which was popular in schools around the world, His career saw him rise to an area superintendent of the Los Angeles Unified School District.

Schachter began a 22-year career moonlighting as an NFL official in 1954, logging about 120,000 air miles a season. He was the head official for the famed "Ice Bowl" in Green Bay, Wisconsin (reading on this follows) between the Dallas Cowboys and the Packers on December 31, 1967. Temperatures were way below zero Fahrenheit and his whistle froze, forcing him and his crew to call the game by voice. Although there were many close calls in the game, Schachter said the best call he made that day was to wear earmuffs.

Frequently referred to as "Number 56" for the number on his back, Schachter refereed 11 NFL Championship games. He was the first to referee a Monday Night Football telecast. Despite once receiving a light-hearted telegram from his eye doctor after a game telling him it was time for new eyeglasses, his outstanding record as an official led the NFL to name him as the referee of the first AFL-NFL Championship on January 15, 1967 (Super Bowl I).

This man of intellect and vast accomplishments went on to referee Super Bowls V and X. The biggest challenge to officiate in the NFL, according to Schachter, was to be in shape to keep up with the quickness of the players and get out of their way.

Select the word for the underlined word or phrase.

1. He's *working* <u>part-time</u>.
2. Did he make the right <u>decision</u>?
3. A lineman's hand size is <u>enormous</u>.
4. The referee is <u>writing down</u> everything.
5. The Packers have a <u>remarkable</u> history.
6. Why don't you wear <u>these</u> in freezing weather?
7. His comments were intended to be <u>humorous</u>.
8. Hard workers <u>get up</u> early.
9. Norm Schachter did <u>great</u> things with his life.
10. An official must be <u>physically fit</u>.

A. legendary
B. light-hearted
C. rise
D. outstanding
E. moonlighting
F. earmuffs
G. vast
H. call
I. in shape
J. logging

"The Ice Bowl"

When the phrase "frozen tundra" is spoken, eyes turn to one place—Lambeau Field, home of the Green Bay Packers. One of the northernmost NFL cities is Green Bay, Wisconsin, known as "Titletown, USA" for its NFL titles. It is also known for its cold days of late autumn. People had better bundle up. But that doesn't stop the Packer faithful.

Just a year before the NFL merger, on December 31, 1967, two powerhouse teams met. The NFL's oldest franchise, the Green Bay Packers, hosted the fledging Dallas Cowboys for the right to go to the second Super Bowl. The game-time temperature was 15° F below zero (−26 °C), with a wind chill that made it seem like −48 °F (−44 °C).

It was so cold that some Green Bay players could not start their cars to get to the game. One player flagged down a passing motorist for a ride. The marching band was scheduled to entertain for pre-game and halftime. However, the woodwind instruments froze and the mouthpieces of brass instruments stuck to the players' lips. A few band members with hypothermia were taken to local hospitals. Still, 50,000 fans, dressed in heavy winter apparel, not only came to the game but most stayed to the end.

It was so cold that at one point during the game CBS announcer Frank Gifford said on air, "I'm going to take a bite of my coffee." The Packers won 21-17.

Fans brave Arctic temperatures at the 'ICE Bowl,' the 1967 NFL championship game between the Dallas Cowboys and the Green Bay Packers, December 31, 1967, in Green Bay, Wisconsin.

We have to be realistic; if we don't win, life will continue.
— Hayden Fry, head coach Univerity of Iowa, et al.

CHAPTER IX

America's Game Matures

Can you name the single event that made football so popular? Do you agree that competition drives success? This chapter will show us what elevated football in popularity and how business competition was good for the game.

Word Preview

Come of age	abundance	exception	bye
Sarcastically	alternated	interconference	
matchups	seeds	round	

The AFC and NFC

When something matures, it is said to "come of age." As we read previously, 1958 is commonly viewed as the year that professional football turned the corner to overtake college football and baseball as America's most popular sports attraction. "The Greatest Game Ever Played" is remembered as the first national telecast of an NFL game and the first game to ever go into "sudden death," where the team that scored first in overtime was the winner. That team was the Colts.

The year 1958 was also a simpler time in America. People in some places didn't lock the doors to their homes; boarding a commercial airliner was simply buying a ticket—no IDs to prove who we were or security lines. In pro football, selecting contestants for the championship game was simple too. There were six teams and two conferences, the East and the West. Teams that finished the season with the best win-loss record in each conference got to play each other for the championship one week after the end of the season in late December. The only exception was in 1958. The Browns and the Giants, tied for

1958 final NFL standings

Tm	W	L	T
East			
New York Giants*	9	3	0
Cleveland Browns*	9	3	0
Pittsburgh Steelers	7	4	1
Washington Redskins	4	7	1
Philadelphia Eagles	2	9	1
Chicago Cardinals	2	9	1
West			
Baltimore Colts*	9	3	0
Chicago Bears	8	4	0
Los Angeles Rams	8	4	0
San Francisco 49ers	6	6	0
Detroit Lions	4	7	1
Green Bay Packers	1	10	1

Graphic: Pro Football Reference

first in the East, needed to decide its representative to the championship tilt in a special playoff game a week later.

There were no mathematic formulas to determine winners like those in use today. Championship games were also played outdoors, alternating each year between the East and West winners, where both players and fans had to cope with the weather, good or bad.

Things have gotten more sophisticated since then. The NFL began a 14-game schedule in 1961, and in 1967 increased to 16 teams in three divisions. One division with five teams gave each team a "bye" or a week of rest.

> A "bye" can be used as a joke when a "good" team plays a "bad" team. The "good" team is said to "get a bye," meaning an automatic win.

The first-ever playoffs among the division winners and the runners-up—the team with next-best won-loss record—would determine the contestants in the title game and the right to advance to the then-called AFL-NFL Championship.

The established teams in the NFL were presumed by many to be superior to AFL teams. After all, Green Bay had whupped its opponents in each of the first two AFL-NFL Championships. The name "Super Bowl" wasn't used until the third championship, on January 12, 1969. That's when questions about superiority were laid to rest.

The heavily favored Baltimore Colts from the NFL were expected to win by more than two touchdowns over the AFL's New York Jets, whose quarterback, Joe Namath, had reportedly "guaranteed" a Jets win. It was no laughing matter, however, after the Jets upset the Colts 16-7.

The NFL and the 10-year-old American Football League (AFL) merged in 1970. The new league, which retained the NFL name, had two conferences, the American Football Conference (AFC) and National Football Conference (NFC). Three former NFL franchises—the Colts, the Browns, and the Steelers—joined the AFC to give each conference 13 teams apiece. Within each conference were divisions (which have been realigned over the years due to expansion and geographic balance). This year also marked the first for scheduling interconference games. In the decade of the 1970s, the AFC won eight out of ten Super Bowls from the old guard, the NFC teams.

First Year NFL merger (1970) final standings

Tm	W	L	T	W-L%	PF	PA	PD	Tm	W	L	T	W-L%	PF	PA	PD
AFC East								**NFC East**							
Baltimore Colts*	11	2	1	.846	321	234	87	Dallas Cowboys*	10	4	0	.714	299	221	78
Miami Dolphins+	10	4	0	.714	297	228	69	New York Giants	9	5	0	.643	301	270	31
New York Jets	4	10	0	.286	255	286	-31	St. Louis Cardinals	8	5	1	.615	325	228	97
Buffalo Bills	3	10	1	.231	204	337	-133	Washington Redskins	6	8	0	.429	297	314	-17
Boston Patriots	2	12	0	.143	149	361	-212	Philadelphia Eagles	3	10	1	.231	241	332	-91
AFC Central								**NFC Central**							
Cincinnati Bengals*	8	6	0	.571	312	255	57	Minnesota Vikings*	12	2	0	.857	335	143	192
Cleveland Browns	7	7	0	.500	286	265	21	Detroit Lions+	10	4	0	.714	347	202	145
Pittsburgh Steelers	5	9	0	.357	210	272	-62	Green Bay Packers	6	8	0	.429	196	293	-97
Houston Oilers	3	10	1	.231	217	352	-135	Chicago Bears	6	8	0	.429	256	261	-5
AFC West								**NFC West**							
Oakland Raiders*	8	4	2	.667	300	293	7	San Francisco 49ers*	10	3	1	.769	352	267	85
Kansas City Chiefs	7	5	2	.583	272	244	28	Los Angeles Rams	9	4	1	.692	325	202	123
San Diego Chargers	5	6	3	.455	282	278	4	Atlanta Falcons	4	8	2	.333	206	261	-55
Denver Broncos	5	8	1	.385	253	264	-11	New Orleans Saints	2	11	1	.154	172	347	-175

Graphic courtesy Pro Football Hall of Fame, Canton, Ohio (* = division winners; += wildcards)

Presently, 32 teams, equally divided into four divisions, play a 16-game schedule spread over 17 weeks. The week a team does not play is called a "bye week." There is an attempt to connect divisions in the league with regions of the nation—North, East, South, and West. Each team plays two regular-season games against each team in its division, once at home and once on the road. The remaining 10 games are against six teams in the same conference and four outside the conference. Computer algorithms, based on each team's previous season's performance, determine the matchups of conference games. For example, a team that finishes 7-9 can expect to face other 7-9 (or close) teams from the last season. Interconference games rotate through the divisions every four years.

Season(s)	Regular Season Games
1935-1936	12 games
1937-1942	11 games
1943-1945	10 games
1946	11 games
1947-1960	12 games
1961-1977	14 games
1978-present	16 games

Note: Prior to the 1935 NFL season, there was not a set number of games played but the league had a minimum a team was required.

When the regular season ends, six teams in each conference qualify for the postseason. This is called "the playoffs." Four division champions and two teams described as "wildcards" (non-division winners with next-best records) compete in a "one-and-done" (a one-game elimination) tournament to reach the NFL title game, the Super Bowl. Each team is called a "seed" and is ranked in order from one to six (best to the least). That means six teams in each division are in the playoffs, while ten are not.

Seeding for Playoffs (each conference) and format

> First seeds have the "home-field advantage." They play all their games at home. If a Number-One falls, the home field is passed on to the highest remaining seed.

Seed 1—conference team with the best overall win-loss record
Seed 2—division winner with the next-best overall record
Seed 3—division winner with the third-best record
Seed 4—division winner with the fourth-best record
Seed 5—non-division-winning team with the best record
Seed 6—non-division-winning team with the second-best record

> "Road Warriors": Six seeds play all games on the road.

Playoff Tie-Breakers

The modern NFL has a tie-breaking formula to determine seeding in each conference. There are 12 steps in all with a coin toss as the last option. (This has never been used.) Here are the first six steps in breaking a tie to determine the seeding, and in some cases, who gets in—or who doesn't—make the playoffs.
1. Head to head results against each other
2. Won-loss percentage in own division
3. Results vs. common opponents
4. Won-loss percentage in own conference
5. Comparison of points scored vs. allowed (points differential)
6. Strength of schedule

Format (Three Rounds Or Stages)

Round One: "Wild card weekend" kicks off, or begins, the playoffs the weekend after the regular season ends. The teams in each conference with the best two records, seeds one and two, have earned a bye, a week off, to allow them to rest and observe their next opponent, one of the seeds three to six.

Round Two: "Divisional Playoffs" place winners from the wildcard games take to the road the following weekend against conference seeds one and two. The lowest remaining seed visits the number-one seed and the higher-seeded first-round survivor visits the number two seed.

Round Three: Conference Championships take place at the home stadium of the highest remaining seed. The winner of this game receives conference trophies: *The George Halas Trophy* (NFC) and *The Lamar Hunt Trophy* (AFC). While Halas was a founder of the NFL, Hunt helped form the AFL, which became the AFC. He also founded the Kansas City Chiefs.

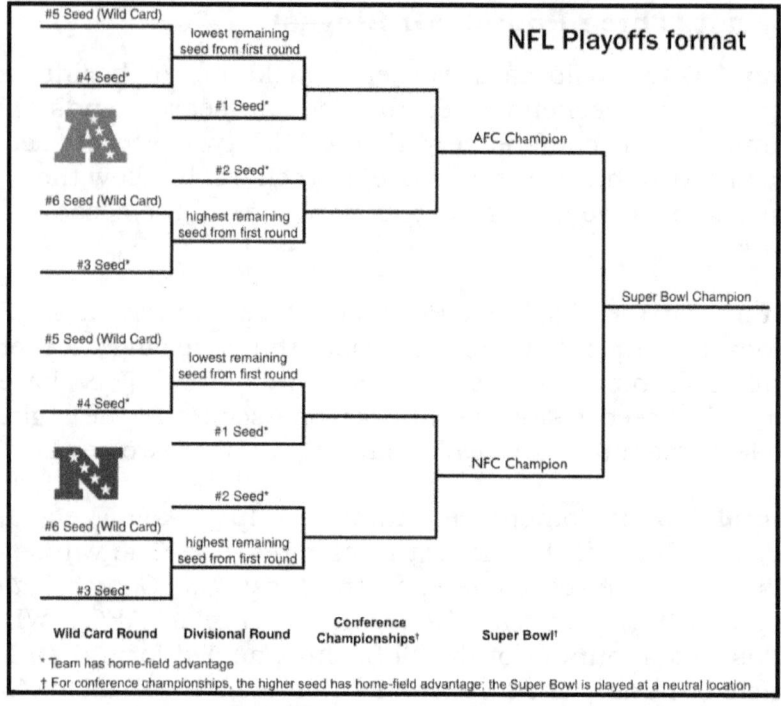

Diagram: Jayron32 at English Wikipedia.

The Super Bowl

The Super Bowl, the ultimate prize for the playoffs, occurs on the first Sunday in February two weeks after the conference championships. Informally, people call this big day "Super Sunday." The site of the game is determined years in advance. Conference representatives alternate each year as the designated "home team." This means they get to choose their uniforms for the game—the home uniform (normally dark jerseys) or the road uniform (usually a white jersey). Due to extremes in weather during this time of year in North America, the location is either in a warmer climate in the Southern region of the United States or a climate-controlled, domed stadium. Only one Super Bowl, in 2014, was played outdoors in a cold climate zone, at MetLife Stadium, in New Jersey.

Footballogy: Elements of American Football for Non-Native Speakers of English

> The origin of the term "Super Bowl" is not certain. However, many believe that Lamar Hunt coined the phrase.
>
> In the 1960s, when pop culture included the Beetles and psychedelic art, new words crept into the culture. Words like "tremendous," "unbelievable" or even "great" were replaced by "groovy" or "super." At the time, there was a small rubber ball that became popular. Labeled the "Super Ball," it could bounce over a three-story building with very little energy. Hunt's children had one. The power of this ball and the fact that it rhymed with "bowl," the established name for a post-season college game, may have inspired Hunt's casual mentions of "Super Bowl" in meetings. The term received attention and by the third AFC-NFC Championship, "Super Bowl" was the official name.

neutral site	coin toss	highest seed
a bye	Green Bay	Lombardi
One week after season		1970
Super Sunday	~~Home field advantage~~	Road warrior

FOOTBALLOGY 6 W'S + H (Who, What, When, Where, Why, Which, How)

I. Match question words & answers in box. See the example.

ex: <u>**What**</u> does the one-seeded playoff team have? <u>**Home-field advantage**</u>

_____ else does the highest seed have? _____

_____ do they call first Sunday on February? _____

_____ is the Super Bowl Trophy named after? _____

_____ is the last step in a tiebreaker? _____

Footballogy: Elements of American Football for Non-Native Speakers of English

_____ is the six seed called? _____

_____ is Wildcard Weekend? _____

_____ is the Super Bowl played? _____

_____ was the ALF-NFL merger? _____

_____ won the first Super Bowl? _____

An Imperfect System

A strong division may have two teams with the same win-loss record tied for best in the conference; however, only one of them can qualify as the division winner. One must be a wild card or at best, the #5 seed. This happened in 2018. The Kansas City Chiefs and Los Angeles Chargers finished 12-4, the best season records in the AFC. Based on the tie-breakers, the Chargers dropped to a five seed, which meant playing an extra week (Wildcard Weekend) with the likelihood of playing all its playoff games as the away team. The New England Patriots (2008 standings listed on the next page), with a very good 11-5 record, did not qualify for the 2008 playoffs due to the tie-breaking formula. The Baltimore Ravens, also 11-5, qualified instead. That year, the Chargers, then in San Diego, won the West Division with an 8-8 record and qualified as a four seed. A similar instance occurred in 2019 when the Cowboys won the NFC East with a dismal record.

Tm	W	L	T	Position
Tennessee Titans (1)	13	3	0	South Champion
Pittsburgh Steelers (2)	12	4	0	North Champion
Miami Dolphins (3)	11	5	0	East Champion
San Diego Chargers (4)	8	8	0	West Champion
Indianapolis Colts (5)	12	4	0	Wild Card #1
Baltimore Ravens (6)	11	5	0	Wild Card #2
New England Patriots	11	5	0	
New York Jets	9	7	0	
Houston Texans	8	8	0	
Denver Broncos	8	8	0	
Buffalo Bills	7	9	0	
Oakland Raiders	5	11	0	
Jacksonville Jaguars	5	11	0	
Cincinnati Bengals	4	11	1	
Cleveland Browns	4	12	0	
Kansas City Chiefs	2	14	0	

Courtesy: Pro Football Reference

Footballogy: Elements of American Football for Non-Native Speakers of English

Tm	W	L	T	W-L%	PF	PA	PD
AFC East							
Miami Dolphins*	11	5	0	.688	345	317	28
New England Patriots	11	5	0	.688	410	309	101
New York Jets	9	7	0	.563	405	356	49
Buffalo Bills	7	9	0	.438	336	342	-6
AFC North							
Pittsburgh Steelers*	12	4	0	.750	347	223	124
Baltimore Ravens+	11	5	0	.688	385	244	141
Cincinnati Bengals	4	11	1	.281	204	364	-160
Cleveland Browns	4	12	0	.250	232	350	-118
AFC South							
Tennessee Titans*	13	3	0	.813	375	234	141
Indianapolis Colts+	12	4	0	.750	377	298	79
Houston Texans	8	8	0	.500	366	394	-28
Jacksonville Jaguars	5	11	0	.313	302	367	-65
AFC West							
San Diego Chargers*	8	8	0	.500	439	347	92
Denver Broncos	8	8	0	.500	370	448	-78
Oakland Raiders	5	11	0	.313	263	388	-125
Kansas City Chiefs	2	14	0	.125	291	440	-149

2008 AFC final standings. Wikipedia.

* = Division Champion
PCT= winning percentage
CONF = Conference
PA = Points Against

+ = Wildcard
DIC = Division
PF = Points for
PD = Points differential

Based on the AFC Final Standings Chart, select your answer.

1. Which team with an 11-5 record did not go to the playoffs?
    a. Ravens   b. Dolphins
    c. Patriots   d. Jaguars

2. Of the information given, why did Denver not win its division?
    a. San Diego won more conference games
    b. San Diego scored more points and allowed fewer
    c. Denver's schedule was easier
    d. Denver lost twice to San Diego in the regular season

3. Select the seeds in order (fill in #1 for top seed to #6)
    __ Baltimore
    __ Miami
    __ Pittsburgh
    __ Tennessee
    __ San Diego
    __ Indianapolis

4. Which team scored the most points?
    a. Kansas City   b. Indianapolis
    c. San Diego   d. New England

5. Which team in the cellar had the best record?
    a. Chiefs   b. Browns
    c. Jaguars   d. Bills

6. Which team had the most point differential?
    a. Tennessee   b. New England
    c. Detroit   d. Oakland

7. Which team allowed the most points?
    a. San Diego   b. Kansas City
    c. Miami   d. New York

"The drive"

In American football, a "drive" has to do with an offensive series. A drive can be one play or several. It can cover just a few yards or the length of the field. It can consume mere seconds off the game clock or several minutes.

One of the most famous drives in NFL history happened on January 11, 1987. In the closing minutes of the AFC Championship game between the Denver Broncos and the Cleveland Browns in Cleveland, Ohio, Denver took over the ball at their own two with just over five minutes left in regulation.

Some say that this game for Denver's young quarterback, John Elway, defined his reputation as a clutch performer—someone who doesn't hyperventilate or get nervous in stressful situations with the game on the line. Elway used the weapons on his offense to mix in a variety of plays, runs, and passes to march the Broncos on a faultless 98-yard drive capped off with a five-yard TD strike to Mark Jackson, which tied the score at 20-20 with 31 seconds remaining. Although the Broncos needed overtime to win the game on a field goal, this game, which brought the AFC Championship to Denver, will always be remembered as "The Drive."

The harder the conflict, the more glorious the triumph.
　　　　　　　　—Thomas Paine, American patriot

CHAPTER X

The National Football League

With respect to the many levels of American football, the top of the pyramid is the National Football League (NFL), where many kids who put on a gridiron uniform dream to play one day. This section provides a picture of each NFL team. How did the team originate? How did it get its name? Its history? Its colors? Included are links to each team's website for the latest in team news, schedules, how to purchase tickets and team merchandise, and information on fan clubs.

Footballogy: Elements of American Football for Non-Native Speakers of English

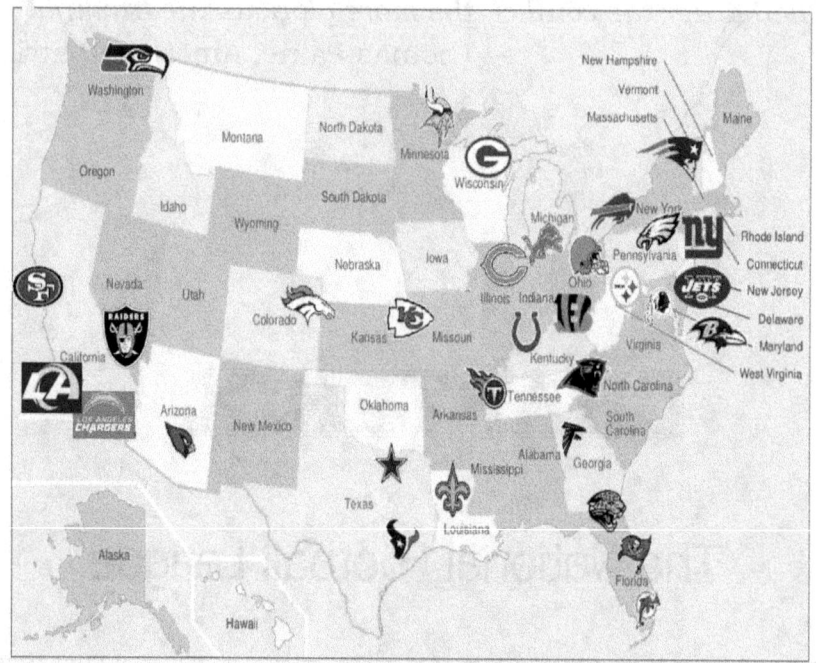

Footballogy Graphic adapted from aarkangel.wordpress.com

All NFL cities are served by major and regional USA airlines and many international carriers offer direct or connecting flights. Game tickets and travel reservations including air, accommodations, and ground transportation can be obtained through any ticket service such as those listed on the following pages.

Footballogy: Elements of American Football for Non-Native Speakers of English

NFL Teams, Websites & General Information

American Football Conference

NFL team and conference logos with permission, Bonnie Jarett/NFL

EAST DIVISION

BUFFALO BILLS
WWW.BUFFALOBILLS.COM

First year: 1960 (AFL); 1970 NFL
Colors: Royal blue, red, and white
Inspiration for name: The only team named after a person—Wild West cowboy and showman Buffalo Bill Cody. The Stadium, Orchard Park, New York (NY). Due to proximity to Lake Erie (one of five US lakes called the Great Lakes), late-season games are famous for being played in "lake-effect" snow conditions, or heavy snowfall.
Home games: Bills Stadium, Orchard Park, New York (NY)
Airport: BUF (Buffalo-Niagara International); in proximity (74 miles; 119 kilometers): ROC (Greater Rochester International)
FYI: The city of Buffalo and pro football date back to the 1890s. It hosted a team in the first nine years of the NFL. The Buffalo Bills own two AFL titles and four straight Super Bowl appearances (1990-93). They hold the record for the biggest comeback in history (Jan. 3, 1993), down 35-3 in the 3rd quarter, and won 41-38. Famous fan club: Bills Mafia.

MIAMI DOLPHINS
WWW.MIAMIDOPHINS.COM

First year: 1966 (AFL); 1970 (NFL)
Colors: Aqua, red, and white
Inspiration for name: From among 20,000 fan entries, the name "Dolphins" was chosen because it was "one of the fastest and smartest creatures in the sea," commented owner Joe Robbie.
Home games: Hard Rock Stadium, Miami Gardens, Florida (FL)
Also known as: The fins; the fish
Airport: MIA (Miami International)
FYI: The youngest team to make the Super Bowl, just five years old (1972). They are the only team with an unbeaten season, counting the Super Bowl (1973). They have five Super Bowl appearances with two wins.

NEW ENGLAND PATRIOTS
WWW.PATRIOTS.COM

First year: 1960 (AFL)
Colors: Navy blue, silver, red, and white
Inspiration for name: Formerly the "Boston Patriots," the name changed to "New England Patriots" in 1971 to represent the entire region in the northeast United States where most of the fighting took place in the American war for independence from England in the late 1700s.
Also known as: The Pats
Home games: Gillette Stadium, Foxboro, Massachusetts (MA)
Airport: BOS (Logan International Airport)
FYI: Since the year 2000, the Patriots have dominated the NFL. They have tied with Pittsburgh for six Super Bowl victories, headed by the winningest coach-quarterback pair Bill Belichick and Tom Brady. Brady was the oldest quarterback (41) to start and win a Super Bowl (2018 season).

NEW YORK JETS
WWW.NEWYORKJETS.COM

First year: 1960 (AFL) as the New York Titans (to "Jets" 1963); 1970 (NFL)
Colors: Green and white
Inspiration for name: In 1963, the team was sold and was about to make Shea Stadium its home. It was close to LaGuardia Airport. "Jets" was suggested to reflect the "modern approach of this team."
Home games: Met Life Stadium, East Rutherford, New Jersey (NJ)
Airport: New York City: JFK (John F Kennedy), LGA (LaGuardia), EWR (Newark, NJ)
FYI: Jets' quarterback Joe Namath, nicknamed "Broadway Joe" for a colorful lifestyle, made the Fu Manchu mustache fashionable. He led his AFL team to an upset of the NFL Baltimore Colts in Super Bowl III (1969) at a time when the more established NFL was thought to be vastly superior.

NORTH DIVISION

BALTIMORE RAVENS
WWW.BALTIMORERAVENS.COM

First year: 1996 (moved from Cleveland, where the team was known as the Browns)
Colors: Black, purple, and gold
Inspiration for name: "The Raven," a poem by Baltimore poet Edgar Allen Poe
Home games: M & T Bank Stadium, Baltimore
Airport: BWI (Baltimore-Washington International)
FYI: Baltimore history with a pro franchise dates to 1946. Ravens' history starts in 1996 when the Browns relocated from Cleveland. After just five years of operation as the Ravens, the team made its first Super Bowl, which it won in 2000.

CINCINNATI BENGALS
WWW.BENGALS.COM

First year: 1968 (AFL); 1970 (NFL)
Colors: Orange, black, and white
Inspiration for name: Link to the past with a former pro team called Bengals (1937-42)
Home games: Paul Brown Stadium, Cincinnati, Ohio (OH)
Airport: CVG (Cincinnati/Northern Kentucky International Airport)
FYI: "No-huddle" and "West Coast" offenses were popularized by the Bengals. Fullback Ickey Woods began the "Ickey Shuffle," a trendsetting touchdown dance routine.

CLEVELAND BROWNS
WWW.CLEVELANDBROWNS.COM

First Year: 1950
Colors: Orange, brown, and white
Inspiration for name: Chosen from a survey of fans to honor popular first coach, Paul Brown
Home games: FirstEnergy Field, Cleveland, Ohio
Airport: CLE (Hopkins International)
FYI: Started in 1944 in the All-America Football Conference by a taxicab company entrepreneur, who laid the groundwork for a modern practice squad. He employed players not on the active roster to drive taxi cabs. One of the greatest players to ever wear a football uniform played for the Browns. Not only was he a Brown, his name was Brown—Jim Brown. The most avid fans call themselves "the dawgs," who sit in a special section of the stadium called "the dawg pound." (A "pound" is a place where stray dogs are kept).

PITTSBURGH STEELERS
WWW.STEELERS.COM

First year: 1933 (Pirates 1933-40)
Colors: Black, gold, and white
Inspiration for name: Prior to 1940, they were named the Pirates (like the city's baseball team). Consecutive losing seasons resulted in a contest for a fresh start. The winning entry honored the town built on steel factories and a blue-collar (hard-working) work ethic.
Home games: Heinz Field, Pittsburgh, Pennsylvania (PA)
Airport: PIT (Pittsburgh International)
FYI: The logo (team symbol) is on one side of the helmet; the other side is a solid color, no logo. They are one of two teams in the NFL with player numbers both on the front and back of the helmet. They dominated the NFL in the 1970s with an overpowering defense called the Steel Curtain and relentless air and ground offensive attacks. They have won six of eight Super Bowl appearances. Fans are called the "Steeler Nation."

SOUTH DIVISION

HOUSTON TEXANS
WWW.TEXANS.COM

First year: 2002
Colors: Dark blue and red
Inspiration for name: The owner selected the name "Texans," which represented "the bravery of Texas natives."
Home games: NRG Stadium, Houston, Texas
Airport: IAH (George Bush International)
FYI: The league's youngest team has won six AFC South Division titles (2011-2019).

INDIANAPOLIS COLTS
WWW.COLTS.COM

First year: 1953 in Baltimore, Maryland (MD). Franchise relocated to Indianapolis, Indiana (IN) in 1984.

Colors: blue and white

Inspiration for name: In a "name-the-team" contest, "Colts" was chosen for the tradition and history of horse breeding and racing in the Baltimore area. The team retained the name in its subsequent relocation to Indianapolis, famous for another kind of racing—automobiles.

Home games: Lucas Oil Stadium, Indianapolis

Airport: IND (Indianapolis International)

FYI: Some of the greatest to ever play the game wore the horseshoe logo, including Johnny Unitas, quarterback in The Greatest Game Ever Played (1958) and Payton Manning. The Colts are the only team to play in the Super Bowl for different conferences (NFL/NFC and AFC).

JACKSONVILLE JAGUARS
WWW.JAGUARS.COM

First year: 1995
Colors: Teal, black, and gold
Inspiration for name: Selected from a fan contest.
Also known as: The Jags
Home games: TIAA Bank Field, Jacksonville
Airport: JAX (Jacksonville International)

FYI: This team qualified for playoffs in just its second year (1996). Since 2013, "the Jags" have had a multi-year agreement to play one home game each season in London.

TENNESSEE TITANS
WWW.TITANS.COM

First year: 1960 (Houston Oilers) relocated to Nashville, Tennessee (TN) in 1996

Colors: Navy blue, light blue, red, silver, and white. Logo contains three red stars, which represent the three major cities in Tennessee—Memphis, Nashville, and Knoxville.

Inspiration for name: (1997) A result of a contest to reflect "strength, leadership, and heroic qualities."

Home games: Nissan Stadium, Nashville

Airport: BNA (Nashville International)

FYI: Won the Divisional Playoff over the Buffalo Bills ("Music City Miracle") on a last-second kickoff return that involved a controversial lateral pass. Nashville is home to titans of another kind: country musicians who perform at the Grand Ole Opry, the premiere venue for Country and Western music.

WEST DIVISION

DENVER BRONCOS
WWW.DENVERBRONCOS.COM

First season: 1960

Colors: Orange, navy blue, and white

Inspiration for name: Acquired from a fan contest (a bronco is a wild horse in the American West).

Home games: Empower Filed at Mile High, Denver, Colorado (CO)

Airport: DEN (Stapleton International)

FYI: The Broncos have three Super Bowl championships. Their "home-field advantage" includes conditioning for a high altitude, which visiting teams must adjust to.

KANSAS CITY CHIEFS
WWW.CHIEFS.COM

First Season: 1960 as Dallas Texans (relocated to Kansas City 1963)
Colors: red, gold, white
Inspiration for name: In honor of the Native Americans who once lived in the area.
Home games: Arrowhead Stadium, Kansas City, Missouri (MO)
Airport: MCI (Kansas City International)
FYI: Represented the AFL before the merger with the NFL in the first "Super Bowl" (January 15, 1967). The stadium is the Truman Sports Complex, named after President Harry Truman (USA 1945-1953). Its most famous imported player is Christian Okoye, also known as "the Nigerian Nightmare" for his hard-running style and ability to fight off tacklers.

LA (LOS ANGELES) CHARGERS
WWW.CHARGERS.COM

First Season: 1960, Los Angeles; 1961 to 2016, San Diego; 2017 to present, Los Angeles
Colors: Navy blue, powder blue, and gold
Inspiration for name: The team's first general manager heard fans yell, "Charge!" at LA Dodgers' baseball games and college football games, and liked the sound of it.
Also known as: The Bolts
Home games: SoFi Stadium, Inglewood, CA. (Shared with LA Rams)
Airport: LAX (Los Angeles International). Also served by regional airports in Burbank (BUR), Ontario (ONT), Anaheim (SNA), and Long Beach (LGB).
FYI: "The Chargers" suggests power, as in electricity. The team has built a reputation for high-powered offenses. Their first season of play was in Los Angeles (1961) but they resided in nearby San Diego until returning to LA in 2017.

LAS VEGAS RAIDERS
WWW.RAIDERS.COM

First year: 1960

Colors: Silver and black

Inspiration for name: Unknown origin. However, like the Hell's Angels motorcycle club headquartered in Oakland, the Raiders' original home, the team has a legacy as outcasts—players not wanted by other teams. "Raiders" sounds ominous or threatening.

Also known as: The Silver and Black

Fans: Raider Nation; the Black Hole

Home games: Allegiant Stadium, Las Vegas, Nevada (NV)

Airport: LAS (McCarron International)

FYI: The Raiders, with a distribution of fans nationwide, enjoy a legacy called "the Raider Mystique," which captures the feeling around the team, where adventure and excitement can erupt at any moment.

National Football Conference (NFC)

EAST DIVISION

DALLAS COWBOYS
WWW.COWBOYS.COM

First year: 1960
Colors: Navy blue, royal blue, silver, and white
Inspiration for name: Texas has long been thought of as a place for cowboys, so the name possibly seemed like a natural fit to team founders.
Also known as: The Boys; America's Team
Home games: AT&T Stadium, Arlington, Texas (TX)
Airport: DFW (Dallas-Fort Worth International)
Trivia: Believed to be the USA's most valuable sports franchise, worth more than $5 billion.
FYI: The Cowboys have eight NFC championships and five Super Bowl championships. The star on their helmets represents the nickname of Texas: "The Lone Star State." Called "America's Team" for its massive fan following in the USA. It is said to be the most recognized team around the world.

NEW YORK GIANTS
WWW.GIANTS.COM

First year: 1925
Colors: Royal blue, red, and white
Inspiration for name: In the early days, it wasn't unusual for football teams to adopt names from baseball teams already in that city. Thus, in early times, the team was known as the "New York Football Giants."
Also known as: The "G" men
Home games: MetLife Stadium, East Rutherford, NJ (shared with the NY Jets)
Airport: JFK, LGA (New York); EWR (New Jersey)
FYI: The Giants are the other contestant in the "Greatest Game Ever Played" (1958). They are the team that spoiled New England's quest for a perfect season in the Super Bowl after the 2007 season. Like the Steelers, they have player numerals on the front and back of their helmets.

PHILADELPHIA EAGLES
WWW.EAGLES.COM

First year: 1933
Colors: Dark green, black, and white
Inspiration for name: The government's recovery program ("the New Deal") from the Great Depression used the bald eagle as its symbol. This seemed appropriate for the mission to soar (fly) to great heights.
Home games: Lincoln Financial Field, Philadelphia, PA
Airport: PHL (Philadelphia International)
FYI: Philadelphia had an NFL team (1924-1932) called the Frankford Yellowjackets, which is not part of Eagles' history. They merged with the Pittsburgh Steelers in 1943 as the "Steagles" due to a player shortage during the Second World War. They are the only team to beat legendary Vince Lombardi, coach of the Green Bay Packers, in the postseason in 1960.

 ## THE WASHINGTON FOOTBALL TEAM
WWW.WASHINGTONFOOTBALLTEAM.COM

First year: 1932

Colors: Burgundy, gold, and white

Inspiration for Name: The original franchise, in Boston, Massachusetts, was the Braves. But Boston already had the Braves—a baseball team. After one year, the organization started play in Fenway Park, home of Boston's other baseball team, the Red Sox. Its change to "Redskins" is said to have been to maintain a connection to "Braves," a term of honor for Native Americans, while avoiding confusion with the name <u>Red</u> Sox. In the team's move to Washington in 1937, it retained the Redskins name, a derogatory reference to Native Americans. Modern sensibilities have demanded a name change, and have caused the name and logo to be retired.

Home games: FedEx Field, Landover, Maryland (MD)

Airport: DCA (Ronald Reagan Washington National Airport); IAD (Washington Dulles International); BWI (Baltimore/Washington International Thurgood Marshall Airport)

FYI: A powerhouse in the 1930s and '40s, the Redskins had to wait until the 1970s to begin to reassert themselves with five Super Bowl appearances and three wins spanning from 1972-91. They are winners of the highest combined score in a game—113 points—72-41—over the New York Giants (1966).

NORTH DIVISION

 ## CHICAGO BEARS
WWW.BEARS.COM

First year: 1920

Colors: Navy blue, burnt orange, white (the color scheme of the University of Illinois)

Inspiration for Name: Chicago had a baseball team

called the Cubs (baby bears). The Bears owner thought "Bears" appropriate because football players are bigger and stronger than baseball players.

Also known as: Da Bears; Monsters of the Midway

Home games: Soldier Field, Chicago, Illinois (IL)

Airports: ORD (O'Hare International); MDW (Midway International)

FYI: The Bears is the team with the most players in the Hall of Fame and the most retired jersey numbers (not used anymore). Originally based in Decatur, IL as "the Staleys," they moved to Chicago in 1921 and became the Bears in 1922. They hold the record for most points scored by a team in a game and the biggest margin of victory: a 73-0 win in the 1940 NFL Championship against Washington. They also tallied 62 points in the mud and rain against San Francisco (1965).

DETROIT LIONS
WWW.DETROITLIONS.COM

First year: 1930 as the Portsmouth (Michigan) Spartans; 1934 to Detroit

Colors: "Honolulu" blue and silver

Inspiration for name: Detroit had the baseball team, the Tigers. Thus, "The lion is the monarch of the jungle, and we hope to be the monarch of the league," explained the first team owner.

Home games: Ford Field, Detroit, Michigan (MI)

Airports: DTW (Detroit Metro Wayne County Airport)

FYI: The Detroit Lions have had a unique association with Thanksgiving since 1934. The biggest Thanksgiving rivalry is with the Packers, who they played 11 straight years (1951-1962). Most famously, they broke up the Packers' undefeated season on Thanksgiving Day 1962. The 1950s was the Lions' decade. They qualified for three NFL Championship matches—all against the Cleveland Browns—and won two.

GREEN BAY PACKERS
WWW.PACKERS.COM

First year: Although their first year in the NFL was 1921, the Packers had begun as an independent in 1919. They are the oldest team in the NFL in the same location.

Colors: green, gold, and white

Inspiration for name: Early team sponsor was a packing company.

Also known as: The Pack

Home games: Lambeau Field, Green Bay, Wisconsin (WI). Named after Curly Lambeau, first Packers' coach. Often heard: "The frozen tundra of Lambeau Field."

Airports: GRB (Green Bay Austin Straubel International); MKE (Milwaukee, WI—about a 2-hour drive).

FYI: Green Bay is called "Titletown, USA" for its abundance of NFL Championship trophies, totaling 13 (9 pre-Super Bowl). Winner of the first two "Super Bowls" (called the AFL-NFL Championship). Fans, who fabricate hats that look like Swiss cheese, are known as "cheeseheads." The "Lambeau Leap" is the tradition of a touchdown-scoring player jumping into the first row of seats to be congratulated by fans. They are the only non-profit, community-owned major sports franchise in the United States.

MINNESOTA VIKINGS
WWW.VIKINGS.COM

First year: 1961

Colors: purple, gold, and white

Inspiration for name: Early settlers to Minnesota were from Scandinavia, home of the seafaring and feared warriors, the Vikings. According to the first general manager, this profile represented "both an aggressive person with the will to win and the Nordic tradition in the northern Midwest."

Also known as: The Vikes

Home games: U.S. Bank Stadium, Minneapolis,

Minnesota (MN)
Airports: MSP (Minneapolis-St. Paul International) (Minneapolis, MS)
FYI: The Vikings were the first team to use the state as the team's designation instead of the city. The "Purple and Gold" fight song was written by Minnesota native Prince.

SOUTH DIVISION

ATLANTA FALCONS
WWW.ATLANTAFALCONS.COM

First year: 1966
Colors: red, silver, black, and white
Inspiration for name: A winning, name-the-team submission by a schoolteacher who suggested, "The falcon is proud and dignified with great courage and fight."
Also known as: The Dirty Birds
Home games: Mercedes-Benz Stadium, Atlanta Georgia (GA). The stadium has a retractable roof.
Airports: ATL (Hartsfield-Jackson International) Atlanta, GA
FYI: The Falcons have two Super Bowl appearances, one in which they blew a big lead in a gut-wrenching (painful) 2017 Super Bowl loss to New England. The Falcon mascot Dirty Bird's celebratory dance was featured in *Rolling Stone* magazine.

CAROLINA PANTHERS
WWW.PANTHERS.COM

First year: 1995
Colors: Black, "Carolina blue (light blue), and silver
Inspiration for name: Suggested by the team's original owner because panthers are "powerful, sleek, and strong."
Home games: Bank of America Stadium, Charlotte, North Carolina (NC)

Airports: CLT (Charlotte-Douglas International) Charlotte, NC

FYI: Their outstanding 15-1 season record in 2015 led to their second Super Bowl appearance. Their mantra (repeated word or phrase) is "keep pounding," which suggests to never give up.

NEW ORLEANS SAINTS
WWW.NEWORLEANSSAINTS.COM

First year: 1967

Colors: black, old gold, and white

Inspiration for name: New Orleans was awarded a franchise on "All Saints Day" (November 1, 1966), which is a Roman Catholic tradition. A popular song at the time by jazz great Louis Armstrong was "When the Saints Come Marching In."

Also known as: The Who Dats; the Black & Gold. In bad years: The Ain'ts ("is nots").

Home games: Mercedes-Benz Superdome, New Orleans, Louisiana (LA)

Airports: MSY (Louis Armstrong International) Kenner, LA

FYI: The year 2009 was a historic season. The Saints won a franchise-record 13 games and won the Super Bowl. They suffered a heartbreaking 2019 NFC championship loss attributed to a pass interference penalty not called against their opponent, which prompted a rule change for the 2019 season.

TAMPA BAY BUCCANEERS
WWW.BUCCANEERS.COM

First year: 1976

Colors: red, orange, black, gray, and pewter

Inspiration for name: A team advisory board selected the name for Jose Gaspar, a mythical buccaneer (pirate) in the Gulf of Mexico. Imagery of a fearless swashbuckler who loves adventure on the sea suited the energy of the new franchise.

Also known as: The Bucs

Home games: Raymond James Stadium, Tampa, Florida (FL); Unlike Green Bay, a city "Tampa Bay" refers to a region on the west coast of Florida.

Airports: TPA (Tampa International); MCO (Orlando International)

FYI: Their inaugural season in 1976 was winless (0-14). They were one of three teams to win their only Super Bowl appearance (2002 season).

WEST DIVISION

ARIZONA CARDINALS
WWW.AZCARDINALS.COM

First year: 1920. Chicago 1920-1959, St. Louis 1960-1987, Phoenix (Arizona) 1988-present. In 1943 only they merged with Pittsburgh to form Card-Pitt, due to player shortages during World War II.

Colors: red, white, and black

Inspiration for name: "Cardinals" has nothing to do with the red bird. The organization, dating back to the 1800s, was originally the Racine Normals, after Normal Park on Racine Street in Chicago. The evolution to Cardinals came about when the team wore faded maroon-colored jerseys, which the owner said was "cardinal red."

Also known as: Big Red, the Cards (when hot: The Cardiac Cards)

Home games: State Farm Stadium, Glendale, Arizona (AZ)

Airport: PHX (Phoenix Sky Harbor International) Phoenix, Arizona (AZ)

FYI: A player named Ernie Nevers set an NFL record of scoring all 40 of the Cardinals' points during a Thanksgiving Day game in 1929.

 **LA (LOS ANGELES) RAMS**
WWW.THERAMS.COM

First year: 1936. To 1945, Cleveland; 1946-94, Los Angeles; 1995-2015, St Louis.
Colors: Millennium blue, century gold (popular alternate: Royal blue and gold)
Inspiration for name: The first owner admired the Fordham University Rams, and so it was.
Home games: SoFi Stadium, Los Angeles, California (CA); Los Angeles
Airports: LAX (Los Angeles International Airport); regional—Burbank (BUR), Ontario (ONT), John Wayne (SNA), Santa Ana, California; and Long Beach (LGB)
FYI: Known as "the greatest show on turf" (1999-2001) for its high-powered offense. Its offense was also pretty potent in 2019 to storm to the Super Bowl under the guidance of the youngest head coach in modern NFL history (Sean McVay, age 33).

 **SAN FRANCISCO 49ERS**
WWW.49ERS.COM

First year: 1946 (AAFC; began play in the NFL in 1949)
Colors: Scarlet red, gold, and white
Inspiration for name: Recognizes the spirit and adventure of the 1849 rush for gold in California's Sierra Nevada mountain range.
Also known as: The Niners
Home games: Levi's Stadium, Santa Clara, California (CA)
Airports: SFO (San Francisco International); alternate: OAK (Oakland International)

FYI: The 49ers were a football dynasty in the '80s and '90s, winning five Super Bowls.

 **SEATTLE SEAHAWKS**
WWW.SEAHAWKS.COM

First year: 1976
Colors: Navy blue, green, gray, and white
Inspiration for name: Fan contest (20,000 entries). The winning name suggests fierce hawks whose main diet is fish. Also called an osprey, the bird has up to a six-foot wingspan.
Also known as: The Hawks
Home games: CenturyLink Field, Seattle, Washington (WA)
Airport: SEA (Seattle-Tacoma International)
FYI: Started in the AFC and switched to the NFC in 1996. They have one Super Bowl win in two appearances.

Footballogy: Elements of American Football for Non-Native Speakers of English

TEAM NICKNAMES

A cheesehead roots for...
(CC-BY-SA)

ACROSS
2. The "Black Hole"
5. Cleveland...St Louis...LA...
8. Early Americans who fought for independence
11. Cat: "King of the Jungle"
12. Another name for "giants"
14. Workers with iron ore
17. Think: voltage...battery
18. Adventurous heroes on horses
19. Near Niagara Falls
20. The National bird of the USA

DOWN
1 The first, da...
3. Sea creatures; mammals (give live birth)
4. Fervent fans in Titletown are known as "Cheeseheads."
6. The origin of name is a color, not a bird.
7. Explorers from Scandinavia
9. Pure, innocent, honest...
10. Young male horses
13. Like an osprey, a bird that fishes
15. Wild horses in the Rocky Mountains
16. Red + blue + yellow =

Footballogy: Elements of American Football for Non-Native Speakers of English

 Multiple choice—based on the chart on NFL teams

1. If we visit the Pro Football Hall of Fame, in Canton, Ohio, what international airport would we likely choose to fly into?
   a. CVG   b. PIT
   c. IND   d. CLE

2. How long is the trip to the Hall of Fame from this city?
   a. One hour by plane   b. One hour by car
   c. two hours   d. four hours

3. Which team is not in the AFC West?
   a. San Diego   b. Kansas City
   c. Arizona   d. Denver

4. Look at graphic at right:

   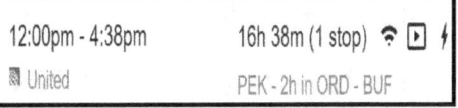

   A. What team does this person plan to see?
      a. Bears   b. Giants   c. Bills   d. 49ers

   B. How long is the layover (time between connecting flights)?
      a. 12:00 PM – 4:38 PM   b. 4:38
      c. two hours   d. data not provided

   C. At what airport the connecting flight?
      a. Orlando   b. Chicago
      c. Ohara   d. Beijing

   D. Travel is completed...
      a. in 14:38   b. in 40:38
      c. in 16:38   d. the same day

5. Which is not an airport for a New York area airport?
   a. JFK
   b. LOG
   c. EWR
   d. LGA

6. I buy a bobblehead football player souvenir whose colors are silver and black.
   a. Saints
   b. Falcons
   c. Raiders
   d. Eagles

7. "Steagles" (which is not true)
   a. One season
   b. Pittsburgh-Philadelphia
   c. 1943
   d. one franchise

8. "America's team...
   a. Wears red, white and blue
   b. has a star on its helmet
   c. is in the nation's capital
   d. is the Patriots

9. A game that begins at 1 PM at Gillette Stadium is shown at _____ in California.
   a. 10 AM
   b. 4 PM
   c. 7 PM
   d. 10 PM

10. Oldest team in one location:
    a. Green Bay
    b. Chicago
    c. Detroit
    d. Arizona

The 1981 season NFC Championship at Candlestick Park in San Francisco, California, featured teams that were accustomed to winning for many years—the Dallas Cowboys and a dynasty in the making, the 49ers. The winner of this game, on January 10, 1982, would go to Super Bowl XVI.

With 58 seconds left in the game and trailing 27-21, the 49ers faced a third-and-three at the Dallas six. Quarterback Joe Montana, taking the snap, was unable to deliver the ball to his primary target, who had slipped, which allowed the Cowboys to cover him against a pass. The intense Cowboy pass rush collapsed 49er protection in a hurry.

Montana had to scramble and appeared like he might go out of bounds and force a fourth-down play. But at the last moment, he did a pump fake (pretended to throw the ball). This caused the 6'9" defensive end chasing him to jump. Then he passed for real—a high, arching strike to tight end Dwight Clark, who made a leaping catch in the back of the end zone. With the extra point, the 49ers won the game 28-27 and the conference crown. This play, called "The Catch" is recognized as a marquee moment in the history of great plays in the NFL.

Nothing's Perfect

It wasn't a pretty catch, but the catch that came to be known as "The Helmet Catch," seen by millions in Super

Bowl XLII on February 2, 2008, had "nothing's perfect" written all over it.

The New England Patriots had completed a perfect 16-0 2007 season and were attempting to become the first team since the 1972 Miami Dolphins to finish unbeaten (including the postseason). The only team to stand in the way was the New York Giants.

Late in the fourth quarter, the Patriots were ahead by four points. The Giants were on the move. At third and five from their own 44-yard line, Giants quarterback Eli Manning barely escaped the grasp of three Patriots defensive players. He managed to stay on his feet and bought himself some time. Scrambling, he spotted receiver David Tyree 32 yards downfield.

But Manning never saw the end of the play. Clobbered just as he released the football, Manning managed to put air under the ball, which means the throw was a little high. Yet Tyree, leaping awkwardly, held on to the ball against his helmet while absorbing brutal impacts from defensive backs as well as the ground. Manning knew the result by the reaction of the Giants' partisans and his teammates.

The first down breathed life into the Giants offense, which completed the drive with a touchdown pass to Plaxico Buress to win 17-14. The stone-cold stats of the day listed Tyree with three catches for 43 yards but do not capture the emotion of this amazing reception, recognized as one of the best plays in Super Bowl history. NFL Films named it "the play of the decade" in the 2000s.

Facts are stubborn things, but statistics are pliable.
— Mark Twain, American author

CHAPTER XI

Passion for Data

When most of us think of data and statistics, we think of a left-brained, rational mind like Mr. Spock in *Star Trek*. But in American football, data and statistics are to get excited about. They are part of what fuels the passion. This section grounds us in the numbers game in American football. To appreciate the game depends on knowing a little about the information in "stat sheets," which appears in media reports, online journals, and broadcasts.

Word Preview

| statistics (stats) | inferences | probability | objectivity |
| hypothesis | cup of tea | defer | unsung hero |

Are you a "stathead"? A stathead is someone who loves statistics. It's OK if stats is not your cup of tea. Numbers and data are not for everybody. Each person has different preferences. Yet to understand some basic statistics adds greater appreciation for and enjoyment of football. How do statistics do this? They aid our ability to:

- Make inferences
- Develop hypotheses
- Project probabilities ("tendencies")

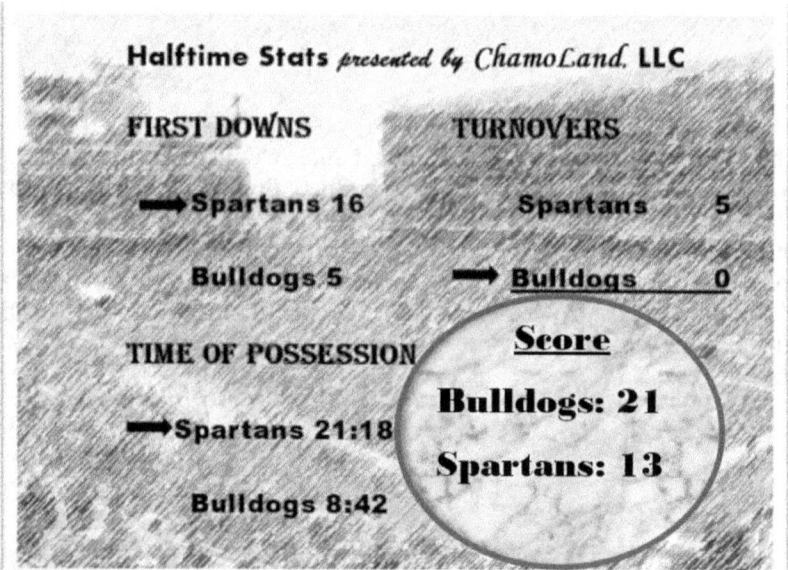

Example of statistics shown on TV screen illustrates how a team can dominate in important statistical categories (first downs, time of possession, etc.), but one in particular—turnovers—can explain why a team is behind in the one statistic that matters most: the score.

Statistics are part of the discussion of football. First, they drive pre-game shows, where experts (usually former players or coaches) give their opinions and make predictions. Stats make up halftime shows, where the first half is analyzed, and based on statistical evidence, predictions are made regarding what adjustments each team might perform to be successful in the second half. Expect stats to appear on the screen now and again between plays during the telecast. Remember, the quiet time between plays is an opportunity to hold viewers' attention with interesting data. Announcers cite statistics frequently.

Finally, to be a fan is to be emotional but statistics are stone-cold facts. They are like Mr. Spock of *Star Trek* fame who did not express feelings, only cerebral objectivity. A 48-yard Hail Mary pass to win the game brings out the emotions of the crowd; however, the stats column in the news source will only state the facts: the pass, from whom, to whom, and at what time of the game.

Statistics come in three forms: individual, team, and game.

Individual statistics cover a season and the career of a player. Mostly, they include measurements of the accomplishments of skills positions players. Not much is recorded on offensive interior linemen except for games played and games started. (That's why tackles, guards, and centers are regarded as "unsung heroes.")

Team statistics are divided into how a team did in a game, in a season, how it did in its series against an opponent, and other areas. This gives people something to talk about and connects the experience of watching a broadcast or attending a game.

Game statistics provide a side-by-side team comparison, from first downs to total yards, passes completed to passes intercepted, sacks, and total yards lost to sacks. A look at the statistics can give a person a sense of what kind of game it was—high scoring or low, dominated by one team or a close game, a balanced attack or mostly passing or rushing, and who won. Occasionally, one team rules the statistics but loses the game. Half the fun is to study the statistics and find out why. Maybe the team fumbled the ball away too many times. Maybe the team's fast-scoring offense was offset by the slow ball control offense of the other team, which wore down the opponent's defense and kept its big-play offense off the field. The factors that contribute to outcomes are many and statistics help us discover them.

 I. Word check: Fill in with one of the words in the Words Preview

1. People who overeat hotdogs more often die of heart attacks, say _____.

2. A low-scoring game is not my _____. I prefer lots of offense.

3. He's from El Salvador. We can make an _____ that he likes pupusas.

4. A team with a bad quarterback has a low _____ of beating a team with an outstanding one.

5. Brave people who don't get credit for their actions are _____.

6. Many theories, or _____, believe that talent + skill + a good work ethic equate to a strong performance.

7. When we look at things with _____, without bias or prejudice, our minds get a better picture of a player or team's strengths and weakness.

8. The decision is not mine; I'll _____ to you.

Team Stats (also called a "yardstick")

II. Mark the appropriate answer X on the line.

	PIT	BAL
First Downs	27	18
Rush-Yds-TDs	27-113-1	16-61-1
Cmp-Att-Yd-TD-INT	29-48-292-2-0	24-38-218-0-0
Sacked-Yards	1-10	2-14
Net Pass Yards	282	204
Total Yards	395	265
Fumbles-Lost	0-0	1-0
Turnovers	0	0
Penalties-Yards	8-103	5-25
Third Down Conv.	10-16	4-12
Fourth Down Conv.	1-1	0-1
Time of Possession	36:29	23:31

PIT=Pittsburgh Steelers   BAL = Baltimore Ravens

1. Which was the visiting team?
    ___Pit   ___Bal

2. Which team attempted 48 passes?
    ___Pit   ___Bal

3. Which team had fewer first downs?
    ___Pit   ___ Bal

4. Which team was successful in turning a fourth down into a first down?
　　___ Pit　　　　　___Bal

5. Which team controlled the game clock?
　　___Pit　　　　　___Bal

6. Which team was sacked more often?
　　___Pit　　　　　___Bal

7. How many times did Pittsburgh do a running play?
　　___ 27　　　　　___ 113

8. How many times was Baltimore flagged?
　　___ 25　　　　　___5

9. How many passes were not completed by Pittsburgh?
　　___ 19　　　　　___29

10. Which team do you think won?
　　___ Bal　　　　　___ Pit

III. Scoring Details

Quarter	Time	Tm	Detail	NWE	MIA
1	8:13	Patriots	James Develin 2 yard rush (Stephen Gostkowski kick failed)	6	0
	5:32	Dolphins	Kenny Stills 7 yard pass from Ryan Tannehill (Jason Sanders kick)	6	7
2	14:14	Patriots	Julian Edelman 2 yard pass from Tom Brady (Stephen Gostkowski kick)	13	7
	13:26	Dolphins	Brandon Bolden 54 yard rush (Jason Sanders kick)	13	14
	10:32	Patriots	Cordarrelle Patterson 37 yard pass from Tom Brady (Stephen Gostkowski kick)	20	14
	7:28	Dolphins	Brandon Bolden 6 yard rush (Jason Sanders kick)	20	21
	3:49	Patriots	Rob Gronkowski 16 yard pass from Tom Brady (Stephen Gostkowski kick)	27	21
3	3:58	Dolphins	Brice Butler 23 yard pass from Ryan Tannehill (Jason Sanders kick)	27	28
4	6:45	Patriots	Stephen Gostkowski 32 yard field goal	30	28
	0:16	Patriots	Stephen Gostkowski 22 yard field goal	33	28
	0:00	Dolphins	Kenyan Drake 69 yard pass from Ryan Tannehill	33	34

1. How many minutes and seconds had passed when James Develin scored?
   ___ 6:47   ___ 8:13

2. How many missed extra points did New England have?
   ___ one   ___ two

3. Which team was ahead at halftime?
   ___ New England ___ Miami

4. Who scored on a six-yard running play?
   ___ Gronkowski   ___ Bolden

5. Which team did Kenny Stills play for?
   ___ New England ___ Miami

6. How many total field goals were in the game?
   ___ two   ___ three

7. What kind of play might the last one have been?
   ___ rushing   ___ Hail Mary

Use this graphic below to answer 8-10

Game Info	
Won Toss	Dolphins (deferred)
Roof	outdoors
Surface	grass
Weather	82 degrees, wind 13 mph
Vegas Line	New England Patriots -9.5
Over/Under	49.5 **(over)**

8. How many points were anticipated?
   ___ 50 or more   ___ under 50

9. Which team kicked off to start the game?
   ___ New England ___ Dolphins

10. Did the underdog or the favorite win?
    ___ favorite   ___ underdog

Player Game Statistics

IV. Questions 1-10: Offense: tm (team); cmp (completed passes); att (pass attempts); yds (yards); int (interceptions); lng (longest); rate (quarterback rating); tgt (targeted – number of times thrown to); fmb (fumbles); Fl (fumbles lost); **Defense**: PD (passes defended); SK (sacks); tackles—solo/ast (assisted) comb (combined); TFL (Tackles for loss of yardage); QB hit (physical contact with QB but not sack); **Special teams:** RT (kick/punt returns); XPA (Extra point attempt; XPM (Extra point Made); FGA (field goal attempt); FGM (field goal made)

Player		Passing								Rushing				Receiving					Fumbles	
	Tm	Cmp	Att	Yds	TD	Int	Sk	Yds	Lng	Rate	Att	Yds	TD	Lng	Tgt	Rec	Yds	TD	Lng	Fmb	FL
Jared Goff	LAR	19	35	295	3	0	5	26	32	111.0	5	7	0	7	0	0	0	0	0	0	0
Johnny Hekker	LAR	1	1	12	0	0	0	0	12	116.7	0	0	0	0	0	0	0	0	0	0	0
Todd Gurley	LAR	0	0	0	0	0	0	0	0		25	114	0	23	7	6	81	1	32	0	0
Brandin Cooks	LAR	0	0	0	0	0	0	0	0		2	9	0	5	8	3	74	0	32	0	0

LAR= Los Angeles Rams

1. Which player had the longest pass completion?
   ___Goff   ___ Hekker

2. Which player had a higher QB rating?
   ___Goff   ___Hekker

3. How many rushing attempts did the Rams make?
   ___130   ___32

4. How many times was the ball thrown to Gurley?
   ___ 7   ___6

		Def Interceptions						Tackles				
Player	Tm	Int	Yds	TD	Lng	PD	Sk	Comb	Solo	Ast	TFL	QBHits
Mark Barron	LAR	0	0	0	0	0	0.0	6	5	1	1	0
Michael Brockers	LAR	0	0	0	0	0	0.0	2	2	0	1	0
Marqui Christian	LAR	0	0	0	0	0	0.0	1	0	1	0	0
Aaron Donald	LAR	0	0	0	0	0	2.0	3	2	1	2	4
Samson Ebukam	LAR	0	0	0	0	0	0.0	4	2	2	0	0
Troy Hill	LAR	0	0	0	0	1	0.0	1	1	0	0	0

Individual statistics (defense)

5. How many interceptions did the Rams as a team get?
   ____ one   ____ none

6. Which player tackled the quarterback behind the line of scrimmage?
   ____ Donald   ____ Brockers

7. How many unassisted tackles did Mark Barron have?
   ____ five   ____ six

8. Troy Hill had one PD (pass defended). The pass was _____.
   ____ completed   ____ knocked down

Footballogy: Elements of American Football for Non-Native Speakers of English

		Kick Returns					Punt Returns				
Player	Tm	Rt	Yds	Y/Rt	TD	Lng	Ret	Yds	Y/R	TD	Lng
Jojo Natson	LAR	1	9	9.0	0	9	2	2	1.0	0	2
Blake Countess	LAR	3	55	18.3	0	25	0	0		0	0

		Scoring				Punting			
Player	Tm	XPM	XPA	FGM	FGA	Pnt	Yds	Y/P	Lng
Greg Zeurlein	LAR	1	1	2	2	0	0		0
Johnny Hekker	LAR					7	316	45.1	52

9. What is the team average yardage per kickoff return?
    __ 6   __ 18.3

10. How many points by Zuerlein?
    __ three   __ seven

Career STATS

Abbreviations in quarterback statistics

Partial compilation of New England quarterback Tom Brady's career statistics (adapted and abridged) from pro-football-reference.com

Year	G	GS	QBrec	Cmp	Att	Cmp%	Yds	TD	Int	Sk	Yds	Rate
2000	1	0		1	3	33.3	6	0	0	0	0	42.4
2001*	15	14	11-3-0	264	413	63.9	2843	18	12	41	216	86.5
2002	16	16	9-7-0	373	601	62.1	3764	28	14	31	190	85.7
2003	16	16	14-2-0	317	527	60.2	3620	23	12	32	219	85.9
2004*	16	16	14-2-0	288	474	60.8	3692	28	14	26	162	92.6
2005*	16	16	10-6-0	334	530	63.0	**4110**	26	14	26	188	92.3
2006	16	16	12-4-0	319	516	61.8	3529	24	12	26	175	87.9
2007*	16	16	16-0-0	398	578	**68.9**	**4806**	**50**	8	21	128	**117.2**
2008	1	1	1-0-0	7	11	63.6	76	0	0	0	0	83.9
2009*	16	16	10-6-0	371	565	65.7	4398	28	13	16	86	96.2
2010*	16	16	14-2-0	324	492	65.9	3900	**36**	4	25	175	**111.0**
2011*	16	16	13-3-0	401	611	65.6	5235	39	12	32	173	105.6
2012*	16	16	12-4-0	401	637	63.0	4827	34	8	27	182	98.7
2013*	16	16	12-4-0	380	628	60.5	4343	25	11	40	256	87.3
2014*	16	16	12-4-0	373	582	64.1	4109	33	9	21	134	97.4
2015*	16	16	12-4-0	402	624	64.4	4770	**36**	7	38	225	102.2
2016*	12	12	11-1-0	291	432	67.4	3554	28	2	15	87	112.2
2017*	16	16	13-3-0	385	**581**	66.3	**4577**	32	8	35	201	102.8
2018*	16	16	11-5-0	375	570	65.8	4355	29	11	21	147	97.7

Att = passes attempted
Comp = passes completed
Fum = number of fumbles
G = games
GS = games started
int = interceptions
Lost = fumbles lost to opposition
Pct = percent completed

QBrec = won-lost record in games started
Rtg/rate – quarterback rating (see QB Rating formula)
sck = number of times sacked
td = touchdowns
y/a = average yards per attempt

V. Brady Stats: Fill in the blank with information based on the chart

1. What season was Tom Brady's best QB rating?
   _____

2. How many total yards did he have in 2011?
   _____

3. What year was he sacked the most?
   _____

4. How many games did he start in 2001?
   _____

5. What was his win-loss record for 2014?
   _____

6. Which season was his team undefeated?
   _____

7. What year was he sacked the second-most?
   _____

8. In what year did he complete the most TD passes?
   _____

9. What percentage of passes did he complete in 2006?
   _____

10. Except 2000 and 2008, what year for fewest interceptions?
    _____

Quarterback Rating (AKA "Passer Rating")

A statistic that announcers talk about is a quarterback's "rating." This can identify how a quarterback did in a single game, a season, and his career. A more accurate description is "passer rating" because the statistics only measure the hard facts of the quarterback, not the intangibles like leadership and play-calling that make a professional quarterback. In the NFL rating, about 86 is average. Anything over 100 is outstanding. The maximum rating in the NFL is 158. As of 2019, Aaron Rogers of the Green Bay Packers held the highest rating for a career, 103.1 and for a single season, 122.5.

The CFL's formula for quarterback rating is like the NFL's, whereas the NCAA applies a different method. The NFL/CFL passer rating formula includes four variables:

- completion percentage
- yards per attempt
- touchdowns per attempt
- interceptions per attempt

FORMULA:

$$a = \left(\frac{COMP}{ATT} - .3\right) \times 5$$

$$b = \left(\frac{YDS}{ATT} - 3\right) \times .25$$

$$c = \left(\frac{TD}{ATT}\right) \times 20$$

$$d = 2.375 - \left(\frac{INT}{ATT} \times 25\right)$$

$$\text{Passer Rating} = \left(\frac{(a+b+c+d)}{6}\right) \times 100$$

ATT = Number of passing attempts
COMP = Number of completions
YDS = Passing yards
TD = Touchdown passes
INT = Interceptions

Football Calculator	
Required Data Entry	
Quarterback Pass Attempts	38
Quarterback Pass Completions	22
Total Passing Yards	302
Completed Touchdown Passes	4
Total Interceptions	1
Calculate Reset	
Calculated Results	
Completion Percentage	57.895
Passing Yards Per Attempt	7.947
Touchdown Passes Percentage	10.526
Intercepted Passes Percentage	2.632
Quarterback Passer Rating	107.566

VI. *You Try It:*

Go to www.CSGNetwork.com (or a quarterback calculator of your choice) and compute the following quarterback rating (or you may use pencil and paper).

Passes attempted: **52**
Passes completed: **31**
Total passing yards: **414**
Touchdown passes: **5**
Total interceptions: **4**

According to the information in the reading, this QB's rating is:

____ below average   ____ average
____ above-average   ____ superior

VII. Verbal Assessment

PF = Points for
PA = Points against
PD = Points difference—"for" and "against"

Tm	W	L	T	W-L%	PF	PA	PD
AFC East							
New England Patriots*	11	5	0	.688	436	325	111
Miami Dolphins	7	9	0	.438	319	433	-114
Buffalo Bills	6	10	0	.375	269	374	-105
New York Jets	4	12	0	.250	333	441	-108

From www.pro-football-reference.com

Choose from the adjectives in word box to complete the exercise about the standings (not all words will be used)

good	bad			few	large
better	worse	more	less	fewer	larger
the best	the worst	the most	the least	the fewest	the largest

1. The Patriots had _____ record in the division.

2. The Bills record was _____ than NY but _____ than Miami.

3. The Dolphins', Jets', and Bills' records were not as ____ as New England's.

4. The Jets had _____ record in the division.

5. The Jets scored ____ points than the Dolphins but ____ than the Patriots.

6. The Patriots scored _____ points.

7. The Dolphins won _____ games than the Patriots.

8. The Patriots had _____ point differential.

9. The Jets' winning percentage was _____ in the Division.

10. The Bills scored _____ points in the AFC.

Footballogy: Elements of American Football for Non-Native Speakers of English

The Game

Complete the crossword puzzle below on elements of the game.

ACROSS
2. color of penalty flag
4. chief official
5. advance ball 10 yard or more (2 words)
9. illegally disrupts receiver
10. ball carrier caught in own end zone
12. pass play—bug/insect in name (2 words)
16. "paydirt"
17. kickoff goes beyond back of end zone
20. number of downs to get a first
21. members for a long time (2 words)

DOWN
1 line of _____
3. extra time
6. member of defense catches the ball
7. 24-24, for example
8. point value of missed PAT
11. three points
12 person who begins a business
13. ball carrier drops the ball
14. pre-game _____ toss
15. They carry 10-yard markers: Chain _____
18. linemen protect ball carriers
19. first word in last second desperation pass.

Great moments

The Fumble

What to call this game depends upon whose side you're on. Philadelphia Eagles fans call it "Miracle in the Meadowlands." But New York Giants fans, who saw a "sure win" go up in smoke (disappear, as if consumed by fire), have another point of view: "Meltdown in the Meadowlands" (of gigantic proportions).

The day's contest, on November 19, 1978, was one of the many wild and unpredictable occurrences in this longstanding rivalry (since 1933) between these present-day NFC East foes. So many meetings had been decided by just one play, as this one would prove to be.

With under two minutes game-time remaining, the Giants, who held a 17-12 lead, had just intercepted the Eagles deep in their own territory. All they needed to do was to run time off the clock to secure the win since the Eagles, who were out of timeouts, were helpless to stop it. Fate was in the hands of the Giants.

To put the sequence about to transpire in perspective, it should be remembered that in those days, a quarterback "taking the knee," or kneeling after the hike to down the ball, was prohibited. The so-called "victory formation," where the offense bunches together at the line of scrimmage to protect the ball carrier (and preserve the win) had not been invented. This meant that the Giants needed to run a bona fide, or authentic, play—a "safe" play.

That play was a handoff but the ball bounced out of the quarterback's hands and off the hips of the running back. It was scooped up by a defensive back, who ran 26 yards untouched for an Eagles' score and an improbable 19-17 win. This game is a glorious reminder once again that in the game of football, nothing is a "sure win" and no lead is safe until the clock reaches 00:00.

The meanings of words are not in the words, they are in us.
—S.I. Hayakawa

CHAPTER XII

Policy, Rules & Decorum

> Rules for the people who play and rules for the ones who watch. Information in this section, taken from stadium policy guidelines, allows us to test our understanding and interpretation of policies that can affect our participation as spectators. This is followed by an unusual look at "polite conversation."

Word Preview

taunting	disruptive behavior
impairment	foul access
harassment	

A Sampling of a General Stadium Policy

Aisle Policy: During the game, please wait at the top of the aisle until the end of a play to return to your seats.

Alcohol Policy: Fans appearing to be less than 30 years old must present a valid ID to purchase alcoholic beverages.
- No alcohol will be sold to fans who appear intoxicated.
- There will be a two-beer limit per transaction.
- Fans passing alcohol to minors (under the age of 21) will be ejected and subject to arrest.

Bag Search: Fans are encouraged to limit the number of items they bring to the stadium. All bags must be clear or plastic and should not exceed 12" x 6" x 12" (about 30 x 15 x 30 centimeters). Examples of allowable bags include:
- One-gallon clear plastic freezer bags (Ziploc bag or similar).
- Small clutch bags, about the size of a hand—not larger than 4.5" x 6.5" (11.5 x 16.5 cm) (An exception can be for medically necessary items after proper inspection.)

Banners and Signs: These and similar items, such as tee-shirts, that have obscene or indecent messages or pictures not event-related or potentially offensive, are prohibited.

Cameras: Still only. Videos are not permitted. Lens must not exceed 6 inches in length or interfere with other fans' enjoyment of the game.

Cell Phones: Cell phones are allowed. No selfie poles. Please be considerate of others.

Disabled Persons: This stadium follows the Americans with Disabilities Act (ADA), a 1990 law that guarantees access to everyone to public facilities. This stadium is equipped with ramps and elevators.

Lost and Found: All fans looking to claim or report lost items during an event should visit one of the Guest Services Centers. Lost items will be kept for one month; those unclaimed after that time will be donated to charity.

Lost Children: Lost children and fans should be taken to one of the Guest Services Centers. Parents looking for a lost child should check with the nearest event staff or security personnel.

Merchandise: For your convenience, all points of sale accept MasterCard, Visa, American Express, Discover, and Travelers Checks.

"My First Game" Certificates: If this is your first game, get a "first game certificate" at the nearest Guest Services Booth. These certificates are for fans of all ages, young and old!

Nursing Rooms: Private locations are provided to mothers to breastfeed their children. Two nursing rooms are connected to the lobby below section 129. Each room can be locked from the inside and is equipped with an electrical outlet, a lounge chair, a small table, and a television.

Parking & Tailgating: Parking areas are open four-and-a-half hours prior to kickoff. In compliance with league policy, and in the interest of public safety, vehicles may be subject to search.

Payphones/TDD Phones: A payphone is located on the main concourse (Section 137). This phone is equipped with TDD capabilities (Telecommunications Device for the Deaf).

A Select List of Prohibited Items/Behaviors

- Abusive, foul or disruptive language or indecent clothing
- Bottles, cans, and beverage containers of any kind, including beverage coolers
- Smoking (including marijuana and e-cigarettes)
- Fighting, taunting, or threatening remarks or gestures
- Displays of affection not appropriate in a public setting
- Intoxication or other signs of impairment related to alcohol or drugs
- Inappropriate signs or banners (vulgar, insulting or not related to the event)
- Laser pointers
- Noisemakers (such as air horns, cowbells, whistles, and instruments)
- Verbal or physical harassment of other guests, including the guest team's fans
- Video cameras and the use of video-capable cell phones for video recording

Persons ejected are required to take an online personal conduct course. Code of Conduct certificates are presented to completers, who must present this before they are allowed to return to the stadium. Issues in the class include:

- Following the instructions of stadium personnel
- The effects of alcohol/substance abuse on responsible behavior

- Controlling emotions/behavior; becoming less impulsive
- Skills in improving empathy or compassion toward others
- Managing stress/anger (Not only at football games but in the game of life!)

I. Multiple Choice: Solve the problem by choosing the correct solution

1. Why should a fan wait at the top of the aisle until the end of a play to return to his/her seat?
    a. To be considerate of others
    b. To buy a hot dog
    c. To see what happens on the play
    d. It's a better view

2. What kind of message on a banner would likely be prohibited?
    a. "Go Raiders"
    b. "Play to Win"
    c. "The Road to the Super Bowl goes through Denver"
    d. "Your mother!"

3. A person attending his or her first game...
    a. is escorted to his/her seat
    b. is given a code of conduct certificate
    c. can obtain a "My First Game" certificate
    d. receives a complimentary beverage

4. Which item is not prohibited in the stadium?
    a. laser pointer
    b. drone airplane
    c. small, clear plastic bag
    d. a can of soda

5. If someone calls me a bozo (a clown) I should
    a. call him a bad name right back—only worse!
    b. ignore his comments
    c. tell him "thank you"
    d. call stadium security

II. True/false

1. I can videotape the action.
    T   F

2. A kiss on the cheek is an inappropriate show of affection.
    T   F

3. I can take selfies at the game.
    T   F

4. Personal conduct classes are for everyone.
    T   F

5. The online class is an attempt to correct bad behavior.
    T   F

Word association: *Draw a line to connect the action with the words*

1. taunting   a. "He's wasted, dead drunk"

2. disruptive behavior b. "Hey, Mister, your team sucks."

3. foul language   c. "That man's acting strange!"

4. access   d. "Please leave me alone, Sir."

5. Harassment   e. "Clean up your mouth, Sir!"

6. Intoxication   f. "She's disabled. Let her sit in the first row."

Whenever two people meet, there are really six people present. There is each man as he sees himself, each man as the other person sees him, and each man as he really is.

— William James
American philosopher (1842-1910)

Please and Thank You

Word Bank

Try to guess the meanings of these words from the context in the content that follows. *Hint: Often the meaning or its synonym is set off by a comma after the word, or after the word "or."*

in-your-face	displeasure	manners	customary
easy-come-easy-go		glance	child-rearing
convey	genuine	sarcasm	impatience
heartfelt	crocodile tears		jeer

Mother used to remind us to "mind our P's and Q's." "Watch your manners," she preached. "Don't forget to say please and thank you." After all, our good conduct was a measure of her job of child-rearing.

On the stage of life, the same words can send different messages or have meanings hidden behind masks. So, as adults, what do we say when we want something? Just as Mom taught: "Please and thank you."
Nothing is so magical. Americans love people who show appreciation. Who doesn't? In formal business relationships or among family and friends, a simple custom means a lot—and it's free. "Good manners," said 19th-century American essayist Ralph Waldo Emerson, "are made up of petty sacrifices."

But as the old American folk song goes, "the old gray mare, she ain't* what she used to be," changes in society have brought changes in acceptable ways of communicating and behaving. In modern times, a "thank you" or a "please" are polite on the surface, but might be a mask for sarcasm, the opposite of the standard intention.

Please

"Please," which adds politeness to a request, can come at the beginning or end of a statement: "Please pass the salt," or "Pass the salt, please." Or part of a question: "Can you please pass the salt?" But "please," when stressed, can show impatience or displeasure. "It can make a question sound urgent, blunt, and even downright rude," says Ben T. Smith, a linguistics and dialects consultant.

We should be aware of how others use "please" and "thank you" and how we express these words to others, at work, in a café, or wherever conversation takes place. Doing so is one small step in empowering us to say what we mean and mean what we say.

So, what's the remedy for a genuine request?

Instead of... *Please, would you come here?* (demand) say...*Would you come here?* (or say it with "please" but do not stress it).

Alternative: *Could I ask you to come here?* (See box below.)

> "A gentleman is one who never unintentionally offends."
> (This applies to ladies, too.)
> — Oscar Wilde, Irish playwright

Option A:

Leave "please" on, but do not stress the word.
- *Can someone please pass me the mustard?* (conveys impatience, irritation)

---

* Colloquial (slang) expression for "isn't"

- Say: *Can someone pass me the mustard?*
- *Will you turn the sound down, please?*
- Say: *Will you turn the sound down?*

Alternative: *Do you mind if I ask you to turn down the sound?* (In this case, a "no" answer means "yes" and a "yes" means "no.")

Option B:

Introduce your request. (Then your question, with or without please, can be gracious.):

- *I hate to bother you, but (your request)...*
- *Sorry to intrude, but...*
- *Sorry for interrupting, but...*
- *Pardon me, but...*
- *Excuse me, but ...*
- *Do you mind if I ask you a question?*
- *May I ask you a question?*
- *Could you do me a favor?*

Examples

- *Pardon me, but could you please tell me the train number for the stadium?*
- *May I ask you a question? Which train goes to the stadium?*
- *Sorry for interrupting, but could you please tell me the price of tickets at midfield?*
- *Could you do me a favor? Would you let me see your Game Day program?*

Thank You

(you're welcome and other expressions of opposite meanings)

Not every "thank you" is equal. It can be pure of heart or maybe contain verbal irony.

- What do you say to a person who slams the door in your face? *Thank you.*
- What does a defensive back tell the quarterback for the easy pick six? *Thank you.*
- What does the wife say to her husband after six hours of watching football when he finally says, "Hi, honey." *Thank you.*
- What would a quarterback like to tell his fullback who missed a blocking assignment that resulted in him being sacked? (But won't because he's the leader of the team.) *Thank you.*
- What did one guy say to the guy who stole his girlfriend? *Thank you.* (This might be sincere!)
- What does a coach whose team has been flagged all afternoon tell the official when, finally, the flag goes against the other team? *Thank you.*
- What do you say to the person who steps in front of you in line without as much as a please or a thank you, excuse me, or a sorry? *You're welcome.*
- What do fans do when their team, with an inept offense and trailing 30-0, avoids a shut-out by nailing a last-second field goal? *They cheer.* (This is called "crocodile cheers.")

Yet some things are heartfelt:

- What do fans do when their inept team reeks, or stinks up, the joint (a place) like Limburger cheese? *They jeer.* (A "booing" sound.)

Excuse Me

When the need arises to, say, interrupt a conversation, who can argue that "excuse me" is proper for the intrusion?

But "excuse me" can also be a bold statement, as if to say: "Out of my way. Can't you see that I'm here?" A polite expression thus expresses rudeness. Second, "excuse me" can be a psychologically imbalanced expression of another's sensitivity, such as taking offense over small, insignificant matters or admitting wrongdoing in an aggressive way.

Sensitive person: Say, Mike, when you get to the game in Philadelphia, you should try the Beef of Weck (*kummelweck*, a hard roll with caraway seeds).

Mike: No! That's in Buffalo! It's Philly cheesesteak where I'm going.

Sensitive person: Well, excuse me!

Sir/Ma'am

How do we address someone we don't know? Traditionally, it is "sir" for a man or "ma'am" for a woman. Life is less formal, however, in this age of forever young. "Sir" and "ma'am" (a reduction of "madam") are intended to show respect or deference to rank, such as in the military. Yet in some corners, people hold that sir or ma'am have the impersonal feeling of a research clinic or laboratory.

"Call me anything, but don't call me sir," a teacher once responded to a student who asked him how he wanted to be addressed. "It makes me sound old and it sounds so sterile."

In the case with this teacher, the solution is easy—just learn his last name and address him as "Mr. —."

For a woman, this would be "Ms." before the last name (British, surname) unless she has a title such as "doctor," "professor," etc. that would be more appropriate.

Ms. does not identify marital status (married or single) like Miss or Mrs.

Stadium employees, for example, have tags with their names on them. Spot it. Use it.

Says Kevin Achtzener, a consultant on using visual strategies, the safe solution to a addressing people is to not use anything. "Instead of, *Yes, ma'am,* just say, *Yes,*" he advises. "If a lady drops her keys, try catching her eye and saying, *Excuse me! You dropped your keys.*"

On the other hand, a woman of any age would not normally object to being called "Miss," a term for a young lady. "Excuse me, Miss, you dropped your keys."

To address a woman as "lady" is impolite; however, if two or more are in the group, "ladies" is permitted.

Not polite: *Hi, lady.*
Polite: *Hi, ladies.*

Similarly, "Mister" (Mr.) without the last name can be a fighting word at worst, disrespectful at best. However, two men together may be addressed "gentlemen."

Additionally, addressing someone you've just met only by last name is not polite. Last-name calling pulls rank: The person being spoken to is deemed inferior.

Finally, ma'am and sir can be caustic (hurtful), suggesting the exact opposite of respect, to signal belligerence, confrontation, or combativeness.

"Sir, you're in my parking space. I suggest you park someplace else, sir."

"Sorry, but I don't see your name on it, sir."

Politeness is not the intent, of course. And "sorry" is clearly not an apology.

Sir and ma'am can appear in a variety of settings—for example, a water-cooler debate over topics of interest where people disagree: "Sir, you don't know what you're talking about!"

Polite discussions on politics or controversial matters can turn into hostile affairs with ample usage of sir or ma'am.

So, is it "sir," "mister," "ma'am," or "miss?" The best answer may be none of the above.

"Hey, you," is rude. So is calling someone we meet for the first time "friend" or "my friend." Although acceptable in other customs, addressing someone on such familiar terms on the first meeting in the USA is not viewed as friendly.

Finally, in these uncertain times over gender identity, an appropriate response might be to ask, "How would you like to be addressed?"

In sum, verbal irony is the part of speech intended to convey emotions or thoughts that are contradictory or the opposite of reality. Here is a sample (underlined words emphasized):

"Oh, <u>really</u>." Not to be believed. (Prove it!)

"<u>Great</u> game." Said when it was a bad game

"Nice day for a game, isn't it?" It's pouring rain, windy and cold.

"Nice going." Said when something is not done right, like an offense that cannot get a first down on 4th and inches.

"Now <u>that's</u> a surprise." Said after hearing expected news, like a 1-10 team losing to a 10-1 team.

"So!" Means what's the problem? No big deal. No sympathy. Example: A player was fined by the league for bad conduct. You say, "So!"

"Sorry!" Can be a sincere apology but can mean: "It's YOUR fault." (I expect YOU to apologize.)

"Take your time…" suggests that you are too slow (Example: Seconds on the clock in the closing seconds of the game, the team behind doesn't hurry while time ticks off)

"<u>Really</u>, Sherlock. <u>Are you sure</u>?" Response to someone who says the obvious: "Alabama is a very good football team."

I. Multiple choice: Circle letter of the best answer

1. Verbal irony expresses _____.
    a. the truth	b. the difference
    c. sincerity	d. sarcasm

2. Which is an example of verbal irony?
    a. To a female officer: "Yes, ma'am."
    b. To the stadium attendant with a name tag: "Mr. Smith, I have a question."
    c. To fellow fans: "Enjoy the game, ladies."
    d. To someone sitting in your place: "Thank you for keeping my seat warm."

3. "Please," "thank you," "excuse me" and "sorry" are
    a. names	b. friendly
    c. used in different ways	d. honest

4. <u>Verbal irony</u> using sir or ma'am can show...
    a. agreement	b. respect
    c. politeness	d. disagreement

5. "You're welcome" can be...
    a. polite	b. sarcastic
    c. either a/b	d. neither a/b

6. Which is not a verbally ironic way to express displeasure with a team's performance?
    a. a cheer	b. "Nice job, bozos!"
    c. a jeer	d. "Next year!"

7. What might someone say to another person who cuts in front of them in the food line?
    a. "You're welcome."	b. "Excuse me."
    c. "Please, go ahead."	d. all of them

8. What might be spoken when the coach of a team with a bad record is fired?
   a. "Now that's a surprise."   b. "Nice going."
   c. "You must be kidding!"   d. A and C

9. Football is played in autumn. (Response to mean "obviously.")
   a. "Really, Sherlock, are you sure?"
   b. "So!"
   c. "Nice going."
   d. "Take your time."

10. "Thank you."
    a. sometimes polite
    b. always polite
    c. always impolite
    d. polite only when spoken in polite company

II. Words: Use words from the word preview to complete this exercise.

At the concessions, it is _____ to wait in line for service. When I first _____ at him, the customer appeared relaxed, you know, ____-____- go. But when he expressed _____ for slow service at a busy time, his __-____- ___ attitude of _____ and _____ made me think someone didn't do a good job of _____-_____, at least with him. I _____my _____ thoughts about his bad _____ to him. He said, "Sir, I'm sorry!" Those _____ did not fool me. He did not make a _____ apology.

That which we call a rose by any other name smells as sweet.

— William Shakespeare, "Romeo & Juliet"

CHAPTER XIII

Differences: Words & Ideas

Part I of this unit shines a light on language and style differences between British English and American English. Is it "pitch" or is it "field"? Can both "color" and "colour" be correct? Do we turn the news pages to the "sport section" or the "sport<u>s</u> section"? The fun ahead puts us on track to making some important distinctions and mastering the talk of American language and football. Part II dispels traditional images of football players by showing non-traditional habits and methods of training.

Part I
British and American English

American football and the football of the rest of the world (known as soccer or association football in the United States) have two distinct differences. First, the terminology in the game; and second, differences in spelling and grammar. Additionally, whether either sport is reported in a British English or American English newspaper results in slight differences in grammar. The chart below compares soccer and football and the way it is reported in news media.

British English (Association football)	American English (American football)
Score: 0-3—away team's score is always first	Score: 3-0—winning team's score is always first
card (red and yellow)	flag (yellow for a penalty; red for a challenge)
chip shot—ball sails over goalie into goal	chip shot—easy field goal (a short distance)
defender	defensive player (informal: "defender")
draw	tie
equalizer (Brit spelling: "equaliser")	tie (the score/points that "even" the game)
even	all (Ex: 7-all = both teams have 7 points)
extra time	overtime
footballer	football player (or "gridder")
friendly	Preseason—pros; non-conference—colleges (see "additional comments" below)
goal	end zone
goal area	red zone
half-line	midfield
match	game
nil	nothing

normal time	regulation
own goal	safety
period (first or second half)	period (quarters)
pitch	field/grid iron
Pk—penalty kick (action)	Pk—place kicker (person)
Sport (section of newspaper)	Sport<u>s</u> (section of newspaper)
shootout (method to break a draw)	shootout—high-scoring game
striker	quarterback (no exact equivalent)
sudden death	sudden death
tele [tell-ee] (The match is on the tele.)	TV (The game is on the TV).
touchline	sideline

Additional Comments

"Friendly" (USA style) — An American football equivalent of "friendly" does not exist. However, the NFL schedules "preseason games," which are a chance for coaches to evaluate players and get their teams tuned-up for the regular season. Preseason games (four in all, beginning in August) do not count in the standings.

At the collegiate level, non-conference games count toward the overall record and subjective national polls (see next section) but do not influence whether a team wins its conference.

Let's say a college team has 12 games. Three of them are with teams from other conferences. It loses all its non-conference games but wins all its conference games (9-0 conference; 9-3 overall). Another team wins all its non-conference games, loses one conference game (8-1 conference; 11-1 overall) but finishes second in the conference.

> **British versus American usage:** British English refers to a team, or its city name, by count. "Arsenal **sign** new player. **They are** a football club in England." (Plural verb and pronoun reference "they.") By contrast, "Chicago **signs** a draft choice. **They are** expected to be improved." Note the irregularity between the noun and verb (singular noun and the subsequent plural pronoun). But, if the nickname is included it's plural: "The Chicago Bears sign a draft choice."

Sport/Sports — As a plural noun, "sport" (Br) signifies all sports and takes a plural verb complement (*Sport are played on all days*). "Sports" is the equivalent in the USA and can be both count and non-count, which can cause confusion. Sports are popular in the USA, each singular one adding up to a plural. Therefore, "A popular sport is football" (one of many). Since "sports" is a count noun, the singular in American English requires an article. However, British English, where "sport" is non-count, has no article: "Do you play sport?" By contrast (USA), "Do you play **a sport**?"/"Do you play sports?"

"Sport" as a person — Both British and American English recognize that "sport" references an athlete's mental attitude or ability to play fairly. ("She's a good [or bad] sport.")

Spelling Comparisons

British	American	British	American
--our (colour)	--or (color)	--re (theatre)	--er (theater
--se (realise, analyse)	--ze (realize, analyze)	--l (enrolment) but "jewelry')	--ll (enrollment) But "jewelry"
--ence (defence)	--ense (defense)	--que (banque) money: (cheque)	--k (bank) check
--gramme (programme)	--gram (program)	--ge (ageing)	--g (aging)

British vs. American Mechanics

Quotation Marks

The **American** style places commas and periods <u>inside</u> the quotation marks, **British** style places unquoted periods and commas <u>outside</u> the quotation marks. Note: **American English** uses double quotation marks (") whereas **British English** uses singles. (')

Example:
American: "I wish," said the coach, "we were able to run the ball better."

British: 'I wish', said the coach, 'we were able to run the ball better".

Titles

American English — Mr., Mrs., Ms., Dr., etc. use a period; **British**, no period.

Time & Date

American English expresses the time with a colon (10:30) and divides a 24-hour day: AM (morning—12 o'clock midnight to 11:59) and PM afternoon/evening (12 noon to 11:59)

Example: 7:15 AM for morning; 7:15 PM for afternoon/evening.

British English uses a period (10.30) and uses both the American preferred method and the 24-hour clock (10.30 PM / 22:30); rail and air timetables use the 24-hour clock.

The **American** method for dates is: Month-Day-Year (October 14, 2020; 10/14/20). In digital form, this is usually expressed with a four-digit year (10/14/2020).

British method: Day-month-year (14 October 2020; note the absence of a comma in this method) or 14-10-20.

> "Evening" may be considered to begin at a point near sunset. "Night" can be any time it is dark outside.

Names (such as found on applications or asked for on the phone):
American: last name is listed first on a document.
British: replaces "last name" with "surname" on a document

Finally, when is football played?

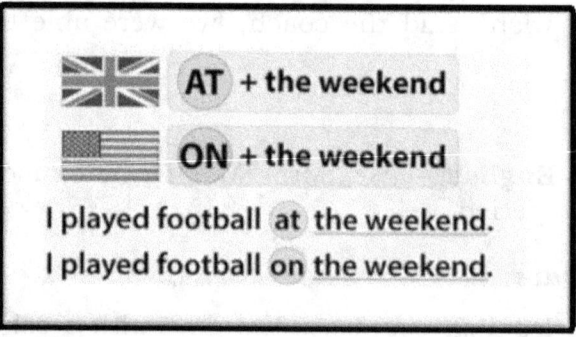

 I. Match the statements below to the right newspaper, British or American (X on line)

	British	American
1. I saw the article in the sports section.	___	___
2. Arizona have played six games.	___	___
3. If Los Angeles wins, I'll not be surprised.	___	___
4. San Francisco has been playing rookies.	___	___
5. I love all sport.	___	___
6. Croatia has many good players.	___	___

Footballogy: Elements of American Football for Non-Native Speakers of English

7. The visiting Lobos lost 13-17. _____ _____

8. The crowd were on their feet. _____ _____

9. What did you do on the weekend? _____ _____

10. He is a good at all sports. _____ _____

Which sport is it, soccer or football?

                                                                             Soccer Football

11. The game was tied at the end of regulation. _____ _____

12. It was the end of regular time. _____ _____

13. The captains met at midfield. _____ _____

14. It was a perfect day for a match. _____ _____

15. A red flag was thrown. _____ _____

16. The team was in the red zone. _____ _____

17. I see many good footballers. _____ _____

18. The pitch was wet. _____ _____

19. The chip shot was made by the PK. _____ _____

20. How long is overtime? _____ _____

21-24 Multiple Choice

21. The Falcons want to try a field goal. Who does it send onto the field for this?
    a. chip shot   b. PK
    c. gridder   d. defender

22. Bucs ball, first-and-10 at the Chargers 12-yard line. Where are they? In the...
    a. red zone
    b. goal area
    c. end zone
    d. nearness

23. Which exemplifies a bad sport?
    a. The winning captain thanked all his teammates.
    b. The losing team credited the victor for a hard-fought victory.
    c. The losing team said the winning team cheated.
    d. The captain of the losing team blamed himself for the loss.

24. The Kansas City Chiefs find themselves at...
    a. midfield
    b. half field
    c. the half-line
    d. red zone

25. Read this passage and put a check √ by the column (A, B, C, D) that lists the <u>correct word order</u>.

With three minutes left in _____, it's 42-____ between the Giants and the Redskins. It's been a _____ between two high-powered offenses. If the game ends in a _____, there will be _____. Each team gets a chance to score unless, on the first possession, one of the contestants scores a touchdown or gets two points on a _____. If neither team scores on its first possession, the contest becomes _____.

A___	B___	C___	D___
overtime	normal time	sudden death	regulation
all	tie	all	all
tie	shootout	overtime	shootout
shootout	sudden death	draw	tie
regulation	safety	safety	overtime
safety	overtime	shootout	safety
sudden death	all	regulation	sudden death

II. Look at this time zone table to answer the questions that follow (* = Next day)

Boston	2:00 PM	Cape Town	8 PM	Dublin	7 PM	Mumbai	11:30 PM
Beijing	2 AM*	Chicago	1 PM	Los Angeles	11 AM	Seoul*	1 AM*
Bogota	12 PM	Denver	12 PM	Mexico City	1 PM	Stockholm	8 PM
Berlin	8 PM	Dubai	11 PM	Moscow	9 PM	Ulaanbaatar*	2 AM

1. The Los Angeles Charger home game starts at 6 PM in LA. I live in Mexico City. What time do I tune in?
   a. 1:00 PM b. 8:00 AM
   c. 8:00 PM d. 5:00 PM

2. Notre Dame is coming to Dublin. Game start: 14:30. I'll watch the game on the big screen back in Chicago. What time?
   a. 9:30 AM b. 8:30 PM
   c. 22.30   d. 8:30 AM

3. A game viewed in Moscow at 7 PM is viewed in Mumbai how many hours later?
   a. 9:30 PM b. 2 ½ hours
   c. 9:00 PM d. 2 hours

4. For a game starting at 1 PM in Boston, what city would NOT view the game in the morning?
   a. Beijing b. Los Angeles
   c. Berlin   d. Ulaanbaatar

5. Seoul is hosting a college game. It starts at 13:00, according to the TV schedule. From my home in Bogota, what kind of food would I eat at that time?
   a. midnight snack b. breakfast
   c. lunch   d. dinner

Part II
Uncommon Roles for Football Players

Knitting

Mike Rivera, a former linebacker, stands 6'2" tall. In his playing days, he exceeded 250 pounds. He contributed 300 tackles as a college football player before going pro with the Green Bay Packers and the Miami Dolphins. Beyond an outstanding football career, something else about Rivera stands out. He is not the traditional picture of a football player. His avocation, or hobby, is crochet (crō´-shā).

Rivera visited an elementary school in the state of Kansas, the breadbasket of the USA. (Wheat fields are a common sight in this area.) He was there to teach students how to crochet. More than a dozen kids showed up for the class and not all of them were girls. Everyone was to learn how to crochet a hat. They weren't told that Rivera was a professional football player, so they were purely interested in the crochet class.

How exactly did a football player like Rivera come to learn how to crochet? He went down to Guatemala to do volunteer work, where he also learned crochet. He says that crocheting is a good way to pass the time, especially when it means that he can help children in need. This class in Kansas that day was his way of passing along his passion for crocheting.

Rivera doesn't stand alone in appreciation for a craft traditionally viewed as something that women do. Roosevelt Grier, a defensive end who anchored the "Fearsome Foursome" defensive line of the LA Rams in the 1960s, was the first to buck gender stereotypes. The all-pro in the NFL Hall of Fame, also an actor and songwriter, is an ordained minister who counsels gang members. He opened the door for other men to take up needlepoint and macramé. He also wrote a book on the topic.

Ballet

What does football have in common with ballet? Let's say it's where art and sports meet—or as the saying goes, "the two make music together." Each uses the same muscle groups and skills. Ballet aids in flexibility, speed and agility, strength, balance, mental focus, and endurance. This makes it an ideal partner in cross-training for players' improved performance on the football field. It should be no surprise that all-stars like tight end Ron Gronkowski and 310-pound defensive tackle Steve McLendon are among the many NFL personalities who sashay (move around) on the ballet floor to get themselves fit for the gridiron. McLendon credits ballet for helping him stay nimble and protect his body from wear-and-tear and injury.

Flexibility: Ballet training produces graceful movements, which helps players avoid tackles and make catches. Legendary Pittsburgh Steeler receiver Lynn Swann, known for his acrobatic catches, credits the high-flying ballet movement, the soute (soo-TAY), for his ability to achieve body control, balance, and a sense of rhythm and timing.

Speed and agility: The difference between a touchdown and a tackle for a loss is often determined by quickness. A running back may be headed in one direction and about to be dumped for a loss of yardage, so he pirouettes (PEER-oh-wet) or cuts back the other way for a gain. Such moves typified Herschel Walker, a legendary running back for the Dallas Cowboys, who took ballet classes.

Strength: An important consideration is that ballet adds strength without adding bulk to the body. This is especially important to players in the "skills positions." For instance, the plié (plee-YAY)—a bending of the knees—helps to strengthen the leg muscles while making the ankles stronger as well. (Weak ankles or feet can cause one to trip and fall or suffer injury.)

Balance: Ballet training helps players snare (catch) passes without losing their footing. Look for an out pattern in football where the player tiptoes along the sidelines to stay inbounds. In ballet, this is called a demi-pointe (de-MEE-point).

Mental focus: Like ballet performers, gridders must follow complex designs, motions, and schemes. They must follow the position and movements of other players both on their team and the opposite team. They need to know where the ball is in the air and make decisions on the fly (spontaneously). A good mental focus can also reduce performance anxiety. In theory, a player could walk across a plank of wood suspended between two skyscrapers just as stress-free as if it were a foot off the ground.

Endurance: Ballet is a kind of aerobic exercise. The muscles used during dance sessions and training require a large amount of oxygen. As a result, the heart, circulatory, and respiratory systems deliver oxygen and nutrients to the player's muscles during periods of intense muscular work. For football players, endurance allows their bodies to run, jump, and face impacts, or collisions, from other players for longer periods without tiring.

Ballet is a beautiful art form with twists and turns, and the intricate moves appear to be effortless. Yet aside from all this loveliness, ballet is quite rigorous. It's the hardest thing player McLendon, who began ballet classes while in college, says he's ever done. Like football players, dancers endure broken toes, broken bones, and pulled tendons. However, the conditioning, strength, and knowledge on topics such as how to take an impact on the knees may be the very tools that cause players like McLendon to continue.

An image of big men in pink slippers and tutus (those fluffy skirts worn by ballerinas) isn't an image associated with football but there is strong evidence that suggests that ballet training makes football players better gridiron performers. "It's helped my body a lot," says McLendon.

I prefer to be a dreamer among the humblest, with visions to be realized, than lord among those without dreams and desires.

—Khalil Gibran, Lebanese poet

CHAPTER XIV

Where Do Football Players Come From?

The stork (illustration) is an ancient allegory or symbol in the Western world for the delivery of infants. This unit explores the structure of the football systems from early life to the production of skilled football players.

Footballogy: Elements of American Football for Non-Native Speakers of English

Word Preview

Try to guess the meanings of the words below from the reading. Be ready to tackle them in the questions that follow.

take up	bumps and bruises	made do	deserted
roomy	made up	call it a day	sandlot on-
the-fly	simultaneously	cleared	youth
innovations	popularized	play-by-play	

Youth

Passion for football starts in the cradle, where football-themed items for babies—bibs, booties, blankets and all—build up to what legendary Buffalo Bills play-by-play announcer Van Miller described as "fandemonium," a combination of "fan" and "pandemonium" (excitement) used mostly for especially dramatic moments in a game.

Early in life, youth take up football, which teaches fair play and teamwork. Although the game is violent, the programs of today promote working together, taking and sharing responsibility, and surviving the bumps and bruises in life.

Once upon a time, young people gathered in the hues of autumn for a fun day of football—no pads, uniforms, strict rules, yard makers or goal posts. Such unplanned activities like the picture at right were known as "sandlot football."

*The "Good Old Days" – Football
Public domain (Wikipedia)*

In the past, in the free spirit of youth, recreation areas, parks, or even deserted parking lots made do as playing surfaces. Rural kids had an extra choice with roomy fields. In either case, the sides were normally the "shirts" and the "skins" (players without shirts). Rules and field dimensions were improvised on the fly, or as the need arose. Matters like keeping track of time, where to spot the ball, and rulings on complete or incomplete passes could present a problem since every player also played the part of an official. The days ended at a score decided upon ahead of time or when it was decided to call it a day.

In a society not as spontaneous as it was formerly, organized youth football is the modern-day method of operation. Two-hand-touch football or flag football can be found in communities from Puerto Rico to Hawaii. *NFL Flag* and the *United States Flag and Touch Football League* provide such a structure for both boys and girls between five and 17 years of age. Flag football participants wear a bright-colored stripe, or flag, attached to their uniform. When the ball carrier's flag is pulled, he or she is "tackled." Touch football requires two hands to simultaneously touch the ball carrier to stop the play.

Pop Warner, a league begun in 1929, emphasizes cooperation and academics. It accepts youth medically cleared to play. Some of these players will one day advance to high-school programs. Those who demonstrate talent and skill may get scholarships that pay for their education while playing football for universities. Others become walk-ons, or athletes not recruited (asked to join). For most, the football journey stops here; making it to pro ball happens to very few. No matter what, all athletes must maintain vigorous discipline for exercise, diet, and physical training. To be good at the sport at all levels demands this.

Pop Warner (real name: Glenn Scobey Warner, 1871-1954) was an American football coach who made several innovations to improve the modern game. These include formations and methods for blocking. A youth football league remains part of his legacy.

Pop Warner (1917)
University of Pittsburgh

The football environment is not limited to the great outdoors. Electronic or video football games, such as Madden NFL, are very popular, not just for children but for adults as well. During the football season, fantasy leagues enable participants to have a virtual experience. They can pretend to be the general managers of gridiron teams from either the National Football League or the Canadian Football League. The competitors choose their team rosters by participating in a "draft" to select names of real players for their roster. Points are based on the actual performances of the players in real-world competition. Two of the biggest organizers of fantasy football are *FanDuel* and *DraftKings*.

I. In other words... Replace the underlined word with the letter of the word in the column.

1. ___I will <u>enroll in</u> *Footballogy* to know football better.
2. ___Some people can run and throw <u>at the same time</u>.
3. ___Stealing a game plan is <u>not honest</u>.
4. ___Eight <u>uninterrupted</u> defeats got the coach fired.
5. ___In close games, teams may do things <u>as they go along.</u>
6. ___The hurt player wasn't <u>given permission to play.</u>
7. ___Our new practice facility is <u>spacious.</u>
8. ___A game can occur in an <u>empty</u> parking lot.
9. ___The <u>unstructured</u> style reminded me of my childhood.
10. ___ It's late. Let's <u>quit</u> and go home.
11. ___ <u>Kids</u> have lots of opportunities.

a. popularized
b. call it a day
c. on the fly
d. simultaneously
e. sandlot
f. deserted
g. cleared
h. play by play
i. take up
j. straight
k. roomy
l. improvised
m. cheating
n. youth
o. bumps & bruises

12. ___A TV commentator does not do the <u>live-action</u>.
13. ___Life is full of <u>difficulties</u>.
14. ___The Isley Brothers' song "Shout" was <u>promoted</u> at Bills' games.
15. ___We didn't have goalposts, so we <u>created</u> them.

II. Details and inferences

True/false or maybe (if the answer is not in the reading).

1. ___ Pop Warner was born in 1929.
2. ___ Fantasy football is like a virtual experience.
3. ___ Fandemonium is a combination of two words.
4. ___ Van Miller worked for WBEN radio.
5. ___ Van Miller played football.

College

Word Preview

aspire	tryout	monitored	comply
full-ride	redshirt	walk-on	catchphrase
pep rally	Power Five/Group of Five		

Young men who aspire to higher levels of football typically play football in high school (ages 14-18). Upon completion, they may choose to continue playing in *college*, a term in the United States for "higher education." While there is Boston *University*, for instance, there is also Boston *College*. Both kinds of schools grant baccalaureate degrees (bachelor's) and higher, earned in four years. When it comes to football, both types of schools are remarkably similar in another aspect: Only 1.6% of the student-athletes will ever get a tryout with an NFL team. And few from this group will make an NFL roster, although some may extend their careers in professional leagues in Canada (CFL) or Europe.

Because the chances are slim to make a career in professional football, students need to concentrate on academics for a better likelihood

> In job interviews, expect the question, "Where did you go to *college*?" (Not *university*.) "College" is a generic, mass noun to mean higher education. (We also say "go to school.")

of a career apart from football. After a student-athlete chooses a major field of study, he must maintain a "C" average to remain eligible to play football.

Academic standards of eligibility in athletics are monitored by the National Collegiate Athletic Association (NCAA), an organization of 1200 schools in all sports, and the National Association of Intercollegiate Athletics (NAIA), about 300 colleges. Each association establishes and enforces rules for its member institutions to ensure fairness in competition and amateur status. For instance, athletes are not supposed to be paid or granted special privileges not available to regular students.

For institutions that do not comply, the NCAA can inflict hardship on their programs. Penalties range from loss of scholarships to probation (schools are not eligible to participate in post-season games). More serious infractions can result in forfeiture of games (wins are recorded as losses). But that's not the worst, which a university in the 1980s found out. In effect, a death penalty was delivered for massive and repeated violations including payments to recruits. Loss of scholarships and cancellation of two seasons left this two-time national champion in ruins.

Divisions

The NCAA has three divisions, which define schools by the level of competition, student enrollment, the resources of their athletic departments, and stadium-seating capacity. The 266 schools in Division I are the most visible (they get the most publicity). The most talented high-school seniors in the nation, rated two-stars to five-stars, are pursued by Division I colleges. Five stars, also called "blue chips," represent about one-tenth of one percent of high-school seniors (students in their last year of high school). They are expected to make the most immediate impact on the teams they choose to join. Recruited athletes traditionally sign a *National Letter of Intent* with the college of their choice in their last year. The universities, in return, award scholarships renewable each year, which helps pay the cost of school and living expenses.

The NCAA allows each Division I football program to grant up to 85 scholarships, 25 of them for freshmen, or first-year students. Those figures are less for schools in lower divisions.

A football recruit receives a scholarship for four years, the usual time it takes to get an undergraduate (baccalaureate) degree. However, he may choose to *redshirt*—a designation that extends his scholarship (and playing time) an extra year. During the redshirt year, he can practice but not play. On the other hand, an underclassman (not yet a senior) who performs very well can declare himself available at the end of the college season for the NFL draft. However, he loses his remaining scholarship even if an NFL team doesn't take him. Therefore, unless he possesses NFL-ready qualities, it is not worth the risk.

There is still hope for non-recruited athletes who dream of playing Division I football. Open tryouts enable a few out of the hundreds of other hopefuls to earn a roster spot as a "walk-on." Punters, kickers, and long snappers are the ones most often discovered in open tryouts. A walk-on does not normally get a scholarship and must find other ways to pay for his education.

Division I

Divided into two subdivisions, Division I comprises the *Football Bowl Subdivision* (FBS) and the *Football Championship Subdivision* (FCS). The FBS is a system of six post-season games, called *bowl games*, where a bowl committee selects participants for each bowl. FBS bowl games occur during the New Year holiday.

Frequently referred to by its old name "1A," the FBS has ten member conferences, the *Power Five* and the *Group of Five* (both are unofficial labels), and a few independents (schools not in a conference). The conference champion in each of the Power Five conferences (see chart A) automatically qualifies for one of the six FBS bowl games (see chart B). Other invited schools, called "at-large," can include an exceptional Group of Five school or a quality team from the Power Five or an independent.

Including FBS bowls, there are over 30 bowls in all that run from mid-December to the New Year holiday in an approximate 2,500-mile (4,000 kilometers) swath across the US Sun Belt (warm weather region) from Southern California to the southeast coast. Invitations by respective bowl committees are made the first week in December. Teams must have at least six regular-season wins to qualify. All bowl games are recognized by their unique names, such as a flower (Rose Bowl) or fruit (Orange Bowl), or condiment (Sugar Bowl). Many are connected to a corporate sponsor, such as the "*Playstation* Fiesta Bowl." Only FBS schools participate in bowls.

> The AP Top 25 Poll is comprised of a nationwide panel of sportswriters and broadcasters with extensive backgrounds in college football who vote on the poll weekly. A team gets 25 points for each first-place vote; 24 for second place, and on down. The team with the most points is ranked number one.

The crowning of a national college champion used to be wholly subjective and was based on the opinions of members in two polls: The Associated Press (AP) and the *USA Today* Coaches Poll. Each week until the conclusion of the bowls, each poll lists its Top 25. The validity could be disputed if each final poll listed two different teams as number one.

The poll that matters in the modern arrangement is the FBS (chart A), published weekly beginning the ninth week of the season by the College Football Playoff committee. It ranks teams' win-loss records, strength of schedule, conference, and point differential (points scored versus allowed) among other variables. For these reasons, Power Five teams, which face tougher opposition, are the usual candidates for the playoffs.

> If you confuse an FBS game with a pro game, you're not alone. First, an FBS game has the look and feel of a pro game. Players at this level are extremely talented, big, strong, and fast. They were the elites among high-school athletes who got recruited to college campuses. FBS stadiums are also big and typically full. Fourteen of the biggest FBS stadiums seat more than the largest NFL stadiums, eight of them over 100,000 spectators, such as the University of Michigan's Wolverine Stadium (107,000) and Penn State University's Beaver Stadium (106,000).

The final poll, revealed with great hype (anticipation) in early December, rewards the top four FBS teams in the College Football Playoffs semi-finals, held on a rotating basis at two of the six FBS New Year bowls. The championship is at a neutral location one week later.

One thing to remember is that all polls are for entertainment. They create hype and give people something to talk about. Besides, part of the fun of college football is school pride and that means knowing how "my school" compares to others. This gives us something to brag about!

Schools in the FCS, formerly known as 1AA, are mostly smaller and more restricted in the scholarships they can offer. Even though they do not have a system of bowls, they do have a 16-team, single-elimination playoff that leads to establishing the national champion.

Playoff games are competitive, which can be quite a contrast to out-of-division games in the early season when Division 1AA schools are paid huge sums of money to play Division I FBS opponents. Although some games can be close, many are lopsided, which sparks controversy. These games count in the official record and inflate the point differential (points scored against point allowed), which can influence poll ranking. Some people sardonically suggest Division IA against Division IAA foes are "practice games," or tune-ups for the "real" season against FBS foes. On a positive note, these games are an opportunity for reserves to see some game action.

Look at the information in the Charts A, B and C. The information is used in an assessment that follows.

Chart A—sample of AP, Coaches and FBS Polls

AP Top 25 (2018)	Coaches' Poll (2018)
1. Clemson Tigers	1. Clemson Tigers
2. Alabama Crimson Tide	2. Alabama Crimson Tide
3. Ohio State Buckeyes	3. Ohio State Buckeyes
4. Oklahoma Sooners	4. Oklahoma Sooners
5. Notre Dame Fighting Irish	5. Notre Dame Fighting Irish
6. LSU Tigers	6. Florida Gators
7. Florida Gators (tie)	7. LSU Tigers

CFP College Playoff

Team	Record	Conference	Prior Week
1. Alabama	13-0	SEC	1
2. Clemson	13-0	ACC	2
3. Notre Dame	12-0	Independent	3
4. Oklahoma	12-1	Big XII	5
5. Georgia	11-2	SEC	4
6. Ohio State	12-1	Big Ten	6
7. Michigan	10-2	Big Ten	7

Chart B—FBS Bowls

Name	First game	Venue/seating	city	Sponsor (as of 2019)
Rose Bowl Game	1902	Rose Bowl/ 92,542	Pasadena, Calif.	Northwestern Mutual
Orange Bowl	1935	Hard Rock Stadium 64,767	Miami, Florida	Capital One
Sugar Bowl	1935	Mercedes-Benz Super Dome/73,208	New Orleans, Louisiana	Allstate
Cotton Bowl Classic	1937	AT & T Stadium 80,000	Arlington, Texas	Goodyear
Peach Bowl	1938	Mercedes-Benz Stadium/71,000	Atlanta, Georgia	Chic-fil-A
Fiesta Bowl	1971	State Farm Stadium 63,400	Glendale, Arizona	PlayStation

Map of all bowl games showing concentration in US "Sun Belt"

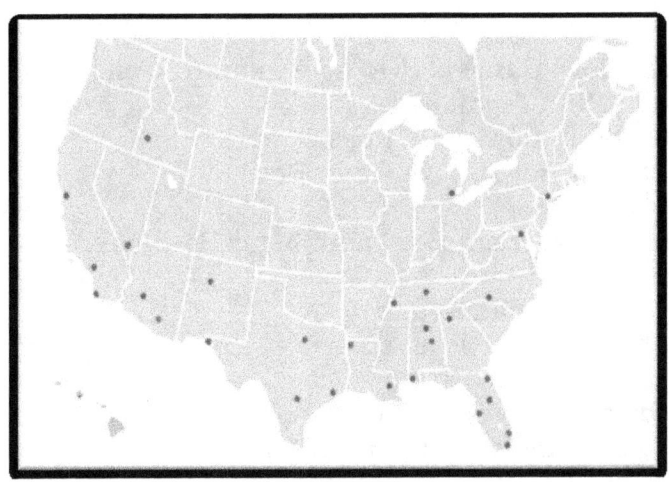

Chart C—Sample of Non-FBS Bowls and year of first game

Sun Bowl (1935)—El Paso, Texas

Gator Bowl (1945)—Jacksonville, Florida

Citrus Bowl (1948)—Orlando, Florida

Liberty Bowl (1959)—Memphis, Tennessee

Holiday Bowl (1978)—San Diego, California

Outback Bowl (1986)—Tampa, Florida

Footballogy: Elements of American Football for Non-Native Speakers of English

I. Chart Smarts (A, B, C + map) Answers to the following questions are in the charts above (requires knowledge from Section IV).

1. Which Bowl Game is NOT held in an NFL city? (refer to section "NFL Teams")
   a. Liberty Bowl   b. Rose Bowl
   c. Sugar Bowl   d. Gator Bowl

2. What do the Peach Bowl and Sugar Bowl have in common?
   a. stadium name   b. city
   c. seating   d. sponsor

3. The biggest crowd can be expected at the...
   a. Sugar Bowl   b. Fiesta Bowl
   c. Rose Bowl   d. Orange Bowl

4. What word best describes why the southern region attracts bowls?
   a. oranges   b. stadiums
   c. traditions   d. warmth

5. A team is invited to the Outback Bowl. To what state are they headed?
   a. Arizona   b. Florida
   c. Texas   d. Tampa

6. Considering there are six CFP bowls, which *rotate* as the host of the two annual semi-final games, how often can a venue expect to host one of these games? Every...
   a. four years   b. other year
   c. three years   d. two years

7. According to chart A, which team replaced Ohio State in the final CFP?
   a. Rutgers   b. Notre Dame
   c. Alabama   d. Clemson

Footballogy: Elements of American Football for Non-Native Speakers of English

8. Winners of the Gator and Sun Bowl play for the national championship.
   T   F

9. The Rose Bowl is the nation's oldest.
   T   F

10. Most bowls take place in northern regions.
    T   F

FBS (Football Bowl Subdivision)
Chart D — NCAA Power Five Conferences* + Independents

ACC Atlantic Coast Conference	Big 12	Big Ten Big Ten (14 teams)	PAC 12 (Pacific 12)	Southeast Conference
Boston College	Baylor Bears	Illinois Fighting Illini	Arizona Wildcats	Alabama Crimson Tide
Clemson	Iowa State Cyclones	Indiana Hoosiers	Arizona State Sun devils	Arkansas Razorbacks
Duke Blue Devils	Kansas Jayhawks	Iowa Hawkeyes	California Golden Bears	Auburn Tigers
Florida State	Kansas State Wildcats	Maryland Terrapins	Colorado Buffaloes	Florida Gators
Georgia Tech	Missouri Tigers	Michigan Wolverines	Oregon Ducks	Georgia Bulldogs
Louisville Cardinals	Oklahoma Sooners	Michigan State Spartans	Oregon State Beavers	Kentucky Wildcats
Massachusetts Minutemen	Oklahoma State Cowboys	Minnesota Golden Gophers	Stanford Cardinal	LSU (Louisiana State) Tigers
Miami	Texas	Nebraska	UCLA	Mississippi

Hurricanes	Longhorns	Cornhuskers	Bruins	Rebels (Also: "Ole Miss")
No Carolina State Wolfpack	Texas Christian Horned Frogs	Northwestern Wildcats	USC Trojans	Mississippi State Bulldogs
North Carolina	Texas Tech Red Raiders	Ohio State Buckeyes	Utah Utes	Missouri Tigers
Pittsburgh	West Virginia Mountaineers	Penn State Nittany Lions	Washington Huskies	South Carolina Gamecocks
Syracuse Orange		Purdue Boilermakers	Washington State Huskies	Tennessee Volunteers
Virginia Cavaliers		Rutgers Scarlet Knights		Texas A & M Aggies
		Wisconsin Badgers		Vanderbilt Commodores

Non-aligned (independent) FBS Schools:

	Brigham Young Cougars	Massachusetts Minutemen	Notre Dame Fighting Irish

*10 schools in Big 12; 14 in Big 10

Division II

Comprised of 167 colleges and universities with football programs, this mid-tier NCAA category still attracts quality athletes. Affiliate schools do not boast as big a student body, sports facilities, or budget, nor can they offer large scholarships. Most athletes need to pay for at least some of their university fees through grants and loans, and academic or needs-based scholarships. Division II stadiums mostly seat 10,000 or less. Early in the season, Division II teams schedule Division I FCS foes.

Teams in the Division have an 11-game schedule. A post-season single-elimination playoff of 28 teams selects the national champion.

Division III

Two-hundred fifty (250) colleges comprise Division III football, the lowermost level of competition in the NCAA. These schools, which have the smallest athletic department budgets and student enrollments, normally schedule ten games. Because athletes in Division III do not get athletic scholarships, they must pay their way through college by academic scholarships and loans. Some perform work-study, for example, where a student-athlete works in the kitchen of a dining hall during the week and on the gridiron on Saturday. Division III has a 32-team playoff system, which concludes in the national championship, the Amos Alonzo Stagg Bowl in Salem, Virginia.

GAME Day & Traditions

College football stadiums are predictably filled with colors, mostly of the home team's school. Fans show pride with apparel, seat cushions, and blankets featuring school colors. While the faces of many are decorated with school decals, cartoon depictions of the college nickname or catchphrase on banners are also popular. "How 'bout them dawgs" is a rallying cry for the University of Georgia Bulldogs. "Hook 'em horns," the University of Texas Longhorns' chant that comes with a hand signal, is among the most recognizable in college football. Such sayings and actions serve a useful purpose of branding a university as well as instilling school pride.

Footballogy: Elements of American Football for Non-Native Speakers of English

The Arizona State University Sundevil mascot; University of Southern California "Tommy Trojan" (insert); and University of Texas "hook 'em horns" (right). Authors unknown: licensed under CC-BY-NC

School mascots breathe life into the schools' nicknames. They are competitively useful—snarling, fighting, ugly, mean, aggressive—while never uttering a word.

The total football experience would be incomplete without marching bands, cheerleaders (alternatively called cheer team or spirit squad), and baton-twirling majorettes who perform before the game and at halftime. In the lead-up to the game during the week, they enliven campus pep rallies (gatherings of people to show their enthusiasm). The most anticipated event is Homecoming Weekend when alumni (graduates) come "home" to renew acquaintances and root for (cheer for) their alma mater.

Contrasting styles: Stanford University Marching Band, billing itself as "The World's Largest Rock and Roll Band" (left—YouTube) and a traditional ensemble, the University of Alabama "Million Dollar" Marching Band (CC Pixabay)

Great moments

"The Play"

"And the Band Played On"
(Name of an 1895 popular tune)

O. Henry was an American short-story writer known for his surprise endings. The season-ending rivalry between the University of California Golden Bears and the Stanford Cardinal should qualify for an O. Henry-like surprise finish. It just took one play in this 85th meeting between these PAC 10 foes to accomplish this. Known affectionately as "The Big Game," here's how this game turned on one big play.

With four seconds left in the game at Memorial Stadium in Berkeley, California, Stanford had just taken the lead 20-19 on a field goal. There was time for one play—the kick-off—and the game would be over. The kick was intentionally "squibbed," where the ball is kicked close to the ground and bounces to make it harder to secure. It also meant the clock started. All Cal could do was take the ball and run with it. Since forward passes are only allowed on scrimmage plays, this also meant the only legal passes were lateral.

As a Cal player with the ball was about to go down, he lateraled, or pitched, it backward to another Cal player. A succession of laterals moved the ball to about the Cardinal 20-yard line, where the last one happened. The runner flipped the ball over his shoulder blindly, hoping for the best. And he got the best outcome imaginable. The new runner would score despite unintended resistance from the Stanford Band, which, thinking the game was over, had prematurely taken the field for the post-game show. Although the band is known for its eccentric and spontaneous performances, this performance was unscripted. The Cal player with the ball moved through the band to the end zone. A conference by the officials determined that the play was legal. Cal was awarded a touchdown and the win before a stunned house.

Music City Miracle

About 12 years later, January 8, 2000, an AFC divisional playoff game between the Buffalo Bills and the Tennessee Titans was thought to be over. The Bills had just gone up 16-15 with 16 seconds left in regulation on a field goal. The hometown crowd in Nashville, Tennessee, the unofficial capital of country and western music—hence, "Music City USA"—was pretty mum. Many fans headed to the exits.

But like an O. Henry tale, a surprise ending lay in store for those who stayed. As the saying goes, "expect the unexpected. The "Music City Miracle" was christened.

The Titans took the ensuing kickoff. The receiver handed off to a faster player. About to be tackled, he heaved the ball across the field to another, who raced behind a wall of blockers untouched for 75 yards to the Bills' end zone. Controversy surrounded whether the last pass was a lateral or forward pass. Video evidence did not confirm that it was a legal pass but the evidence that it *wasn't* was insufficient for the referee to reverse the decision on the field. The score was upheld. The Titans were to survive the playoffs for a Super Bowl encounter with the Rams (then based in St. Louis) but fell short of a game-winning score on the game's last play by one yard. No miracle that day.

We aim above the mark to hit the mark.
— Ralph Waldo Emerson, American essayist

CHAPTER XV
The Draft

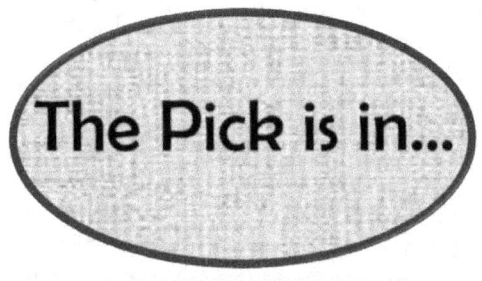

Many dream but few get chosen to put on a uniform of a professional football team, This unit discusses the final steps to becoming a professional football player and a look at a few legends in the game.

In February, college athletes gather for a week in Indianapolis, Indiana, for the NFL Scouting Combine. Mostly—but certainly not always—this event involves college seniors. Players perform physical and mental tasks in front of NFL coaches, general managers, and scouts, who assess each candidate for the NFL draft (or selection) of college talent in late April.

> Considering the market-like atmosphere, it's no surprise that during the season, sports announcers refer to a player as "a product" of the institution that produced him.

The draft is seven rounds, or cycles, over three days. Teams assemble in an NFL city, the location of which rotates annually. Each team drafts in the reverse order of its finish the previous season. The one that had the worst record drafts first; the Super Bowl winner last. The first player chosen is thought to be either the best player in the draft or the best at his position, depending on the focus of the team selecting him.

Like a chess match, there is lots of strategy resembling a commodities exchange. Team executives trade and negotiate, weigh benefits and liabilities, and try to anticipate other teams' needs and maneuvers. "It's something you have to figure out to get the players to play in your system," says the New England Patriots' Coach Bill Belichick, who has used the draft to build Super Bowl teams. Veteran players might be traded in exchange for a draft pick. Draft positions in a round can be negotiated in exchange for a higher order,

> Player evaluation also ranks intangibles, also known as "soft skills" such as work ethic and moral character. This includes the Wonderlic Cognitive Ability Test to measure intelligence. (Wonderlic is also a tool used by hiring departments in some companies in the USA). Players need to be quick mentally to prioritize and make important decisions instantly on the field. Wonderlic is a reliable indicator of this.

which can happen if a team senses a special player it greatly wants may not be available when its turn to draft comes.

All eyes are on the first player selected, the number-one overall draft pick. But history has shown that the draft is as much luck as it is a science. Number ones don't always pan out (prove to be the best choice).

In the years to come, a first pick gains notoriety if he is a "bust"—a player who performs below expectations. On the other hand, there are late draft choices who shine in the NFL. A most famous example is a 2000 sixth-round draft choice (199th overall) by the name of Tom Brady, who was to lead the New England Patriots to six NFL titles and earn the nickname GOAT—Greatest of All Time.

On the third and final day, the last player selected in the last round gets media attention too, in a jocular or lighthearted way. This individual gets to carry the label "Mr. Irrelevant." He is celebrated not as being the last one chosen but for the good fortune of being selected at all.

Players not drafted may keep their dreams alive with an invitation from a team to try out. Such players are called "undrafted free agents" or UFAs. Their chances of making the final team roster are slimmer than drafted players although everyone, drafted or not, must work hard to earn a roster spot. Unlike regular life, where who you know is important for getting and keeping a job, the NFL is all about what you can do. Job uncertainty affects even veteran players, who can be cut from a roster before or during the season. (A team's needs, as well as individual performance, are both factors.)

> Job security applies to coaches and management, who are judged by a team's performance on the field.

UFAs and drafted players, called "rookies," gather with veteran players in July for a difficult, weeks-long session known as training camp. By August, teams are conditioned to begin a four-game schedule of preseason games, which starts with the Hall of Fame game in Canton, Ohio. These games—like "friendlies" in soccer—don't mean anything toward the outcome of the season but they allow coaches an opportunity to evaluate players and finalize team rosters for the season, which starts the second week in September. Rosters that began with about 90 players must be reduced to the league limit of 53 by the start of the regular season. In addition to the 53, teams have a practice squad—a ten-man roster for young or inexperienced players who can practice with the team but do not put on a uniform on game day.

One of those on the practice squad is a player from the NFL's International Pathways Program, which began in 2017. This program recognizes emerging international talent, which allows teams to add an 11th player to the practice squad. Unlike other practice squad members, a Pathway member cannot be put on the regular roster when opportunities arise during the season due to injuries, cuts, trades, or team needs. Instead, he has a full year on the practice squad to adjust to the quickness and elite skills of NFL play without fear of being cut.

Players cut, or waived, are free to join another team or professional leagues in Canada and around the world. Some become coaches while others get a "day" job to pay the bills. Who knows, the NFL may come calling again someday...

American Dream: Kurt Warner, a University of Northern Iowa product, knows a thing or two about the expression "come calling." Undrafted and rejected by many NFL teams, he was working as a store clerk in Iowa, a state in America's heartland (middle), when the Rams (then in St Louis) knocked on his door. The strong-armed quarterback, a product of the University of Northern Iowa, turned the Rams' offense into "The Greatest Show on Turf." He led the team to a Super Bowl win in 2000 and was named the game's Most Valuable Player. He also led the Arizona Cardinals to a Super Bowl. Warner's rise to fame typifies the American Dream—to never accept defeat and to keep your dreams alive against the greatest of odds.

I. Write "T" (true) or "F" (false)

1. ____ UFAs are players not selected in the draft.

2. ____ The American Dream means to be successful.

3. ____ "Waive" is to release (let go of) a player.

4. ____ The NFL has a program to develop talent from other countries.

5. ____ Pro football is like any other business.

6. ____ The 53-man NFL roster includes a 10-player practice squad.

7. ____ The team that makes the last draft selection is "Mr. Irrelevant."

8. ____ To be jocular is to be humorous and to smile.

9. ____ The only thing that matters to pro scouts is a player's speed and strength.

10. ____ "Round" means the number of times or chances.

II. Main idea, details, and inferences. Circle your answer choice.

1. Which statement best reflects the main idea of this passage?
    a. Football players start in Pop Warner.
    b. The journey to playing pro football is long, difficult, and uncertain.
    c. Pro football in America has players of many talents and backgrounds.
    d. To make it to the NFL, you must begin playing football early in life.

2. Which league is the least competitive?
   a. Pop Warner   b. college
   c. NFL   d. high school

3. Which game determines the Division III national college football?
   a. FBS   b. CFP
   c. FCS   d. Amos Alonzo, Stagg Bowl

4. Which is not a feature of the International Pathway Program?
   a. A player cannot be cut.
   b. A player must have experience as a college player.
   c. A player is on the practice squad.
   d. A player cannot play in a game during his first season.

5. An NFL team that finishes a season in last place...
   a. drafts first
   b. drafts last
   c. must play last year's college national champion in an exhibition game
   d. gets first choice on all free agents

6. Which is an example of non-contact football?
   a. touch   b. flag
   c. neither a/b   d. both a/b

7. Why were the Rams called "The Greatest Show on Turf"?
   a. ground game   b. offense
   c. Kurt Warner   d. defense

8. Which college division is played for the love of the sport, not to impress pro scouts?
   a. Division III   b. NAIA
   c. FCS   d. Division II

9. Rookies are...
    a. undrafted free agents
    b. first-year players
    c. veterans
    d. reserves

10. Soft skill means to...
    a. leap high   b. run fast
    c. hit hard   d. anticipate

Chart E—individual college player awards

Look at the information in Chart E and F to do the assessment that follows.. Chart E is college football's highest honors, presented annually to one outstanding athlete in each category. Recipients can expect to hear their names called on the first day of the NFL draft. Chart F is a comparison of college and professional football.

Maxwell Award	Best Player
Walter Camp Award	Best Player
Jim Thorpe Award	Best Defensive Back
Davey O'Brien Award	Best Quarterback
Rimington Trophy	Best Center
Lou Groza Award	Best Placekicker
Butkis Award	Best Linebacker
Doak Walker Award	Best Running Back
John Mackey Award	Best Tight End
Outland Trophy	Best Interior Lineman
Ray Guy Award	Best Punter
Bednarik Award	Best Defensive Player
Nagurski Trophy	Best Defensive Player

Footballogy: Elements of American Football for Non-Native Speakers of English

Chart F—comparison of major differences—college and pro (NFL) football

Area	NFL	College
completed catch	both feet down inbound	one foot down inbound
Fair catch	Ball is placed at spot of signal for fair catch no matter where	Fair catch signal inside 25 is considered a touchback. Ball is spotted for paly at
roster	53 (46 active on game day)	unlimited (can be over 100!)
jersey numbers	unique # set by position	any number (duplicate OK)
clock on 1st downs	keeps going	stops while officials reset chains
hash marks	18' 6" apart	40' apart
names on back of jerseys	Mandatory	Optional (though most do)
overtime (OT)	Regular-season games can end in a tie; One possession for each team after kickoff unless TD is scored on first possession (by offense, defense or special teams); a safety can also win; tie score after 10-minute OT (regular season), game is official, a tie; post season is "Sudden Death"—play goes on until one wins.	Games can never end in a tie; untimed period(s); no kickoff; ball is placed on 25-yard line (red zone); each team gets chance to score; game continues until tie is broken.

III. College and pro comparisons. The following questions deal with Charts E and F. Select your answer from the choices provided.

1. What are the most points that could occur for OT in the NFL to end in a tie?
    a. three
    b. six (TD)
    c. six (two field goals)
    d. zero

2. Adam West plays guard for a Division I team. What award might he win?
   a. Outland
   b. Mackey
   c. Heisman
   d. Rimington

3. (Involves previous knowledge on formations and plays.) The hash marks, farther apart in college ball, mean that the marks are closer to the sidelines. When the ball is spotted at or near a hash mark, how might this be an advantage to a college team over an NFL team?
   a. Running the ball on a sweep
   b. Passing the ball long
   c. Screen pass
   d. Off-tackle run

4. Jersey number 46...
   a. could be a defensive lineman in college, but not the NFL.
   b. could be a running back in the NFL and college.
   c. neither A nor B
   d. Both A and B

5. The OT rule when the first team that scores wins is called...
   a. sudden death
   b. overtime challenge
   c. red zone
   d. one possession rule

6. How can a team end an NFL game in overtime without possessing the ball?
   a. A kickoff return for a TD
   b. An interception or fumble return for a TD
   c. A safety
   d. All of the above

7. What's the minimum number of points a team in the NFL can score in OT to win?
   a. three
   b. six
   c. two
   d. one

8. A receiver but <u>not a wide receiver</u> can win this collegiate award:
   a. Butkus
   b. Mackey
   c. Bednarik
   d. Heisman

9. The Lou Groza award is probably named after...
   a. a kicker
   b. a punter
   c. a lineman
   d. a coach

10. One foot down inbounds (inside the playing field)
    a. is a completed catch in the NFL but not college.
    b. is a completed pass in both the NFL and college.
    c. is not a completed pass in either the NFL or college.
    d. is not a completion in the NFL but is in college.

IV. Matching — Place the letter from the word in the box with its definition

1. ___ enemy; opponent
2. ___ an audition; a trial
3. ___ supervised
4. ___ motto; fancy expression
5. ___ random
6. ___ completely paid for
7. ___ FBS schools
8. ___ sit out; not play for a year
9. ___ athlete not recruited
10. ___ event to energize school spirit/pride
11. ___ publicize
12. ___ aim; desire
13. ___ someone chosen to play for a pro team
14. ___ changes; alternates
15. ___ obey; fulfill

a.	catchphrase
b.	at-large
c.	pep rally
d.	draft pick
e.	redshirt
f.	tryout
g.	foe
h.	Power Five/Group of Five
i.	monitored
j.	rotates
k.	stepping-stone
l.	walk on
m.	hype
n.	full ride
o.	aspire
p.	comply

V. Combining Sentences: Subordinating conjunctions connect clauses to make a sentence. (Such clauses are used in the readings above.) Each clause shows a relationship.

Instructions: 1. Place letter of clause group (A, B, C, D) in the blanks. 2. Circle yes (Y) if a comma is needed; no (N) for no comma. 3. If a comma is needed, insert it in the proper place.

because as since	**A**	**Cause and effect** I am happy because (since/as) my team won. Since (because/as) my team won, I am happy. (w/comma)
while whereas	**B**	**Compare** The Lions run the ball while (whereas) the Tigers pass it. Whereas (while) the Lions run the ball, the Tigers pass it. (w/comma)
although though even though	**C**	**Contrast** They lost even though (though, although) they played well. Although (though, even though) they lost, they played well. (w/comma)
when after as soon as	**D**	**Now (as soon as = exactly, when = about)** I turned on the TV as soon as (after/when) I got home. When (as soon as/after) I got home, I turned on the TV. (w/comma)

Ex: __D__ 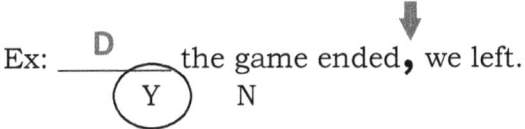 the game ended**,** we left.
        (Y)   N

1. _____ the score was 40-7 the team didn't quit.
        Y   N

2. _____ I went to Kansas State my sister went to Clemson.

        Y   N

3. The team played hard _____ they were well-coached.

        Y   N

4. _____ they are a national powerhouse many of their players are drafted by the NFL.

        Y   N

5. Winning isn't "everything" _____ some people think it is.

        Y   N

6. _____ the Rose Bowl ends we'll watch the Orange Bowl.

        Y   N

7. He played college ball _____ he never played in high school.

        Y   N

8. Linemen are big _____ running backs are fast.

        Y   N

Footballogy: Elements of American Football for Non-Native Speakers of English

Word Search—Colleges & Universities

```
L W O B E S O R W D Y H V V Y
N Y Y H V B Q W H N P Q S D M
F A S S H I J N S E Z V T E E
G K M S F Q F F E T M Y I T C
I D B S L G W J H G P C U N N
Q X P P I S D F A I L W R E E
A H P I N E K B X B A A C L R
L W R H T T H S Z O Y L E A E
A N T C R I G C W Y O K R T F
V Z N E I H F C N Y F O E R N
M L Q U H A N N Q C F N A Q O
J N G L S Z I G X T A L L B C
W Y O B D P A A E F Z A B U Y
A I O R E N R N N T N H X C S
A L E V R N W J X G E T Y K P
```

BIGTEN   HEISMAN   RECRUIT   WALKON
BLUECHIP   NAIA   REDSHIRT
CONFERENCE   NCAA   ROSEBOWL
FBS   PLAYOFF   TALENTED

American football may not be a religion, although the passion for the sport can make it seem that way at times. That said, the sport does not lack references to religious terms. "Immaculate Reception" is borrowed from the Catholic liturgy "Immaculate Conception," to mean pure or without defect. Indeed, it may have seemed like Divine intervention on December 23, 1972 at Three Rivers Stadium in Pittsburgh, Pennsylvania. Depending on one's point of view, it was either a battle of strong defenses or inept offenses. The Raiders had just scored the first touchdown of the afternoon to take a 7-6 lead with 1:17 left in the game. The Steelers were unable to move the ball after the ensuing kickoff, and with 22 seconds remaining and out of timeouts, they faced 4th and 10 from their own 40-yard line.

The Raider defense, clearly aware that this was a do-or-die or a desperate last gasp for the Steelers, applied a great pass rush on quarterback Terry Bradshaw. The quarterback spotted his target, Frenchy Fuqua, at the Raiders 35. But as the ball arrived, he and the defender collided. The ball bounced backward. Just before it hit the ground (which would have made it an incomplete pass and the ball would have been turned over to the Raiders to run out the clock for the win), fullback Franco Harris scooped up the ball and rambled to the end zone for a Steelers win 13-7. This team—whose black-and-gold uniforms resemble Darth Vader more than anything holy—advanced in the playoffs, resulting in its first of six Super Bowl wins, thanks in no small part to the pass that came to be called the "Immaculate Reception."

Hail Mary, a prayer in the Catholic faith, is used in all levels of football to describe a wish for a last-second miracle to reward the team with a win. In such a circumstance, the time has expired once the play begins. So, whatever happens will spell the end of the game unless it's a defensive penalty, where the offense did not produce a touchdown. The way it works is the quarterback "throws up a Hail Mary"—a long pass in the direction of the end zone—hoping (praying) that a teammate comes down in possession of the ball. All eligible receivers bunch together in the end zone and are surrounded by almost all the other team's defenders.

Boston College is remembered for a Hail Mary that occurred on Thanksgiving weekend, 1984. Six seconds remained in a high-scoring slugfest with the defending national champion, the University of Miami. The Eagles trailed the Hurricanes by four points and desperately needed a touchdown. After a short scramble, quarterback Doug Flutie (considered too short at 5'10" by many schools to even recruit him), put a 64-yard bomb in the air. It was as if it had been telegraphed to receiver Gerald Phelan, who nabbed the spiral in the end zone over the outstretched arms of defenders. Boston College had just done the unimaginable. Not only had they knocked off the best team in the nation but they did it dramatically. Although Flute had had a great season, this one play, some believe, secured him the Heisman Trophy, which is given annually to the most outstanding college football player.

Bonus Feature

NFL Champs Vs. College All-Stars 1934-1976

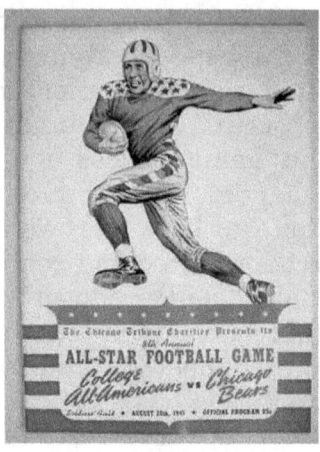

From 1934 to 1976, the exhibition season began with a game between a team of the last year's college all-stars against the defending NFL Champion. The game, a benefit for charity, was played at Soldier Field in Chicago. The first contest, which attracted a crowd of 79,000, was a **stalemate** (0-0 tie). The second year, won by the Bears 5-0 is remembered for a *guard* from the University of Michigan, Gerald R. Ford, who became the 38th **president** of the United States (1974-77). These preseason events attracted as many as 105,000 persons in their prime of popularity. Games were competitive, although the pros held the edge in series 32-9 with two ties.

The final college victory was in 1963, 20-17 over one of the best teams ever, the Green Bay Packers. Although popular with the fans, there were many risks since the all-stars were the property of the NFL club that drafted them. Coaches became **reluctant** to let their rookies play in a **meaningless** exhibition and possibly be injured. This fear was grounded in an incident in 1949 where a drafted player suffered a career-ending injury.

The series concluded in 1976 with the four-time Super Bowl Champion Pittsburgh Steelers **dominating** 24-0 in a heavy rainstorm that was called, or terminated, at halftime.

VI. Use words in the bonus feature to complete the following sentences:

1. A team that keeps winning is _____.

2. Winning a preseason game is _____.

3. Gerald Ford played _____.

4. Gerald Ford was _____ of the USA.

5. When you're at the top, you're in your _____.

6. When neither side scores, it's a _____.

7. Someone not eager to do something is _____.

A Few Of The Many Historical Names in College Football

Bear Bryant: Bryant coached from 1945 to 1982. He is best remembered for his 25 years at the University of Alabama, winning 325 games, including 15 bowl games and six titles.

Doc Blanchard and Glen Davis: Known as Mr. Inside and Mr. Outside, Blanchard and Davis were two of the most prolific running backs in college football history. They led the undefeated teams at the US Military Academy at West Point, NY from 1944-46. Davis, Mr. Outside, earned his reputation for blazing speed. Mr. Inside, Blanchard, punished those who stood in his path.

Grantland Rice (1880-1954): College football is not complete without a sportswriter in the conversation. Rice, known for his elegant prose and poetry, had a 50-year career in print and broadcasting. A former bowl game was named in his honor as well as scholarships and football awards.

Joe Paterno: Paterno coached 46 years at Penn State guiding the Nittany Lions to almost 400 victories with 24 wins in bowl games.

Knute Rockne (1888-1931): The most iconic name in college football, Rockne was a player but gained fame as a coach at the University of Notre Dame from 1918-1930. Rockne, whose life was cut short by a plane crash, holds the highest percentage (.881) of wins among Division I coaches. Rockne popularized the forward pass that made the Fightin' Irish a major factor in college football. He was coach of **the Four Horsemen**, a legendary backfield that trampled opponents and lost only two games in three years.

Photo by Unknown Author. Licensed under CC- BY-SA

Red Grange: Better known as the Galloping Ghost, Grange played halfback for the University of Illinois (1923-25) and professionally, mostly for the Chicago Bears. He is a charter member of both the college and professional Halls of Fame.

Woody Hayes: A passionate coach and educator for the Ohio State University Buckeyes for 28 years, Hayes claims 238 wins, 13 Big-Ten Championships, and five national titles.

Red Grange—public domain

> "Win one for the Gipper" is a line from the movie *Knute Rockne: All American* (1940), starring Ronald Reagan (who became the 40th president of the United States). George Gipp, who lay dying, asked Rockne to inspire the team with this famous line. It's playfully referred to today for motivation.

 VII. Who am I? (one is "what") Not all responses can be used.

1. ___ If I didn't cover (write about) sports, I'd write novels.
2. ___ You can't see me on that speeding horse.
3. ___ My last wish was for my teammates.
4. ___ I run with power and strength.
5. ___ You know nothing about college football if you don't know me.
6. ___ We're the best backfield in Notre Dame history.
7. ___ A lion, a tiger, and a...
8. ___ Who can speak Ohio State football without mention of my name?
9. ___ Fast like a young horse, a car is named after me.
10. ___ Agile, I run with speed.

a. The Gipper
b. Lee Iacocca
c. Knute Rockne
d. Red Grange
e. Joe Paterno
f. Mr. Outside
g. mustang
h. Woody Hayes
i. Grantland Rice
j. Four Horsemen
k. Mr. Inside
l. Bear Bryant

Footballogy: Elements of American Football for Non-Native Speakers of English

Crossword—Elements

ACROSS
1. Things babies wear on their feet
5. Games before the season
9. The _____ squad does not suit up
10. A state in the American Midwest
11. The result of something
12. Initials for an undrafted free agent
13. A list of players on a team

DOWN
2. General, comprehensive, global
3. football by children, not organized
4. Wonderlic test evaluates or measures this
6. To be successful = American _____
7. Choose; select
8. Cut or release a player
9. A commodity

Without our traditions, our lives would be...shaky...
— from the musical "Fiddler on the Roof"

CHAPTER XVI

Traditions

Football, more than a game, is an experience. The pages that follow show us how to make our preparations and visit to a football game connect.

The Great American Halftime show

Word Preview

regroup	belt out	baton twirlers	strike up
made up of	feisty	formations	alma mater
bring in	brought back	onlookers	

Halftime shows like this are an important part of the autumn experience of American football. (Unknown author, CC-BY-SA)

After thirty minutes of game action, both teams get a short rest period of about 12 minutes. The intermission lets teams rest and regroup, plan for the second half of the game, and gives fans a break.

Yet, there is action on the field—the halftime show. This traditional spectacle features school bands that march in brilliant formations on the field. They spell out words and create designs while striking up hit tunes of the day as well as traditional songs.

Footballogy: Elements of American Football for Non-Native Speakers of English

> A band can range in size up to several hundred members. Situated in a section of the stadium during the game, it may strike up a few notes of the school fight song after scores, first downs, long gains, sacks—anything! Fans who support the other team, however, may not appreciate this.

The color guard, which bears flags, and high-stepping majorettes twirling batons, heighten the extravaganza. At some interval, we'll hear the school fight song.

High-stepping drum majors and majorettes are popular at halftime shows. (Photo by Unknown Author, CC-BY-SA)

Sample of University Fight Songs:

On Iowa – University of Iowa

Victors Valiant – University of Michigan

Conquest – University of Southern California

Anchors Away! - US Naval Academy

Victory March - University of Notre Dame

Suggestion: Search "college fight song" on YouTube and listen as you read this

Origin of Halftime

The halftime show started in the 1920s. Historians mostly credit mid-game entertainment to Walter Lingo, founder of one of the first NFL teams, the Oorang Indians, made up of Native Americans. (This is the team Jim Thorpe played for.) Noted for his special talent for publicity, Lingo would lure, or bring in, audiences to games with the promise of an extraordinary halftime show rather than the promise of a good football game. Entertainment was provided by the players along with Lingo's Airedale dogs, known for their intelligence and sporty look. The dogs retrieved or brought back targets while Indian dances and tomahawk and knife-throwing demonstrations delighted onlookers. Evidence suggests that women's tackle football was a halftime exhibition as far back as 1926.

Tomahawk image: Pixabay

For many years, professional football halftimes featured traditional shows with local talent. High-school bands and drum and bugle corps performed, which television stations would show. Even the early Super Bowls were a picture of tradition. The Marching Tiger Band of Grambling State University and an ultra-clean-cut singing group called "Up with People" were mild compared to today's trendy performances with pyrotechnics and celebrity performers. The reality is that broadcast rights for football are high stakes, about money. Lady Gaga, say, commands a wide following and keeps viewers tuned in but that's not the case with unknown band members in plumed outfits. Stars cost a lot but their fame brings in revenue.

For viewers at home, halftime television broadcasts—or "telecasts"—open a window for trips to the kitchen. Unless the occasion features a trendy recording artist, most regular-season telecasts don't televise the halftime show. Instead, viewers can keep up with scores and highlights from other games around the league. The moment is also a chance for fans to match wits with those of the game hosts, who make "expert" game strategies and predictions for the second half of the game.

I. Multiple tasks: fill-in-the-blanks, multiple choice, true/false

1. (origin/originate/original) Flights that _____ in Dallas are usually on time. What is your place of _____? My _____ plan was to celebrate with my friends.

2. (pride/proud/proudly) Most students show their _____ with school colors. They are _____ of their team's accomplishments. They _____ tell others.

3. (perform/performance/performer) The _____ will _____ this weekend at a _____ after the game.

4. (tradition/traditional) Our family _____ is to eat _____ food at the holidays.

5. Bear and twirl:
   a. show and spin
   b carry and spin
   c. carry and show
   d. wear and carry

6. Pyrotechnics has to do with:
   a. water
   b. fire
   c. air
   d. dance

7. Trendy (antonym):
   a. old
   b. modern
   c. avant-garde
   d. soft

8. "Broadcast" can mean "telecast."
   T   F

9. "Tomahawk" is to "tool" as Airedale is to _____.
   a. Missile
   b. Native American
   c. dog
   d. halftime

10. How does one feel when he/she hears the playing of the alma mater?
    a. playful
    b. heartbroken
    c. sentimental
    d. angry

11. To be feisty is to be
    a. strong   b. energetic
    c. sentimental   d. angry

II. Separable verbs

Two-word verbs appear in *Footballogy*, including the above reading about halftime shows. Some are separable, some are inseparable. Use your knowledge of two- and three-word verbs by rewriting the following sentences with the correct pronoun. (Hint: Separable verbs have pronouns for separation; inseparable verbs do not.)

>Ex: (separable) *I filled up the car with gas. I filled it up.*
>Ex: (inseparable) *She looked through the telephone book. She looked through it.*

1. Will you please bring back Robert?

   _____

2. A football is made up of many particles.

   _____

3. The band director decided to speed up the tempo.

   _____

4. We struck up a friendly conversation.

   _____

5. The performer belted out the popular melody.

   _____

6. She ran into Tom and Mary at the game.

   _____

7. I <u>looked up the statistics</u> online.

_____

8. Tom <u>called up his mother</u>.

_____

9. We <u>picked up the tickets</u> at Will Call.

_____

10. I <u>can't stand two-word verbs</u>.

_____

The Great American Tailgate Party

The great pastime of tailgating at a football game.
(Unknown Author, CC-BY-SA)

Word Preview

canopy	banned	toss (around)	cushions
perishable	SUV	RV	obnoxious	designated
driver	curb	restrictions	regulations

The word "tailgating" suggests following another car too closely. This can cause rear-end accidents—an awkward way to make friends. However, tailgating has a whole new meaning at a football game. It's a social event around the backside of a motor vehicle, its tailgate (the flap on hatchbacks, pick-up trucks, and SUVs) or under the canopy at the side of an RV. Tailgaters in the stadium or nearby parking lots make new friends and celebrate in a festive atmosphere while chowing-down (eating) on scrumptious barbecued food.

A tailgate party can be fancy with tables and décor or it can be simple. A grill and a cooler for food and drinks are the necessities. Hot dogs and hamburgers are common, of course, and depending on the region of the country, there will be diverse offerings such as Polish sausage (kielbasa), carne asada, Philly cheesesteak, chicken wings, and Boston baked beans. Whiskey and similar "hard drinks" are banned although beer can be OK. Selling food is not allowed since food is available for purchase just a few steps away inside the stadium.

The parking lot can be a sea of vehicles with team banners and bumper stickers. Fans wear hats and apparel bearing the logo and colors of their favorite teams, normally dominated by the home team. Seat cushions, folding chairs, table coverings, and umbrellas are among the many products on exhibit. A tailgate party is a place for light recreation for young and old to toss around beach balls and footballs if there is space.

Graphics: CC-BY-SA (Wiki)

Want to start your own tailgate party? Here's how. *(Adapted from WikiHow)*

1. Invite friends and family who think a tailgate party is a good idea. Trucks are best for this. After all, "tailgate" means the flap at the back of the truck, called a tailgate. Vans and SUVs are also good. You could use a folding picnic table instead of a tailgate.
2. Ensure that at least one person has a car large enough to cope with all the things you're likely to need: Folding furniture, containers for beer, soda, etc. Blankets, tablecloths, cooking utensils, and seat cushions are also useful.
3. Make a list of food, drinks, and other items that people will be bringing.
   - Check the rules of the stadium about bringing alcohol. If there are children, make sure to have non-alcoholic drinks.
   - Bring plenty of trash bags.
   - Bring condiments—mustard, sauces, and salt and pepper, etc.
   - Bring a cooler for beverages and perishable foods.
   - Bring lights in case of a night game or dark weather games (remember, American football is played in all kinds of weather!).
   - And don't forget the grill and self-lighting charcoal (lighter fluid may not be allowed).
4. Plan the food. KISS—Keep It Simple, Stupid—just quick and easy stuff to fix. Barbecued steak, chicken, hot dogs, sausages, hamburgers, kebabs (skewers), one-pot-meals (chili, macaroni and cheese, baked beans), Buffalo wings, pretzels, potato chips, and coffee, hot chocolate or tea for cold weather. Where possible, prepare foods like salads ahead of time.
5. Get to the parking lot early. It's nice if two vehicles come together and pick parking spaces right next to each other. Call the people who are coming and tell them where you are if they're not already with you.
6. Set up any equipment. Start the barbecue grill so that when people show up, the charcoal will be ready to cook right away.
7. Have fun, get into conversations with other tailgaters, and enjoy the party. Play your favorite music, toss a miniature football around (there won't be much space for this so be considerate of

others). Display your team's logo and colors! Don't drink too much, for obnoxious, drunken behavior can ruin the fun for others. And have an autograph book nearby. Sometimes retired football stars come by looking for a free meal. For a fee, you might even get team cheerleaders to come by for a photo opportunity.

8. Clean up after the party. If you didn't manage to get into the event, have a TV or radio with a DC (direct current) power converter so that you can continue to enjoy the game from your tailgate party, if permitted.

Warnings!

- ➢ Have a designated driver.
- ➢ It's a good idea to have an instant stain removal spray on hand in case of spills on the car's interior.
- ➢ Drink responsibly.
- ➢ Follow the regulations of the venue; failure to do so can result in a fine or even arrest.
- ➢ The best things in life may still be free but many NFL and major college teams now require a paid subscription to access an area in the parking lot designated as a tailgate zone.

I. Matching: Place the letter from column B next to the number in Column A.

<u>**COLUMN A**</u>

1. ___designated driver
2. ___cushion
3. ___regulations
4. ___perishable
5. ___banned
6. ___canopy
7. ___restrictions
8. ___SUV
9. ___obnoxious
10. ___RV

<u>**COLUMN B**</u>

a. limits
b. rules
c. covering
d. non-drinking person to drive
e. prohibited
f. recreation vehicle
g. Sport Utility Vehicle
h. something soft to sit on
i. bad behavior
j. fresh; not preserved

Footballogy: Elements of American Football for Non-Native Speakers of English

Leading the Cheer

We've got the S-P-I-R-I-T
We've got the spirit
So let's hear it!

Cheerleaders, strong and athletic, work in all kinds of weather (photo left John Harrison WikiCommons SA BY 3.0)

    The loud and energetic "rah-rah" at the game is led by the cheerleaders—both male and female—who must be athletic, muscle-toned, and agile to dazzle audiences with routines that include gymnastics and modern dance. Their animated presence adds to the total sensory experience of American football. They wave pompoms (decorative balls made of fiber) during player introductions and perform anything from cartwheels to stylish dances and acrobatics during game breaks. Demands are on cheerleaders to be always "on." Even when things are not going well for their team, their faces are reliably lit-up—bright and smiling—a comforting reminder that the event is only a game, not a serious life-or-death matter.

    In high schools and colleges, where the preferred term is "cheer team," young men commonly are a part of the group. When this happens, the team is said to be "co-ed." Everyone must match up in their abilities to do acts that involve creating pyramids and tumbling, to do rhythmic chants, jump up and down, and perform cartwheels, high kicks, and choreographed dances after their team makes a good play, scores, and during timeouts. Embedded in the cheer team is the team mascot, who represents the nickname of the team. A team named "the Tigers" would obviously have a mascot dressed as a tiger. The mascot waves at fans and performs amusing antics like a clown at a circus.

To become a cheerleader is very competitive. Many are called but few are chosen. In addition to physical appearance and athletic ability, cheerleading requires intelligence and outgoing personalities as well as strong moral character. After all, cheerleaders represent their school or organization not just on game day, but at social functions and special events.

In the NFL, cheerleaders work games as an avocation or a hobby that normally lasts a few short years. It's not uncommon for cheerleaders to be accountants, teachers, lawyers, architects, or to have unusual professions like sign language interpreters. Many are in STEM (Science, Technology, Engineering, and Math) fields, like a 49er cheerleader who is also a degree-holder from MIT (Massachusetts Institute of Technology) in chemical engineering. A former Washington Redskins cheerleader became a lawyer and a medical doctor (see her interview later in this chapter). "Cheerleaders are an incredible source of inspiration to millions of young women," says Darlene Cavalier, founder of "Science Cheerleader," an organization of cheerleaders in STEM fields.

Twenty-six of the 32 NFL teams have their own cheerleaders although the community-owned Green Bay Packers utilize the services of the cheerleading squad from nearby St. Norbert's College. Like the players, cheerleaders "play" in all kinds of weather, from supremely hot to rain, snow, and ice.

NFL cheerleaders carry the torch, representing their team at charity events. They have a significant role in promoting causes like Hispanic Heritage Month and Breast Cancer Awareness. They serve food at homeless shelters, bring gifts to needy children, and support programs for handicapped individuals such as the Special Olympics.

Los Angeles Rams Cheerleaders and mascot "Rampage" serving traditional Thanksgiving dinner at A Place Called Home in Los Angeles, Calif. Photo: Timothy Wahl

 I. True/false and multiple choice

1. Men don't become cheerleaders.
    T   F

2. Halftime shows were the main attraction at the first professional football games.
    T   F

3. Which would you probably <u>not</u> see at a tailgate party?
    a. hot dogs   b. a tablecloth
    c. Zinfandel   d. beer

4. Mustard is for...
    a. hot dogs   b. a plant
    c. a beverage   d. a chair

5. "rah-rah" =
    a. a pompom   b. a cheer
    c. a majorette   d. a name

6. Cheerleading teams do not attend charitable activities.
    T   F

7. Food is sold at tailgate parties.
    T   F

8. Cheerleaders can
    a. dance   b. do charity events
    c. become doctors   d. all—a, b &

9. Which is not a requirement to be a cheerleader?
    a. good moral character   b. intelligence
    c. athleticism   d. being tall

10. Not all NFL teams have cheer teams.
    T   F

Interpreting Fact Sheets

Some professional football organizations, upon request, will provide cheerleader appearances at special corporate events, occasions like birthdays, meeting you and your guests in your private box seat at the stadium, or will join you at your tailgate party. Whatever the reason, the appearance of NFL cheerleaders can deliver lasting memories.

Read the cheer team request information and description of services below, then test your understanding in the questions that follow.

Cheerleader Appearance Request Fact Sheet

- **Appearances at business and corporate events (meet-and-greet)**
    - Fee: $200.00 per person/per hour, with a 2-person/1 hour minimum.
- **Appearances at business and corporate events (with performances)**
    - Fee: $300.00 per person/per hour, with a 4-person/1 hour minimum.
- **Appearance at non-profit organizations (churches, civic groups, charity events)**
    - Fee: $75 per person/per hour, with a 2-person/1-hour minimum.
    - Restriction: All proceeds (money) must go toward charity.
- **Appearances for youth birthday parties, ages 1 to 13 years**
    - Fee: $100.00 per person/per hour, with a 2-person/1 hour minimum.

Requirements

- Reservations must be made three (3) weeks in advance.
- Payment must be paid in full at the time of the event by
- check or credit card, not cash.
- For travel in a 25-75-mile radius, a charge of 58.5 cents
- per mile beyond 25 miles is charged.
- Travel beyond 75 miles must include one night's lodging
- plus two meals.
- Appearances must not have or promote alcoholic
- beverages.
- Cheerleaders will appear in public places only.

I. True or False; multiple choice.

1. Based on the chart, I can infer that an event hosted in someone's home is not OK.
    a. True   b. False

2. "Meet-and-greet" involves shaking hands and short conversations.
    a. True   b. False

3. Travel costs to an event 35 miles away will amount to _____.
    a. $58.50   b. $0.00
    c. $5.80   d. $58

4. Little Tommy turns 14 years old. Does he qualify for a youth party?
    a. yes   b. no

5. You want an event on November 24. When is the latest date to make a reservation?
   a. November 3   b. November 10
   c. November 17   d. date of event

6. Cheerleaders will come to a private box seat but not to my tailgate party.
   a. True   b. False

7. What's the minimum fee for a corporate event with a performance?
   a. $300   b. one hour
   c. $1200   d. 4 cheerleaders

8. I want to promote a new kind of beer at an event attended by cheerleaders.
   a. OK   b. Not OK

9. "Suite" sounds like "sweet"...
   a. True   b. False

10. Four cheerleaders for two hours for a cost of $600 is which event?
    a. Non-profit
    b. corporate meet-and-greet
    c. corporate performance
    d. youth

11. Who benefits from an appearance at a non-profit?
    a. The NFL team   b. a charity
    c. the Uber driver   d. youth

Interview: Regina Bailey, MD

Footballogy caught up with former NFL cheerleader, Regina Bailey, who has earned recognition as a medical doctor and an attorney-at-law. As a patent attorney, she has fought for the rights of generic drug companies to get their lower-priced drugs on the market. She's done biomedical research at Yale and Stanford, two of the world's top universities, and has been published in scholarly journals. She's appeared as an expert guest in the area of health and fitness on TV shows and at public venues. Dr. Bailey, who serves as an Emergency Room (ER) physician in Houston, Texas, also owns a medical spa, where she gives out healthful lifestyle solutions to clients, many of them women. She has a line of nutritional supplements called Fit & Fine. Dr. Bailey, in her forties, still competes in beauty pageants—and wins!

Regina Bailey, medical doctor and attorney-at-law, scholar, health and fitness expert, and former cheerleader. Twitter photo

Reported Speech

"Reported speech" is when we talk about (report) what somebody else said.

Direct Speech: "I've been to three games this year."
Reported Speech: *She said (that) she'd been to three games this year.*

The reporting verb in the above example is "said," the past tense of "say." When the reporting verb is in the past, we also change the verb tense in the structure that follows. Thus, "have been" (or "was") becomes "had been" in a reported statement; is/are → was/were, etc.)

A few examples of reporting verbs:
observed	added	believed	thought
exclaimed	explained	claimed	answered

Reported Speech Capsule

Notice how the pronoun changes in conversation from direct to reported.

DIRECT SPEECH	REPORTED SPEECH	EXAMPLE
Simple present	Simple past	"I **want** to eat a hot dog." She said (that) she **wanted** to eat a hot dog.
Present continuous	Past continuous	"**I'm enjoying** the game." She said (that) she **was enjoying** the game.
Simple past	Past perfect	"I saw the game on TV." She said (that) she**'d seen the** game on TV.
past continuous	Past perfect continuous	My son **was talking** to me at kickoff. She said (that) her son **had been talking** to her at kickoff.
Present perfect	Past perfect	"**I've** just **done** my exercises." She said (that) she**'d** just **done** her exercises
Modal (future)	will	My friends **will make** the game. She said (that) her friends **would make** the game.
Modal (ability)	can	"My brother **can play** guard." She said (that) her brother **could play** guard.

The modals *could, should, ought to, had better* do not change. *Must* becomes *had to.*

Footballogy: Elements of American Football for Non-Native Speakers of English

 I. Instructions: Follow the example below and report Dr. Bailey's answer. Remember to use the proper verb tense and pronoun.

Footballogy = FB   Dr. Regina Bailey = DRB

FB: When you were a little girl, what did you dream of becoming when you grew up?

DRB: *I dreamed of being a doctor and a cheerleader.*

> *Example: Dr. Bailey said that she had dreamed of being a doctor and a cheerleader.*

TW: What are the best things about being an NFL cheerleader?

DRB: *My favorite part is being on the field and close to the game.*

> A.) Dr. Bailey said that _____
> _____.

FB: What are the special challenges of being an NFL cheerleader?

DRB: *It's a lot like being on a Broadway chorus line with so many costume changes, drills, and dances to rehearse.*

> B) Dr. Bailey said (that)_____
> _____.

FB: Cheerleaders ALWAYS have smiles—even when their team is way behind or during tense moments of a game. How is this possible?

DRB: *We are there to keep the spirits of the fans up even when things may not be going how we want.*

C) Dr. Bailey replied that they _____
_____.

FB: What's your secret to accomplishing so much in your young life?

DRB: *I have always been very good at multitasking and I get bored very easily. The combination of those two elements has helped me reach all my accomplishments so far.*

D) Dr. Bailey answered _____
_____.

FB: How has your training as a cheerleader supported your success in law and medicine?

DRB: *Cheerleading helped me with self-confidence.*

E) Dr. Bailey said that _____
_____.

DRB: *Before cheerleading, I was very shy, but cheerleading helped me break out of that.*

F) Dr. Bailey added _____
_____.

DRB: *Cheerleading has been very helpful with enhancing my communication skills that are necessary in law and medicine.*

G) In addition, Dr. Bailey claimed _____
_____.

FB: What do you do to stay healthy and fit?

DRB: *I exercise two to three hours every day and eat a very healthy diet.*

H) (Add your own reporting verb) Dr. Bailey _____
_____ .

DRB: *After my mother died from complications of diabetes and hypertension, it became necessary for me to change my life around, lose weight, and become healthier.*

I) Dr. Bailey _____
_____ .

DRB: *I realized that to be around for my young daughter, I had to develop healthier habits.*

J) She _____
_____ .

DRB: *I have also discovered that staying physically healthy keeps me mentally healthy.*

K) _____ .

> "I want to empower women to not let anything stop them from pursuing their dreams," she states. "Sometimes, after we age, we become very hard on ourselves. I like to show women that you can still pursue your dreams at any age!"

Report this here:

_____

_____

_____ .

Special Feature: The Heidi Game

CC-BY-SA   Public Domain

The following story is about a famous game that changed the way football games are broadcast on television. At the end of the story is a test, which includes the vocabulary below.

Word Preview

pre-empted	going at it	flashy	go at it
back-and-forth	air	powers	barely
humorist	counterpart	debacle	determined

What could a little girl with braids in the Swiss Alps have to do with American football? On November 17, 1968, what she did was unforgettable. If TV viewers hadn't heard of "preempted" by that date, they were in for a lesson.

Two old American Football League powers, the New York Jets and the Oakland Raiders, were going at it in a late game at 4:00 PM (Eastern time zone), in Oakland, California. Joe Namath, named "Broadway Joe" for his flashy lifestyle, quarterbacked for the Jets, a team destined for the Super Bowl that year. Strong-armed Darryl Lamonica, the so-called "Mad Bomber" for his deep throws, was his counterpart for the Raiders. The contest, which featured 10 future Hall of Famers, including Namath and Lamonica, had the makings of a classic. The teams had traded leads eight times. There wasn't any quit in either team and each was determined to fight to the end.

In a perfect world, a football game lasts not more than three hours. For that reason, the National Broadcasting Company (NBC), which televised the game, calculated that the 4 PM game would finish by 7 PM, and the evening's entertainment would continue as scheduled. *Heidi*, a much-anticipated movie for children, was set to air. But the hard-hitting, back-and-forth contest with excessive penalties and timeouts was running long. With 65 seconds left, the Jets scored to go up 32-29. Seven o'clock was near.

The network had to make a hard decision in a short time of what to do about *Heidi*. Should it show the rest of the game and join *Heidi* in progress, or should it leave the game and show the movie from the beginning? Whatever the decision, some viewers would be happy, others not. One matter to consider was that early Sunday evenings traditionally were for children's viewing, so the first option made sense.

After the late Jets score, the Raiders had barely enough time to come back. The law of probability said that they wouldn't. But this was the NFL, where the law of "any given Sunday" applied.

Fifty seconds remained when the Raiders crossed midfield on what was to be their winning drive. NBC, looking to its contractual obligation with *Heidi's* sponsor to show the movie in its entirety, couldn't wait a second more. Viewers were shown the opening credits of *Heidi* and images of a little girl in braids climbing the Alps with her grandfather.

Said Delbert Mann, *Heidi's* director in an interview years after the airing, "There was a considerable amount of plot information early in the film that was absolutely essential to understanding it."

Twenty minutes into the film, the network presented the final score at the bottom of the TV screen. Who could have predicted such an exciting finish? The Raiders made two quick scores in nine seconds to win 43-32.

Mann, too, was upset—but for another reason. Showing the score, he said, "interrupted a dramatic point in the film."

Many callers expressed their unhappiness to NBC, some connecting with organizations like the *New York Times* and New York Police Department that had nothing to do with the game. Some even complained to their local telephone company.

Art Buchwald, a humorist for the *Washington Post*, offered a witty observation: "Men who would not get out of their armchairs for earthquakes made their way to the phone to call in to NBC."

The immediate result of the *Heidi* debacle was an apology from NBC. The incident was also responsible for a new policy with TV networks to show future games from start to finish. Shows scheduled to follow would not be preempted but started after the game.

This famous Jets and Raiders game, called the "Heidi Game," rests in football folklore. In 1997, it was voted the most memorable regular-season game in pro football history.

 I. Vocabulary. Replace the underlined word with one from the word bank.

1. The game went <u>one way and then the other</u>. _____

2. Come to LA, where movie stars wear <u>bright and stylish</u> clothes. _____

3. The game is scheduled to <u>broadcast</u> at 1:30. _____

4. A <u>disaster</u> occurred because the team was not prepared. _____

5. Never again will the show be <u>replaced</u> by another.
   _____

6. That guy wants to be funny but he'll never be a <u>comic</u>.
   _____

7. The vice president of the Rams joined his <u>opposite</u> with the Chargers. _____

8. They will <u>fight hard</u> until one of them wins. _____

9. I have <u>hardly</u> time to get ready. Ten minutes isn't enough! _____

II. Main idea, details, and inferences. Circle the correct answer.

1. Which of the following best describes the main idea of the passage?
   a. It happened one Sunday.
   b. Outrage over a movie changed the way football is shown on television.
   c. The *Heidi* movie was not well-timed.
   d. A football game and a movie do not mix.

2. In addition to the local phone company, the *Washington Post* was one non-essential organization people complained to.
       T   F

3. Besides Namath and Lamonica, how many other future Hall of Famers were in the game?
       a. 10   b. 8
       c. 6   d. 12

4. What was the main factor that motivated the switch to the movie?
       a. money   b. children
       c. football fans   d. no chance for a Raiders win

5. Who suggests that a football game is more important than a natural disaster?
   a. Joe Namath   b. Darryl Lamonica
   c. Delbert Mann   d. Art Buchwald

6. Did the team that won the *Heidi* game play in the Super Bowl?
   Y   N

7. The game was played in the state of California.
   T   F

III. Parts of Speech

1. hard: difficult as hardly: (   )
   a. not any   b. easy
   c. barely   d. only just

2. hardly: adverb: hard: (   )
   a. adverb   b. adjective
   c. preposition   d. noun

3. The rule for *fast* in "he runs fast" is:
   a. Adjective describes noun
   b. Adverb modifies adjective
   c. Adverb modifies verb
   d. Adverb modifies adverb

4. The rule for fast in "He is a fast runner" is:
   a. Adjective describes noun
   b. Adverb modifies adjective
   c. Adverb modifies verb
   d. Adverb modifies adverb.

5. A humorist is a person who speaks _____.
   a. laughingly   b. humor
   c. humorously   d. satirically

*If you cannot do great things,
do small things in a great way.*
—Napoleon Hill

CHAPTER XVII
Insiders

To be an insider means to be close to the source of information—to be "inside." This chapter presents a discussion with a football insider. Along the way is a discovery of "insiders," so to speak, in speech.

Embedded Speech/Noun Clauses

English does not have the familiar (personal) or formal "you" form. Languages that have a formal "you" and informal "you" make it easy when addressing another person. We'd use a different pronoun when talking to a professor or doctor than to our friends. Since English does not have this ability to distinguish between formal or informal, it uses embedded speech or "indirect speech" for this purpose. Embedded speech asks a question in a friendly way. It makes the question "softer" or polite. (Grammar teachers call this structure a "noun clause.")

For example, if a person asks, "Where's the bathroom?" it can sound abrupt and unfriendly. This could cause pushback or a not-too-friendly response in return, such as: "Excuse me?" (See verbal irony.)

However, heading your question with a phrase such as those listed in Chart I below will likely lead to a friendly response.

Chart I – Introduction to the noun clause*

can you tell me + noun clause	Do you have any idea...?
Could you tell me ...?	I'd like to know...
Could you possibly tell me...?	I wonder...
Do you know...?	I was wondering...
Please tell me...	Could you explain...?
I was thinking...	Would you be so kind as to tell me...?
Do you believe...?	Do you happen to know...?
Can I ask you...?	Do you by chance know...?

*The heading (beginning) is followed by a question word ("if" for yes/no), then the question being asked—<u>but in sentence word order</u> (subject + verb), not question word order. Notice that not all embedded questions are questions at all, but a statement that still requires a response.

Direct question: Where is the bathroom?
Embedded question: "Can you tell me **where** the bathroom is?

The noun clause, which begins with "where" or any other question word, is followed by statement word (subject + verb).: "where the bathroom is?"

Statement form: I wonder where the bathroom is. (No question mark.)

Chart II shows questions with tenses, including "to be" (when using an auxiliary or "helping" verb), do, does or did. In a direct question, omit the auxiliary in reported embedded speech but be sure to use the correct tense of the main verb (if it's present—"he," "she," "it") and use the past form if the question is past.

CHART II—embedded/indirect speech

Information Questions	Start of noun clause	Question word	subject	verb	More info/end mark	
Why are they late?	Do you know	why	they	are	late	?
What is he doing?	Can you explain	what	he	is doing		?
Where do you buy tickets?	Can you tell me	how much	tickets	cost		?
When does the bus go?	Can I ask you	when	the plane	goes		?
What time will it start?	I wonder	what time	it	will start		.
Who saw him?	I'd like to know	who		saw	him	.
Who did you see?	Please tell me	who(m)	you	saw		.
Where has she been?	Can I ask you	where	she	has been		?
What should we do?	Please explain	what	we	should do		.

When else to use embedded questions

1. <u>When discussing someone not in the conversation:</u>

    Direct: *Will he pass the ball?* You turn to someone: *Do you think <u>he will pass the ball?</u>*

2. <u>When reporting a person's response to a question</u>. This looks like reported speech. However, in place of that, which is optional in reported speech, we must use a question word in reporting the question asked.

    When does the game start? (Can you tell me when the game starts?)
    She told me when the game start<u>ed</u>.
    Reported speech: *She said that it started at one o'clock.*

Practice: Complete these noun clauses. Be sure to include the correct end mark (punctuation).

Direct Question	**Indirect**
What is his name?	Can you tell me what _____
Where can I exchange my money?	Do you know where_____
When does the game start?	Is it possible for you to tell me _____
Where should we sit?	I wonder _____

Direct question	**Indirect**
What is his name?	Can you tell me what _____
Where can I exchange my money?	Do you know where_____
When does the game start?	Is it possible for you to tell me _____

Where should we sit?　　　　　　　I wonder _____
  [Answers: *what his name is; where I can exchange money; when the game starts; where we should eat*]

Yes/No Questions

The question word can be replaced by "if" or whether" (less common).
Ex: Is the game over? *I wonder if the game is over.*

Direct Question	**Indirect question**
Is she a student?	Do you know _____?
Can he swim	Do you have any idea _____?
Are the tickets sold out?	Would you please tell me _____?
Will they come with us?	I'd like to know _____.

[Answers: *if she is a student; if he can swim; if the tickets are sold out; whether they will come with us*]

For your information

Embedded speech questions may indicate an optional "yes" or "no" response before the "real" answer.

Example: *Do you know what time it is?*
Yes, I do. (Yes, I know what time it is.) It's 10:30.

Reporting this reply to your companion:

Yes, she <u>knew</u> what time it was. (embedded speech)
 She <u>said</u> that it <u>was</u> 10:30. (reported speech)
Remember reporting imperatives ("stay"; "see me"). Use "to":
She asked me **to stay.**
She asked me **to see <u>her</u>.**

Footballogy: Elements of American Football for Non-Native Speakers of English

The transcript that follows is a discussion with Chris Brown of the Buffalo Bills organization. While Chris, embedded with the Bills, takes us inside his unique job, our job is to get inside a sentence with embedded speech. This involves the use of noun clauses, which typically start with a question word or an "if."

Chris Brown, Buffalo Bills Insider (retrieved from Twitter @ChrisBrownBills)

 I. Instructions 1-10: Put an "X" is the space provided next to the correct embedded structure.

1. Footballogy (FB): let's begin by my asking you…
    a. ____who do you work for?
    b. ____who you work for.

2. Can you tell me…?
    a. ___ what your job title is?
    b. ___ what is your job title?

3. FB: Please tell me...?
    a. ___ where your job is located?
    b. ___ where is your job located?

4. FB: Do you mind telling me...?
    a. ___ have you worked there very long?
    b. ___ if you have worked there very long?

5. FB: Can you explain...?
    a. ___ what are your job duties?
    b. ___ what your job duties are?

6. FB: Let me ask you...
    a. ___ what you like most about your job.
    b. ___ what do you like most about your job?

7. FB: Do you have any idea...?
    a. ___ why football is a popular sport?
    b. ___ why is football a popular sport?

8. Would you be so kind as to share...?
    a. ___ what has been your proudest accomplishment?
    b. ___ what your proudest accomplishment has been.

9. Could you possibly share with our readers...?
    a. ___ what like you most about your job?
    b. ___ what you like most about your job?

10. Can you let us in on...?
    a. ___ what the most stressful part of your job is?
    b. ___ what is the most stressful part of your job?

Questions 11-15: You finish

Example: ("What is your job title") Let's begin by my asking **What your job title is.**

11. ("What does 'football Insider' mean?")
    Please explain _____.
12. ("Describe your duties as multi-media reporter?")
    Can you _____?
13. ("What is your proudest moment?")
    Can you share _____?
14. ("What's the best part of your job?")
    I'd like to know _____.
15. ("Do you ever discuss football with people whose first language is not English?)
    Could you please tell me _____?

16-30 Chris' replies. Fill in the spaces (NOTE: most follow indirect/embedded speech; however, four blanks do not change verb tense or pronoun due to direct speech.)

Chris said that his job title *Bills Insider* **16.** (mean) _____ that he **17.** (serve) _____ as the lead reporter for the Buffalo Bills' website. He described the best part of his job **18.** (to be) ___ game day. "Nothing **19.** (beat)_____ being at the game and reporting on what **20.** (unfold) _____," he reports. Chris noted that pressure, or stress, **21.** (can happen) _____ when he **22.** (have)_____ a tight deadline and **23.** (need) _____ to deliver fast-breaking news quickly.

Chris talked about his proudest moment, a feature story **24.** (I) ____ **25.** (put) ___ ___ together on Robert Woods (a wide receiver) and his older sister, who sadly **26.** (died) ___ ___ after a battle with cancer when both were in high school. He was honored to be able to tell their story in a way that **27.** (to be) ___ appreciated by their parents. "It was some of the most rewarding work I've done," he says.

Chris stated that **28.** (my)___ most memorable moment **29.** (come) _____ at the end of the 2017 season. "I was in Miami and **30.** (to be/cover) _____ the jubilant Bills locker room when they **31.** (qualify) ___ for the playoffs." It was their first in 17 years.

II. MATCHING. Place the letter of the description (column B) next to word(s) from the reading (A).

A	B
1. __beat	a. to report on a news story
2. __breaking news	b. the basic elements; kind or sort of something
3. __to cover	c. informal for someone who's embedded
4. __insider	d. very happy
5. __jubilant	e. a set, fixed time that something must be finished
6. __nature (the)	f. to develop, reveal, become clear
7. __stressful	g. News territory assigned to a reporter
8. __tight deadline	h. an unfriendly response
9. __pushback	i. information that's happening now
10. __unfold	j. full of tension

A "Wild" Wild Card Game

On January 3, 1993, the Buffalo Bills hosted the sixth seed, the Houston Oilers (now the Tennessee Titans) in the Wildcard round. The Bills were aiming to make a run to their third straight Super Bowl. But they had to do it without their starting quarterback, Jim Kelly, leader of the potent Bills' offense (known as the K-gun), who was out due to injury. The afternoon's quarterback duties rested in the hands of veteran backup Frank Reich. By halftime, Reich and the Bills faced a 25-point deficit. Strangely coincidental, Reich had been in this situation before as a college player in a game that had a favorable turn of events.

A locker-room tongue-lashing (scolding) by defensive coordinator Walt Cory and the motivating words of head coach Marv Levy—a philosopher-like coach with a master's degree in English literature—sent the Bills back onto the field for the second half, which didn't start well for them. Just over a minute into the third quarter, the Oilers tacked on another touchdown to up the score to 35-3.

Fans, resigned to an embarrassing defeat of their beloved team, began to leave the stadium. Broadcast announcers were hard-pressed to say anything to maintain viewer interest. It appeared to be time for reserve players on both sides to come in and "mop up," to get experience in a game whose outcome was not in doubt.

Backups were not an option with the Bills but a necessity. The fact that star running back Thurman

Thomas had been injured on the Bills' first drive of the third quarter meant that for the team to do anything positive, they'd need to do it with a second-string back, Kenneth Davis, in addition to Kelly's replacement, Frank Reich.

Instead of the Bills unraveling, or falling apart even more, like a symphony, all its parts came together—the offense, the defense, and the special teams. What began to occur was the biggest come-from-behind win in NFL history. The Bills scored 28 points in the third quarter and took the lead in the fourth. But a Houston field goal forced overtime. After an interception on Houston's opening drive, a field goal sealed the win for the Bills and etched this game in NFL history. Frank Reich was proclaimed Frank "Lloyd" Reich, the "Architect of Comebacks"—a reference to the famous American architect Frank Lloyd Wright. Clearly, this game put a spin on the word "wild" in wildcard.

Tough to Top a Dynasty

Super Bowl LI (51) featured the perennial powerhouse, the AFC's New England Patriots, against the NFC's Atlanta Falcons, making just their second appearance in the Super Bowl. For nearly 45 minutes, the Falcons dominated the Patriots, building a 28-3 lead. But the Patriots, who had four Super Bowl wins to their credit at that time, led by creative play-calling and risk-taking, fought their way back into the contest. Quarterback Tom Brady marched the Patriots down the field time after time and before long, the Patriots evened the score 28-all, helped in part by successful gambles on two, two-point conversions.

The Patriots didn't just win the coin toss to begin overtime—they made the most of the opportunity on the opening drive. The Falcons were unable to stop the Patriots, who drove 75 yards in eight plays capped off with James White's two-yard TD run, which guaranteed further glory in the victory parade in downtown Boston, Massachusetts two days later. The win also secured an invitation to the White House as guests of the President of the United States, an annual tradition for Super Bowl champs.

I ain't got nothin' to say; I just wanna play football.
—Marshawn Lynch, NFL running back

CHAPTER XVIII
Global Football

We might guess that "global" means "around the world." As this concluding unit attempts to show, football is global, indeed, involving multiple nations. But global means a little bit more. The material in this chapter covers accessibility and uncommon participants in football. It leaves us with links to how each of us can participate as a player, coach, or fan.

PLAYING WITH DISABILITIES

Record-setting	unwavering	impairment
ASL a blow	blows	stomps

Trivia question: Who invented the huddle?
Read on to find out...

Athletes come in many shapes and sizes and include players with disabilities. Among them are Derrick Coleman, a running back for the 2014 Super Bowl champions the Seattle Seahawks; and Larry Brown, a record-setting rusher for the Washington Redskins spanning the 1960s and '70s. Something that they share with other notables in football is hearing loss.

A strong work ethic and unwavering positive attitude helped them be successful. Add a little wit: "If someone was yelling at me," says Coleman in his 2015 memoir *No Excuses*, "and told me I was 'no good,' I never listened. You know what I mean?"

Hearing impairment is a way of life at Gallaudet University in Washington, DC, whose charter was signed in 1864 by US President Abraham Lincoln. Its football team, the Bisons, plays in Division III in the Eastern Collegiate Football Conference. At Bison home games, cheering isn't performed by the cheer squad in the traditional sense, nor is the national anthem sung. Not that there isn't enthusiasm—there is plenty. Cheering and singing are communicated in American Sign Language (ASL). Gallaudet is a university for the deaf and hard of hearing but its football players play the game just like anybody else.

At Gallaudet, coaches, widely known for yelling, communicate to players in sign language. Player huddles, of course, are also in sign language. In fact, it is documented that Gallaudet invented the huddle in the 1890s when the team formed "a tight circle" to prevent its opponent, another team of deaf players, from stealing signs.

Charles Goldstein, who learned ASL when hired as Gallaudet's 36th head coach in 2009, explains to *Footballogy* that players begin action at the snap of the ball, not the traditional snap count of the quarterback. The quarterback taps the center on the back to let him know when to hike the ball. On field goals, punts, or shotgun formations, the player waiting for the snap waves his hand or stomps his foot to give the hike signal.

Coach Goldstein adds that occasionally not hearing an official's whistle can be a problem, such as when he blows a play dead, but the action continues. "[T]he worst is when we have to take a running back out for a blow (rest) because he just ran 80 yards for a touchdown that didn't count because he didn't hear the whistle," says Coach Goldstein.

Gallaudet supporters know that hearing loss is not a disability on the gridiron. There has been plenty to cheer about, although victory celebrations at Gallaudet are silent by most standards. In 2013, the Bisons won the league championship with a 9-1 record and qualified for the national Division III playoff tournament.

Div. III Gallaudet University in Washington, DC, for deaf and hard-of-hearing students, fields a competitive football team. (CC-BY-2.0 Wikimedia)

I. True, False, or Maybe (if it is not in the reading)

1. "A blow" is an opportunity to relax.
    T   F   M

2. The huddle was invented by the NFL in 1926.
    T   F   M

3. A deaf player has never played in the Super Bowl.
    T   F   M

4. Gallaudet is in Division II.
    T   F   M

5. Gallaudet plays Alfred State College.
    T   F   M

6. Coach Goldstein probably uses ASL with players.
    T   F   M

Footballogy: Elements of American Football for Non-Native Speakers of English

Wristbands: An essential aid in the huddle

> Necessity is the mother of invention   secret codes   chuckled
>
> abandoned   simplified   runner-up   banged up

Wristbands contain coded information to help quarterbacks call plays. (See left arm of Seattle Seahawks QB Russell Wilson.) Photo by Larry Mauer, CC-BY-20 Wiki

Like Gallaudet, which found a solution to opponents who tried to steal signals, necessity was the mother of invention for an NFL team when a team ran out of quarterbacks. This caused the creation of the wristband, common in the modern era of football. Even veteran quarterbacks wear a wristband, which contains secret codes to assist him in making play choices. The codes tell the linemen their blocking assignments and receivers and backs their patterns. It tells the type of play—a run or a pass.

Teams in the pre-Super Bowl era, however, didn't have the luxury of wristbands. If the starter got hurt, the system was simplified for the replacement, who hadn't had time to practice the plays in the playbook. It could be a disaster for a team to lose its starter. Imagine how it was if a team lost both its starter and his backup!

This was the case in the 1965 season. The then-Baltimore Colts found themselves in a bind when both quarterbacks—starter Johnny Unitas and backup Gary Cuozzo—were injured and couldn't play. Without another quarterback on the roster, the Colts turned to Tom Matte (pronounced "măt-tay"), a reserve running back with no professional experience as a quarterback.

Fortunately, the team had two of the game's sharpest football minds, Head Coach Don Shula and his offensive coordinator, Don McCafferty. But as good as they were, it was Matte's wife, Judy, who had a solution. In tiny script, she wrote the Colts' playbook on a piece of paper, which she slipped inside a transparent band on her husband's wrist. Scaled down, consisting mostly of draw plays and handoffs, it was a gem!

Matte executed the plays on the wristband well enough during the last game of the season to defeat the Los Angeles Rams—a game that must have embarrassed the Rams organization enough that it fired its head coach.

Tied for first place in the NFL's West Division, Matte led the Colts into Green Bay in a playoff game to decide the conference winner. The Packers were led by four future Hall of Fame players and Hall of Fame coach Vince Lombardi, the namesake of the Super Bowl trophy. Still, Matte and the banged-up Colts put up a fight. Although he completed just five of 12 passes in the loss, a week later, in a game called the Runner-up Bowl—a championship of sorts for the divisional second-place finishers—he triumphed in a big way in a win against the Dallas Cowboys. Matte passed for two touchdowns and was named that game's Most Valuable Player. His statistics were not logged, however, since this post-season event, long since abandoned by the NFL, was cast as an "exhibition game."

Nonetheless, Matte had gained respect from the nation and etched a niche in football lore. His wristband, now at the Pro Football Hall of Fame in Canton, Ohio, was a trendsetter. Even the great quarterbacks of today's NFL can be seen peeking at their wristband playbook between downs.

No one needs to look further than Judy Matte to thank for her husband's achievement. "She's in the Hall of Fame," Matte once chuckled to the *Baltimore Sun* about his wife's contribution to his moment in the sun as a pro quarterback. Her one iota has become a big part of the biggest game in American sports.

Footballogy: Elements of American Football for Non-Native Speakers of English

 I. Multiple Choice. Select the answer that best matches the meaning.

1. "Necessity is the mother of invention" means
    a. "do-or-die"
    b. "live, eat and be merry"
    c. "necessary evil"
    d. "do the necessary"

2. What are signals?
    a. the motherboard
    b. Don Shula
    c. the referee
    d. secret codes

3. The "banged-up Colts" ...
    a. had many injured players
    b. did a good, or bang-up job
    c. had healthy players in key positions
    d. hit opponents hard

4. "Simplified" means
    a. made easy   b. coded
    c. developed   d. done over

5. A wristband contains...
    a. the team's list of plays
    b. padding to protect from injury
    c. diagrams of each play
    d. the count number to hike the ball

6. Who was the first to wear a wristband?
    a. Eli Manning   b. Joe Montana
    c. Don Shula   d. Tom Matte

7. Where is the first wristband today?
    a. On Display at the Hall of Fame in Canton, Ohio
    b. On Display at the Hall of Fame in Cooperstown, NY

c. In a trophy case of the Green Bay Packers
d. Under the watchful eye of Tom Matte's wife

8. What is meant by "etched a niche"?
    a. made a lasting mark
    b. left an eternal impression
    c. Neither A nor B
    d. Both A and B

9. Judy Matte played an iota in football history.
    a. A small but significant part
    b. A big role
    c. Got women interested in the game
    d. Helped the Colts win a championship

10. A runner-up can be classified as
    a. a last-place team
    b. The player who runs in plays from the sideline
    c. the signal-caller
    d. a good team but not the best

11. Matte "chuckled."
    a. smiled   b. said
    c. laughed   d. wondered

Women in Football

unthinkable	crowned	irreverent	powder puff
strongholds	prominent	dues	he-man

Probably unthinkable a generation ago, girls in high school are now participating on male teams. About 2,401 played varsity football in 2017, says the National Federation of State High School Associations (NFHS). Most play the "non-contact" position of placekicker but there are exceptions. Erin DiMeglio, quarterback for her high school team in South Florida, made a game-winning pass in her first game in 2012. Five-foot-five-inch Lisa Spangler, a starter on the boys' team in Washington state, earned high praise from her coach. "I never expected to have a girl be my middle linebacker but my job is to get the best 11 on the field, and she's one of the best," he says. In 2018, a Mississippi girl, Kaylee Foster, kicked a game-deciding extra point. That same night she was crowned queen for the school's homecoming.

"State of Mississippi high school student Kaylee Foster, crowned Homecoming Queen and kicked the winning field goal on the same night. With permission: The Mississippi Press.

Evidence suggests that women in tackle football in the USA date back to 1926. Irreverent labels like "powder puff" were depicted in the news media. One newspaper proclaimed this to be an invasion of "one of the last strongholds of masculinity."

Not much is recorded about the early activity of women's football; however, *Smithsonian* magazine called it "hard, fast" regulation football.

"Ladies of the Gridiron: He-man sport suffers Powder Puff invasion" Headline in Click magazine, January 1940. With permission: OldMagazineArticles.com

Today, there are seven women's professional contact (tackle) football leagues in the United States. The most prominent is the Women's Football Alliance, a spring league that has over 60 teams. Participants need to pay annual dues and practice multiple times per week, mostly nights after work from their full-time jobs. The league, which uses NFL rules (except for smaller footballs), stages their national championship playoffs in July.

Draw a line to match the vocabulary word from the reading (column A) with the word closest in meaning (column b)

A	B
prominent	very masculine
powder puff	name; honored
irreverent	not likely or probable
unthinkable	disrespectful
strongholds	(old slang) feminine
he-man	money for membership
dues	noticeable
crowned	fortresses; bastions

Global Opportunities

There is a world of ways to experience American football, which has also long prospered in Canada and Mexico, countries more noted for hockey and soccer preferences. The Canadian Football League season starts in July and ends with the highly regarded Gray Cup in November.

All but lost in history is that a university in Mexico was once a contestant in a US bowl game, the Sun Bowl, in El Paso, Texas, in 1945. For several decades Mexico has had youth-to-college activities under its *Organización Nacional Estudiantil de Fútbol Americano*. Universities with football programs in Mexico compare to US Division III programs. People in Mexico can take pride Mexico's Monterrey Tech defeated a US junior college team with future Heisman winner and NFL number-one draft pick, Cam Newton.

Presently, US colleges and the NFL stage games at world venues. Mexico City hosts an annual NFL contest, which sells out the 87,000-seat Azteca Stadium. The city of London also hosts a series NFL games each season.

The International Federation of American Football (IFAF), based in Paris, manages a worldwide program in 103 countries. Leagues include both contact (tackle) and non-contact (flag) football for men, women, and children. The IFAF, structured after FIFA, organizer of the World Cup, has its own World-Cup-style tournament every four years in one of its member countries.

Members of IFAF have their own leagues and league championships annually. The Israel Football League (IFL), one of the many IFAF members, stages the IsraBowl. Japan's X league, which integrates American ex-pats on their rosters (like teams from other nations) has an eight-team X Bowl playoff tournament. Other nations have something of their own: the Desert Bowl (United Arab Emirates), Kimchi Bowl (South Korea), and Impact Bowl (Ivory Coast).

Of Europe's 50 countries, 41 have American football with an estimated 1,500 teams spread throughout these countries, according to Brussels-based The Growth of the Game, which advocates American football in Europe and offers football skills camps. Germany alone has over 200 men and 40 women's teams (21 countries host approximately 200 women's teams).

The place of the biggest growth for organized American football might be China. The China Arena Football League (CAFL) plays indoors on a 50 x 35-yard field with an eight-man lineup. It is headed by Ed Wang, a star offensive tackle at Virginia Tech who was the first player of Chinese heritage to be drafted by the NFL. The American Football League of China (AFLC), co-founded by former University of Michigan tight end Chris McLaurin in 2013, has grown from a small recreational league into a showcase for American football and culture in China. Most players, whose income is from other employment, are from China or are of Chinese descent. In a country where American entertainment is popular, players cite that their interest in the sport emerged from American movies such as Adam Sandler's *The Waterboy*, as well as NFL games online. Though the language in the game is Chinese, teams have adopted American-sounding nicknames like the Lions, Nighthawks, and Titans.

Will the growth of American football point to global support for the game becoming an Olympic sport? American football was an Olympic demonstration sport in the 1932 Olympics in Los Angeles but if it is to gain status as an Olympic sport for competition, the IFAF, recognized by the International Olympic Committee, may be the one to carry the torch.

*American Football League China 2015 championship game.
Photo courtesy of Chris McLaurin, AFLC*

Useful Sources for News, Information, and Live Streaming

American Football International
www.americanfootballinternational.com
News and information, live game streaming.

Canadian Football League
https://www.cfl.ca/tryouts/
Interested in playing in the CFL? Its teams travel across North America on scouting trips. Please contact individual teams to learn more about their scouting camps.

Fuel Up to Play 60
https://www.fueluptoplay60.com
Launched by the NFL and National Dairy Council, this program helps youths, with the cooperation of parents and schools, to set health, nutrition and exercise goals.

International Federation of American Football (IFAF)
www.ifaf.org
Maintains links to teams websites, which includes information about competitions, future games, and how to try out or coach.

International Women's Flag Football Association
https://www.iwffa.com
Around since 1995, this association organizes worldwide tournaments and clinics for coaches, players, and officials.

NCAA
www.ncaa.org
Information on all sports at all of its schools in each division (schedules, rankings, records, statistics); links to school websites.

NFL Flag
www.nflflag.com
For boys and girls 5-17 in the United States. Connects to existing clubs in the USA and shows how to start a club.

National Football League
www.NFL.com
Latest news and information on NFL teams and players, game highlights (videos), statistics, schedules, scores, and team information.

NFL Operations
https://operations.nfl.com
Complete explanations, pictures, and videos that include rules and penalties, officials' hand signals, types of plays, player positions, ways to play, youth football, and more.

Pro Football Reference
www.pro-football-reference.com
Contains comprehensive statistics and facts on every team—historical and present—every game and every player in professional football in the United States.

The Growth of a Game
www.growthofagame.com
News and information about European football organizations; helps people interested in learning football, player techniques, and how to start clubs.

USA Football
www.usafootball.com
The national governing body for amateur American football in the United States. This organization conducts training events and education programs for coaches and game officials, and develops training, skills, and nutrition habits for youth in local communities.

Pro Football Hall of Fame
www.profootballhof.com
If you cannot visit the Hall of Fame in Canton, Ohio, the next best thing is to visit its web site. Established in 1963, the Hall of Fame enshrines, or brings in, exceptional figures in the sport of professional football—players, coaches, franchise owners, and front-office personnel such as general managers, and even owners who have made

exemplary (great) contributions to the game. Players must wait five years after retirement to be enshrined. The induction, or ceremony, takes place at the Hall of Fame Game, a special game in August, one week before the NFL pre-season.

The College Football Hall of Fame
www.cfbhall.com
Founded in 1951, this is a popular attraction in Atlanta, Georgia, that memorializes the greatest to ever put on a college football uniform.

Footballogy: Elements of American Football for Non-Native Speakers of English

from Great Moments

ACROSS
1. First name: Ice Bowl ref
3. Visiting team in Ice Bowl
5. He threw a Hail Mary in college
10. Undefeated 2007 season
11. David Tyree: Catch. Super Bowl
13. Fumble, final play, won game
16. Embarrassed 73-0
18. Winning team of "the drive"
19. Winner of 1940 Championship

DOWN
2. The "architect" of comebacks
4. Winner Immaculate Reception game
6. Biggest-ever NFL comeback
7. Victims: "the pick"
8. The Big Game and the band played on.
9. Victim: Immaculate Reception
10. Host team in the Ice Bowl
12. Victor: Music City Miracle
14. QB of famed 98-yard drive
15. He caught the Immaculate Reception
17. Remembered for intercepting Sipe

Answer Key

Chapter I
I. True/false-multiple choice
1-y, 2-n, 3-y, 4-y, 5a-m, 5b-f, 5c-f, 5d-f, 5e-t, 5f-t, 6-d, 7-b, 8-a

II. Crossword on heritage

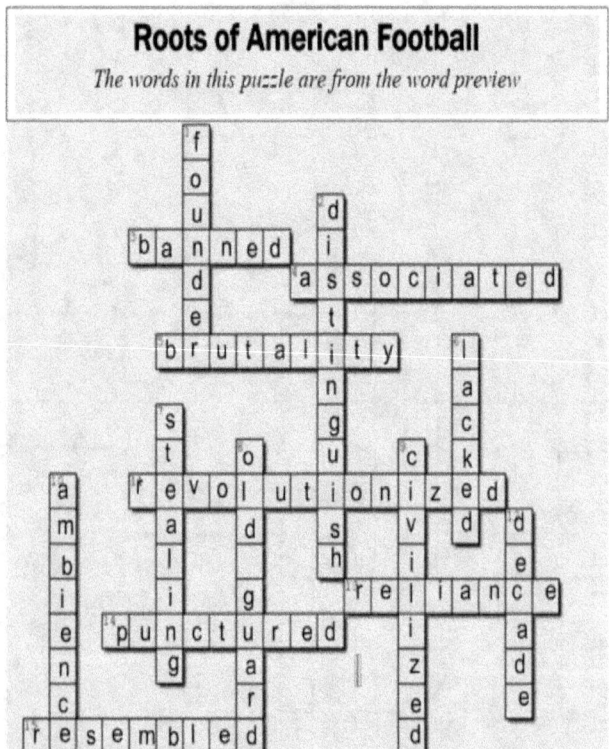

I. America's first football star
1-a, 2-d, 3-b, 4-a, 5-a, 6-d

Chapter II
I. Check Your Understanding
1-d, 2-b, 3-t, 4-d, 5-c, 6-a

7 - traditionally, traditional, tradition, traditional, tradition, traditional, tradition, traditionally 8 - Rival, rivalry, rivalry, rival;

9 - Scoring, score, scoring, score, score, score, scoring; 10-d 11-a 12-a 13-d

II. Matching — Antonyms
1-d, 2-b, 3-f, 4-k, 5-I, 6-h, 7-j, 8-c, 9-e, 10-a, 11-g

III. Modals
1-might celebrate, 2- might fly, 3-might take, 4- might find, 5-might be

IV. mechanics (placement of punctuation, capital letters)
1. "Tryouts will be held next Monday at 10 AM," the coach said, "so don't be late."

2. "Will you come to my Super Bowl party?" she asked.

3. "My feeling is that the Rams should win this game," he stated.

4. The poster stated: "Under no circumstances can alcohol be brought with you to the game."

5. "The guard appeared to be holding," the announcer insisted, "but the officials missed it.

Reading: "Greatest Game..."
I. 1-c, 2-a, 3-d, 4-b, 5-c, 6-b, 7-a, 8-b, 9-a, 10-c

II. 1-b, 2-d, 3-c, 4-g, 5-a, 6-h, 7-I, 8-j, 9-f, 10-e

Chapter III
I. Vocabulary check
1-d, 2-b, 3-d, 4-c, 5-c, 6-a, 7-a, 8-d. 9-c

II. Parts of Speech
1, adj., 2, n, 3, adj, 4-n, 5-v, 6-adj, 7-n, 8-n, 9-v, 10-n

Sights at the game
I. true / false
1-t. 2-t, 3 -f, 4-t, 5-f, 6-f, 7-t, 8-f, 9-t, 10-t

Footballogy: Elements of American Football for Non-Native Speakers of English

Chapter IV

I. true/false: 1-f, 2-t, 3-f, 4-f, 5-t, 6-f, 7-t, 8-t, 9-t, 10-t

II. Plays

1-c 2-b, 3-b, 4-a, 5-d, 6-b, 7-c, 8-c, 9-a 10- draw, bootleg, end around, trap, off tackle, reverse

III. Iron Man

1. durability 2. Remarkably 3. tough 4. undersized 5. calling 6. fit right in 7. nagged 8. mystique

Chapter V

Positions on a team

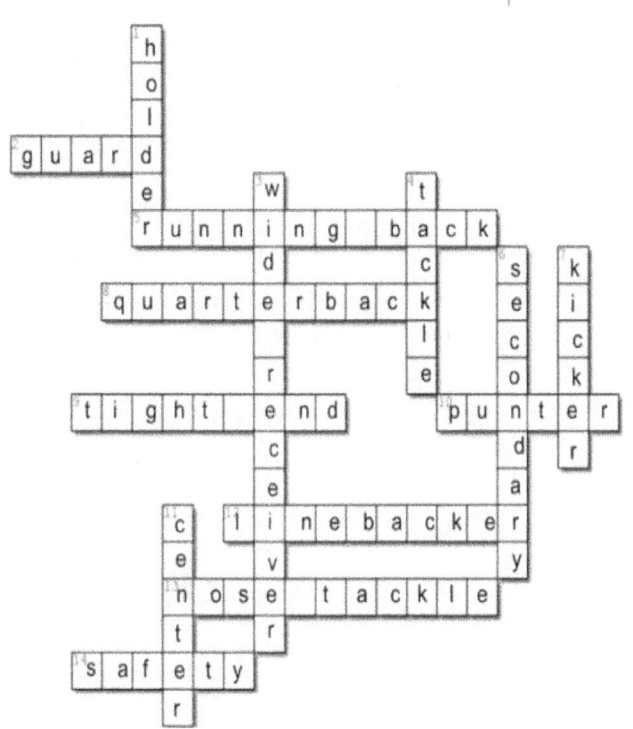

I. Interpreting the program
1-a, 2-d, 3-c, 4-c, 5-a, 6-b 7-c, 8-b, 9-c, 10-d

II. Numbers (crossword)

Legends of the Game
I. Matching
1-k, 2-a, 3-c, 4-j, 5-g, 6-b, 7, l, 8-f, 9-h, 10- i, 11-d, 12-e

II. Comprehension
1-f, 2-t, 3-d, 4-a. 5-f, 6-a, 7-a, 8-b, 9-f, 10-t

III. Find/correct errors
1. Is considered, 2- the most, 3-played, 4-Lane's, 5- whose, 6-to face/facing, 7- playing, 8-play, 9-players, 10 plays

Chapter VI
I. Sentence-clause transitions
1-NC, C; 2-C, D; 3-C, D; 4-NC, B; 5-C, E; 6-C, A; 7- NC, A; 8- C, A; 9- NC, C; 10- NC, C

Chapter VII
I . Multiple choice
1-a, 2-d, 3-b, 4-b, 5-c, 6-d, 7-a, 8-c, 9-d, 10-c, 11-d, 12-a, 13-c, 14-a

II. To do/to make
To do: 1-done 2-did, 3-doing 4-doing, 5-do, 6-do, 7-do, 8-do, 9-done, 10-do/done

To make: 1-make, 2-makes, 3-make, 4-made, 5-make, 6-made, 7-made, 8-make, 9-made, 10-make

To do/make: 1-did, 2-making/do, 3-make, 4-makes/made, 5-made/do, 6-made, 7-do, 8-makes, 9-make, 10-made/making, 11 do/makes

AD LIBS
The game of American [noun]**football** is played on a **gridiron** 100 yards [adverb] **long** and 45 [plural noun] **yards** wide. There [linking verb] **are** [number] **eleven** players [preposition] **on** each side. The objective of the offense is to [verb] **score** points. The job of the [noun] **defense** is to [verb] **stop** the offense, which [verb] **has** four opportunities, called downs, to make a [ordinal number] **first** down and keep the ball. Sometimes a team's drive stalls (stopped by the defense), [conjunction] **and** a [ordinal number] **fourth** down forces it to [verb] **punt** the ball to the other [noun] **side**.

The [color] **red** zone is when a team moves the [noun] **football** inside the [number] **twenty**-yard line. If it doesn't score a [noun] **touchdown**, worth [number] **six** points, it can try a [noun as adjective] **field** goal for [number] **three** points. After a [initials] **TD**, a team can try [article] **an** [adjective] **extra** point. A way for the defense to score is a [noun] **safety**, which counts for two [plural noun]. [article] **The** (or **A**) game is [number] **sixty** minutes, [conjunction] **but** can go into an extra period, called [noun] **overtime** if both teams are even, or [adjective] **tied** at the end of regulation. A game that [linking verb] **is** tied at the end of OT is recorded as a [noun] **tie**.

Chapter VIII
I. 1-c, 2-d, 3-f, 4-c, 5-a, 6-b, 7-c, 8-a
II. 1-p, 2-p, 3-uc, 4-ur, 5-pf, 6-s, 7-uc, 8-ps, 9-p, 10-pf, 11-ps, 12-t, 13-pf, 14-uc, 15-ps
III. 1-illegal formation; 2- false start; 3-holding; 4-roughing the kicker; 5-pass interference; 6-offside; 7-half-the-distance; 8-intentional grounding; 9-unsportsmanlike conduct

IV. Words from preview
I. blink of an eye; 2. depiction; 3. prejudice; 4. pressure; 5. infraction; 6. litigious

Norm Schachter
Matching: 1- e, 2-h, 3-g, 4-j, 5-a, 6-f, 7-b, 8-c, 9-d, 10-i
True / false: 1-f, 2-f, 3-t, 4-t, 5-t

Chapter IX
I. 6 W's + H 1-what/ a bye 2- What (or how)/Super Sunday 3-Who/Vince Lombardi 4-How/coin toss 5- What/road warrior 6-When/one week after the season 7-Where/neutral site 8-When/1970 9-Which (or what)/Green Bay 10- Who/Lamar Hunt

II. Final Standings
1-c; 2-b; 3-(6,3, 2, 1, 4, 5); 4-c 5-d 6-a 7-a

Footballogy: Elements of American Football for Non-Native Speakers of English

Chapter X
Teams crossword

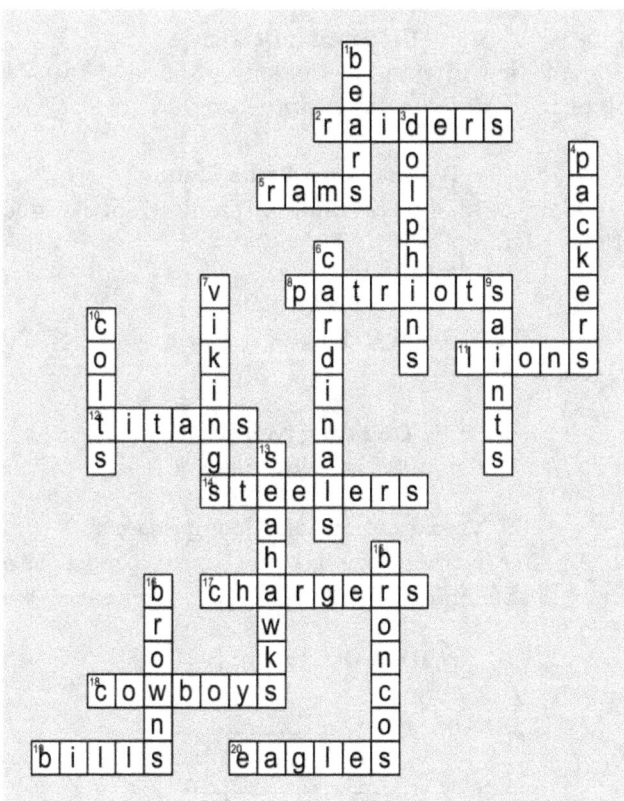

I. multiple choice
1-d, 2-b, 3-c, 4A-c; B-c; C-b; D-c; 5-b, 6-c 7-d 8-B 9-a 10-a

Chapter XI
I. Fill in the blanks
1-statistics; 2-cup of tea; 3-inference; 4- probability; 5-unsung heroes; 6-hypotheses; 7-objectivity; 8-defer

Footballogy: Elements of American Football for Non-Native Speakers of English

II. Stats
1-pit; 2-pit; 3-bal; 4-pit; 5-pit; 6-bal; 7-27; 8-5; 9-19; 10- Pit (23-16)

III. Scoring Details
1-6:47; 2-one; 3-New England; 4-Bolden; 5-Miami; 6-two; 7-Hail Mary; 8-50 or more; 9-Patriots; 10-underdog

IV. Individual Game Stats
1-Goff; 2-Hekker; 3-32; 4-7; 5-none; 6. Donald; 7-5; 8--knocked down; 9-18.3; 10-seven

V. Brady Stats
1-2007; 2-4806; 3 2015; 4-14; 5-12-4; 6-2007; 7-2013; 8-2007; 9-61.8; 10-2016

VI. QB rating (you try it)
84.936 is below average

VII. Verbal assessments (comparisons)
1-the best; 2-better/worse; 3-good; 4-the worst; 5-more/fewer; 6-the most; 7-fewer; 8-the largest; 9-the least; 10-the fewest

The Game

Chapter XII
I. Multiple Choice
1-a, 2-d, 3-c, 4-c, 5-b

II. True false
1-f, 2-f, 3-t, 4-f, 5-t

III. Matching (draw line)

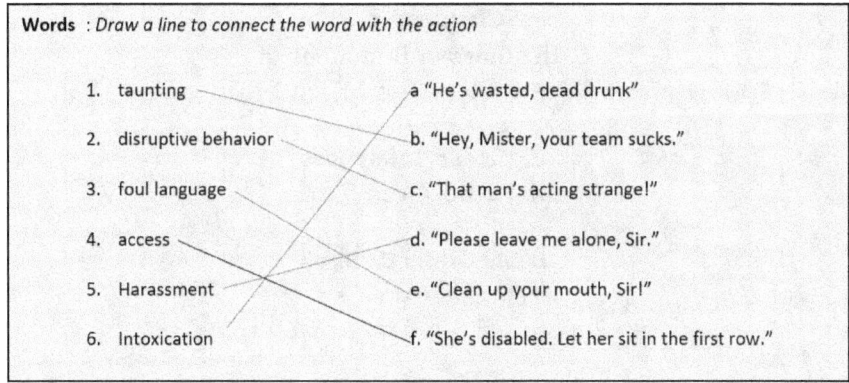

Words : *Draw a line to connect the word with the action*

1. taunting — a "He's wasted, dead drunk"
2. disruptive behavior — b. "Hey, Mister, your team sucks."
3. foul language — c. "That man's acting strange!"
4. access — d. "Please leave me alone, Sir."
5. Harassment — e. "Clean up your mouth, Sir!"
6. Intoxication — f. "She's disabled. Let her sit in the first row."

Please And Thank You
I. Multiple choice
1-d 2-d 3-c 4-d 5-c 6-c 7-d 8-d 9-a 10-a

II. Words
Use words from words preview to complete this exercise.
At the concessions, it is **customary** to wait in a line for service. When I first **glanced** at him, the customer appeared relaxed, you know, **easy-come-easy** go. But when he expressed **displeasure** for slow service at a busy time, his **in-your-face** attitude of **impatience** and **sarcasm** made me think someone didn't do a good job of **child-rearing**, at least with him. I **conveyed** my **heartfelt (or genuine)** thoughts about his bad **manners** to him. He said, "Sir, I'm sorry!" Him pretending to cry—those **crocodile tears** did not fool me. He did not make a **genuine** (or **heartfelt**) apology.

Chapter XIII

I. 1-AM 2-BR 3-AM 4-AM 5-BR 6-AM 7-BR 8-BR 9-AM 10-AM 11-ftb 12-soc 13-ftb 14-soc 15-ftb 16-soc 17-soc 18-soc 19-ftb 20-ftb 21-b 22-a 23-c 24-a 25-column d

II. Time zones
1-c 2-d 3-b 4-c 5-a

Chapter XIV
I. In other words (matching)
1-i 2-d 3-m 4-j 5-c 6-g 7-k 8-f 9-e 10-b 11-n 12-h 13-o 14-a 15-l

II. Details/Inferences
1-f 2-t 3-t 4-m 5-m

Subheading: Colleges
I. Chart smarts
1-b 2-a 3-c 4-d 5-b 6-c 7-b 8-f 9-t 10-f

Chapter XV
I. true/false
1-T; 2-T;3-T;4-T;5-T;6-T;7-T;8-T;9-F;10-T

II. Multiple choice—main idea, details, inferences
1-b; 2-a; 3-d; 4-b; 5-a; 6-d, 7-b, 8-a, 9-b, 10-d

III. COLLEGE&PRO COMPARISONS
1-c, 2-a, 3-a, 4-d, 5-a, 6-d, 7-c, 8-b, 9-a, 10-d

IV. MATCHING
1-g, 2-f, 3-i, 4-a, 5-b, 6-n, 7-h, 8-e,
9-l, 10-c, 11-m, 12-o, 13-d, 14-j, 15-p

V. SENTENCE COMPARISONS
1-c-y, 2-b-y, 3-a, n, 4-a-y, 5-c-n, 6-d-y, 7-c-n, 8-b-n

Footballogy: Elements of American Football for Non-Native Speakers of English

```
L W O B E S O R · · · · · · ·
N · · · · · · · N · · · D ·
· A · · · · · · E · · T E E
· · M · · · · · T · · I T C
· · · S · · · · G P · U N N
· · · P I · · F · I L W R E E
· · · I · E · B · B A A C L R
· · · H T · H S · · Y L E A E
· · · C R · · · · · O K R T F
· · · E I · · · N · F O · · N
· · · U H A · · · C F N · · O
· · · L S · I · · · A · · · C
· · · B D · · A · · · A · · ·
· · · · E · · · N · · · · · ·
· · · · R · · · · · · · · · ·
```

BIGTEN (10, 7, N)	HEISMAN (7, 8, NW)	RECRUIT (13, 9, N)	WALKON (12, 6, S)
BLUECHIP (4, 13, N)	NAIA (9, 14, NW)	REDSHIRT (5, 15, N)	
CONFERENCE (15, 12, N)	NCAA (9, 10, SE)	ROSEBOWL (8, 1, W)	
FBS (8, 6, S)	PLAYOFF (11, 5, S)	TALENTED (14, 9, N)	

VI. Words — bonus feature

1-dominating, 2-meaningless, 3-guard, 4-president, 5-prime, 6-stalemate, 7-reluctant

VII. Who am I?

1-i, 2-d, 3-a, 4-k, 5-c, 6-j, 7-l, 8-h, 9-g, 10-f

Footballogy: Elements of American Football for Non-Native Speakers of English

Crossword "Where do football players come from?"

Chapter XVI
I. multiple tasks

1-originate, origin, original; 2-pride, proud, proudly; 3-performer, perform, performance; 4-tradition, traditional; 5-b, 6-b, 7-a, 8-t, 9-c, 10-c, 11-b

Meanings
II. sep/insep verbs

1-bring him back, 2-made up of them, 3-speed it up, 4-struck it up, 5-belted it out, 6-ran into them, 7-looked them up, 8-called her up, 9-picked them up, 10-can't stand them

"Tailgating"
III. Matching
1-d, 2-h, 3-b, 4-j, 5-e, 6-c, 7-a, 8-g, 9-i, 10- f

"Cheerleading"
IV. Multiple choice/T-F
1-f, 2-t, 3-c, 4-a, 5-b, 6-f, 7-f, 8-d, 9-d, 10-t

V. T/F & multiple choice:
1-t, 2-t, 3-c, 4-n, 5-a, 6-t, 7-c, 8-b, 9-a, 10-a 11-b

Dr. Regina Bailey Interview/reported speech

A. <u>her</u> favorite part <u>was</u> being on the field close to the game. . .
B. it <u>was </u>a lot like being on a Broadway chorus line with so many costume changes, drills and dances to rehearse.
C. <u>they were</u> there to keep the spirits of the fans up even when things may <u>not have been</u> going how <u>they wanted</u>.
D. <u>she had</u> always been very good at multitasking and <u>she got</u> bored very easily. The combination of those two elements <u>had</u> helped <u>her</u> reach all <u>her</u> accomplishments.
E. cheerleading <u>had</u> helped <u>her</u> with self-confidence.
F. before cheerleading, <u>she had been</u> very shy, but cheerleading <u>had</u> helped <u>her</u> break out of that.
G. cheerleading <u>had </u>been very helpful with enhancing <u>her</u> communication skills that <u>were</u> necessary in law and medicine.
H. <u>said that she</u> <u>exercised </u>two to three hours every day and <u>ate</u> a very healthy diet.
I. <u>added that </u>after <u>her</u> mother <u>had </u>died from complications of Diabetes and Hypertension, it <u>had become</u> necessary for <u>her</u> to change <u>her</u> life around, lose weight and become healthier.
J. noted that <u>she had</u> realized that to be around for <u>her</u> young daughter, <u>she</u> had to develop healthier habits.
K. She concluded by saying that <u>she had</u> also discovered that staying physically healthy <u>kept her </u>mentally healthy.

Text box: She wanted to empower women to not let anything stop them from pursuing their dreams, she stated. Sometimes, after women [suggestion] age, they become very hard on themselves. She liked to show women that they could still pursue their dreams at any age.

"Heidi Game"
I. Vocabulary—fill in the blank

1-back-and-forth, 2- flashy, 3-air, 4-debacle, 5-pre-empted, 6-humorist, 7-counterpart, 8-go at it 9-going at it, 10-barely, 11-determined

II. Main idea/inferences
1-b, 2-f, 3-b, 4-a, 5-d, 6-n, 7-t

III. Parts of Speech
1-c, 2-b, 3-c, 4-a, 5-c

Chapter XVII
Buffalo Bills Insider

Insiders Part I 1-31
1-b; 2-a; 3-a; 4-b; 5-b; 6-a; 7-a; 8-b; 9-b; 10-a
11. what *football insider* means
12. describe your duties as multi-media reporter (co change)
13. what your proudest moment is
14. what the best part of your job is
15. if you ever discuss football with people whose first language is not English
16. meant; 17. served; 18. was; 19. beats; 20. unfolds; 21. could happen; 22. had; 23. needed; 24. he 25. had put; 26. had died; 27. was; 28. his; 29. had come; 30. was covering 31. qualified

II. matching
1-g, 2-i, 3-a, 4-c, 5-d, 6-b, 7-j, 8-e, 9-h, 10-f

Chapter XVIII
I. true /false
Gallaudet: 1-t, 2-f, 3-f, 4-f, 5-m, 6-t

II. Multiple choice (wristbands)
1-a, 2-d, 3-a, 4-a, 5-a, 6-d, 7-a, 8-d, 9-a, 10-d, 11-c

Footballogy: Elements of American Football for Non-Native Speakers of English

III. Matching

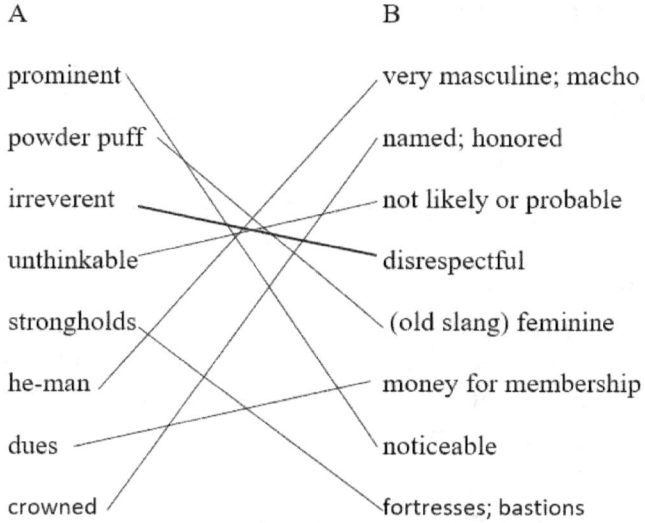

Great Moments

Glossary

Terms and Idioms

All-purpose yardage — (abbreviation: APY) The sum of all yards gained by a player rushing, receiving, punt and kickoff returns; (team) sum of all yards passing, receiving, punt and kickoff returns.

Audible — A play called by the quarterback at the line of scrimmage to change the play that was called in the huddle.

Barnyard brawl — The barnyard is where livestock is kept; the soil is normally soggy and brackish (dark). Two strong farm kids go at it in a fist fight, each bloodying the other's nose and more. Football has the same meaning, two teams playing each other tough.

Bend-but-don't-break — Characterizes a defense that stiffens (becomes stronger) when it's defending the goal from inside its own 20-yard line.

Blitz — On defense, when one or more linebackers or defensive backs, who normally remain behind the line of scrimmage, charge into the opponent's backfield. When a safety does it, it's called a **safety blitz**. Archaic usage: **red dog.**

Blocker — (n.) One who blocks or knocks opposing players out of the way to help the player with the ball pick-up or gain yardage.

Block — (v.) A passing or rushing situation in which players, commonly offensive linemen, knock defensive players out of the way to protect the player carrying the ball or to protect the quarterback if it's a passing play (without using hands or it's a penalty).

Bootleg — The quarterback runs with the ball toward either side behind the line of scrimmage before running upfield or giving the ball to a running back.

Broken play — An unplanned play. *The quarterback improvised after the missed handoff but the broken play managed to get his team a first down.*

"Bulls his way" — An expression made by sportscasters to describe a runner, big and strong, who carries or drags defenders with him.

Cannon arm — A strong-armed quarterback. Both Josh Allen and Patrick Mahomes have cannon arms.

Chain gang — The crew of two on the sidelines whose role is to maintain two poles separated by a chain ten yards in length to keep track of the exact distance from the present down and yards to go for a first down. They may be called upon to bring their markers onto the field to measure for a first down when the placement of the ball is too close for the referee to call.

Check down — A short pass from the quarterback to a receiver when all other passing options are covered downfield. A tailback typically serves as the receiver in this situation (see "safety valve"). *The quarterback couldn't find an open receiver downfield and checked down for a short gain.*

Chip shot — A short field goal attempt about the distance of an extra point.

Chop block — Blocking below the knees. An illegal block that comes with substantial risk of injury and carries a 15-yard penalty.

Clock it — A tactic in the final seconds of a half or game where a team wants to score while preserving time on the game clock without using a timeout. With the clock running, the quarterback spikes the ball (immediately throws the ball to the ground). This stops the clock and enables the field goal team to set up for a three-point attempt or the offense the opportunity for another play.

Clothesline (also: horse collar) — An illegal tackle where the tackler pulls the ball carrier down by the neck.

Coffin corner — A punt that lands near the corner of the field of play close to the goal line. The team about to go on offense thus begins play with its back to its own goal line.

Corner route — The receiver runs deep down the center of the field and cuts across toward the corner of the end zone.

Cover 2—a defense in which the two safeties drop far down the field to guard against deep passes.

Cut — 1) A team drops a player from the roster; 2) The action of a ball carrier to turn sharply.

Crackback block — An illegal block delivered below the opponent's waist by an offensive player.

Dead-ball foul — A penalty by either the offense or defense before or after a play. Illegal procedure on offense or offside on defense are examples.

Down by contact — The knee or another part of the player carrying the ball hits the ground after hitting a defensive player, even if only slightly.

Down lineman — A player on offense stationed at the line of scrimmage whose role is to pass protect or run block.

Draw first blood — To score first. *The Raiders drew first blood with a 33-yard field goal.*

Draw play — The quarterback drops back as if to pass, then hands off to a running back. In some cases, he may run with the ball himself.

Drive — A continuous set of offensive plays. Example: A long drive consumes many minutes from the clock, and gains a lot of yardage and a first down. A successful drive leads to points.

Dump-off — A short pass a few yards behind or ahead of the line of scrimmage (see "screen pass").

Edge (also: squeak by) — (v.) To beat an opponent by a small margin. *The Raiders edged the Jaguars 21-20.*

Edge rusher — A defensive end or player who runs toward the offensive backfield from his outside—or "edge"—position.

End around — When an offensive end comes behind the line of scrimmage to take a handoff and attempts to carry the ball around the opposite flank. Business: To not let obstacles interfere. *Human resources won't let us hire anyone, so we'll need to do an end-around and bring in an outside contractor.*

Face mask — Protective bars at the front of a helmet. *The defensive end drew a penalty for grabbing the running back's face mask.*

Face off (also see "square off") — When two teams play against each other. *The hometown rivals faced off.*

Fair catch — The catch of a punt in which the player expecting to catch the ball extends and waves his arms to wave off defenders from tackling him. The receiver of the kick may not advance the ball. The ball is marked at the spot the catch is made. Note: If the fair catch is made in the final seconds of a half or game, the receiving team may attempt a free kick for a field goal.

Field goal — Three points are scored by kicking the ball between the uprights at the end of the opponent's end zone.

Field position — The measure of how many yards a team must travel at the start of the drive in order to score. "Good field position" suggests the offense has less distance to cover; "bad field position" means it starts deep in its own end of the field.

Flat — An area, covered by linebackers, up to ten yards beyond the line of scrimmage. This is an area where quarterbacks will find a receiver on short-passing routes or a running back on a screen pass.

Flea flicker — One of the most exciting plays in the game in which a quarterback hands off to the running back, who flips a backward pass back to the quarterback, who then throws a long pass to a wide receiver or tight end.

Football move — The action of a receiver, in the eyes of the officials, that determines whether or not he catches the ball. Normally, the ball is secure in his grasp and he takes one step (or move) with it.

Forward progress — The spot where the referee places the ball after a ball carrier was stopped and pushed back.

Full-house backfield — The quarterback, two half backs, and one full back. Also called the "T" formation, believed to have been invented by Walter Camp. One of the oldest but seldom-used formations.

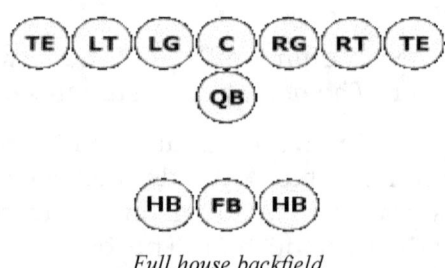

Full house backfield
CC-BY-SA

Fumble — When the player in possession of the ball drops it.

Game of inches — Describes football where a few inches can make a difference between success or failure

Go all out — Teams do their maximum to win or an individual player is at his peak performance for his team.

Go at it — To fight.

Go route (aka "fly route") — When a speedy receiver runs as fast and as far as possible to get by the defensive back to catch a deep pass (see "long bomb").

Goal-line stand — When a defense does not let the opponent, who is close to the goal line, score a touchdown.

Gridiron — Another name for the football field.

Gridder — A person who plays American football.

Ground game — A rushing or running attack by the offense. *The Bills had the most powerful ground of any team in 2016.*

Gun — (n.) The sound that ends each half of the game.

Gunners — Players on the punt team at the end of the lines who run down the field to get to the punt returner.

Gunslinger — A quarterback with a reputation for throwing a lot and taking high risks.

Hail Mary — A last-second, long-distance desperation pass to a receiver yards away in the end zone. *Aaron Rogers lifted the Green Bay Packers past the Detroit Lions, 27-23, when he heaved a 60-yard Hail Mary, caught in the end zone by Richard Rogers, as the gun sounded.* (YouTube: search: hail Mary + NFL)

Handoff — (hand-off, v.) **Football**: A ball handed directly from the quarterback (usually) to another player, usually a running back. **Business**: To give the issue to another person or department. *She decided to hand-off to Roberto, whose expertise might bring results.*

Hands team — Players on special teams (kickoff or punt) who are accustomed to handling the ball (i.e., running backs, receivers). *Anticipating an onside kick, the Browns had their hands team on the field.* **Business**: A team of negotiators with its most specialized performers. *The Daggert Company sent their hands team to the meeting.*

Hard count — The quarterback uses irregular, accented sounds (counts) at the line of scrimmage with the desired result to draw the defense offside. *Payton Manning was good at drawing teams offside with a hard count.*

Hash marks — Dash-like lines between which the ball begins each play. The lines are parallel to and a distance in from the sidelines. If a play is blown dead while the ball is between the hash marks, the ball is spotted where it is blown dead. If the play ends outside the hash marks, the ball is placed at the closest hash mark.

Headed — Football: To lead in the game. *The Steelers went up 7-3 and were never headed after that.* **Business:** To lead. *The team is headed by Peter, Paul, and Mary.*

Heave — To throw the football either long, aimlessly, or both. *Bledsoe scrambled and heaved the ball out of bounds.*

Heave-ho (give the) — To be ejected from the game. *He was given the heave-ho for fighting.*

High octane (high-powered) — An offense with explosive potential. *The high-octane offenses got together in a high-scoring affair won by the Rams 54-51.*

Hike (aka "snap") — When the center passes the ball back between his legs to the quarterback to start the play.

Hole — An open area for a runner to run through. A gaping hole—a big hole. *Derrick Coleman found a hole for pay dirt.*

Home field advantage — A condition where the home field favors the home team due to familiarity with the environment and the enthusiasm of its supporters.

Home stand — When a team plays a series of consecutive games in its own stadium.

Hook route (aka "hitch route") — When a receiver runs a few steps and quickly turns to the quarterback for a short pass.

Hurries — A statistical category for defensive players who force a quarterback to throw the ball sooner than he wants (to "hurry" the throw).

Hurry-up offense — When the team on offense does not huddle (see "no-huddle offense").

Intangibles — An athlete's characteristics beyond football skills such as intelligence and instinct.

Interception — When a passed ball is caught by a defensive player.

Interference — An act that interferes, obstructs, impedes. **Football**: 1) blocking: *On the screen pass, their four blockers* *were leading the interference.* 2) Catching the ball: *The safety was flagged for pass interference.* **Business**: Often, a member of an advanced team who does the initial work for the agenda at negotiations. *"We're counting on you, Emilio, to lead the interference."*

Iron man — A player with a long history of playing without injury. *Jim Otto was an iron man who never missed a game in his career.*

Journeyman — In sports, characterizes a player whose skills are steady and reliable but not outstanding.

Juke — (v.) To evade tacklers by quick moves. *The running back juked to the left and found an opening for a long run.*

Kneel down (see "victory formation") — With seconds remaining in the half or the game, the quarterback takes the snap from the center and puts his knee on the ground to run time off the clock. *John Brodie knees down and runs out the clock.*

Knock on the door (at the doorstep)—characterizes a team that is close to the opponent's end zone. *The Chargers, at the Chief's seven, are knocking on the door/at the doorstep.*

Lateral — A backward pass. Note: If the ball is dropped by the receiver, it is not an incomplete pass but a fumble, a live ball, which may be recovered by the defense.

Long bomb — The ball is thrown a long distance (see "air it out").

Man in motion — Before the ball is snapped, one player on offense, a running back or receiver, may run parallel to or backward from the line of scrimmage. The objective is to make the defense adjust.

Man-to-man coverage — Each player on defense is assigned an offensive player to cover (opposite: "zone coverage").

Misdirection — The blockers head one way to get the defenders to move in the same direction while the ball carrier heads the opposite direction.

Momentum — Describes a game event when a team begins to assert control of its own destiny. (This can shift back and forth from one team to another.)

Muff (muffed punt) — When a player drops a punt without ever having possession. The team that recovers gets the ball on offense.

Nail-biter — A game that is very close, usually decided in the last seconds. *The Seahawks-49ers game was a nail biter, wasn't it?*

Net yards — A statistical measurement for a team for all yards gained, passing and receiving (gross) minus plays that resulted in a loss of yardage. *Although the Tar Heels gained 354 yards, three sacks for 16 yards left them with 338 net yards.* (This yardage is subtracted from the team total.)

No huddle — Between plays, the offense does not huddle. (The play had been previously decided or is sent to the quarterback by hand signal from the sideline.) This fast pace is designed to fatigue the defense and to keep it off-balance.

Off tackle — When the running back follows the blocking of the right or left tackle.

Offsetting penalties — A penalty or penalties on each team that cancel each other. The previous down is replayed.

Onside kick — A strategy in which the kicking team on the kickoff tries to recover the kick.

Option — (See RPO)

Out (route) — When the receiver sprints straight upfield and abruptly turns to the sideline and attempts to catch the ball, which has already been thrown. (Timing and communication between the quarterback and receiver are integral to the success of this play.)

Out of bounds — When the ball lands at the side of the field of play on a kickoff or a punt, or the player with the ball steps outside the field of play. The ball is usually marked at that spot.

Over the top — On short-yardage situations, teams try for a first down or a touchdown when the runner jumps over the pile of linemen and defenders at the line of scrimmage.

Pass happy — Suggests a team that passes the ball a lot. *The San Diego Chargers, under Don "Air" Coryell, was a pass-happy team.*

Pass interference — A penalty that is called when a defensive player contacts the receiver before the ball reaches him.

Pass rush — A defensive maneuver to go after the quarterback and sack him.

Pass rusher — A defensive player who rushes or tries to get at the quarterback and sack him before he releases the ball. *Deacon Jones, who coined the term "sack," is considered among the top all-time pass rushers in the NFL with 173 career sacks.*

Passing attack — A team's game strategy for passing the football.

PAT—Point-after-touchdown. After a touchdown has been scored, a 1-pt. PAT is a kick between the uprights; a 2-pt. PAT occurs when the offense runs or completes a pass across the goal line.

Pick (aka "pick-off") — An interception of a pass. (v.) *The safety picked-off the pass.* (n.) *The safety has two picks.*

Pick six — An interception returned for a touchdown. *Charles Woodson stepped in front of the receiver to grab an easy 30-yard pick six.*

Pitch out — When the quarterback takes the hike from the center and tosses the ball to a running back in motion to the right or left.

Play fake (play action) — When the start of play looks like a run play as the quarterback pretends to hand-off but instead, drops back to pass.

"Plus" territory — When a team takes possession of the ball on the opponent's side of the field. *The poor punt enabled the Hawkeyes take over the ball in **plus territory**, at the Nittany Lions' 44.*

Pocket (also known as "tackle box") — The area in the backfield protected by the offensive line for the quarterback when he drops back to pass the ball.

Pocket presence — Describes a quarterback who is alert and makes intelligent decisions while under pressure in the pocket.

Pooch kick — (n.) A deliberately short kick designed to prevent the ball from rolling into the end zone for a touchback or to limit the ability of the receiving team for a return.

Post route — A receiver runs a short distance (10-15 yards) and cuts across toward the center of the field (hence, in line with the goalposts).

Prevent defense — A strategy on defense in the closing minutes of a half or game for deep zone coverage, which may allow short or medium passing gains but prevents long, devastating ones.

Pull — After the snap, a member of the offensive line takes a step back and moves laterally to block somewhere else. Pulling can be done on both pass and run plays.

Pulling guard — When an offensive guard drops back (or "pulls") and leads the blocking to the left or the right of the line of scrimmage. *Some say that Jerry Kramer was the best pulling guard there ever was.*

Pump fake — When the quarterback pretends to throw, tricking defenders to unnecessarily leap, which obstructs the defenders' timing to block or intercept a pass.

Pylon — A flexible, brightly colored cone at each corner of the end zone to facilitate judgments of close plays.

Quarterback keeper — A designed play where the quarterback keeps the ball and runs.

Quarterback sneak — A short-yardage situation where the quarterback tries to gain the necessary yardage for a first down or a touchdown behind the push of the interior line.

Red zone — (n.) The area between the 20-yard line and the opponent's goal line for the team with the ball.

Reverse (also called double reverse) — A trick play designed to keep the defense off-balance where the ball is handed off to a player (usually a receiver) headed one way in back of the line of scrimmage, who then hands it off to another player (usually a second receiver) headed in the opposite direction. The hope is for a long-distance rushing play.

Riverboat gambler — Describes a head coach with a reputation for taking risks.

Rout (raʊt) — (n.) An overwhelming defeat. *Leading by 24 points in the third quarter, the rout was on.* (v.) To defeat an opponent by a wide margin. (also wallop, clobber, whip). *The Chargers routed the Cowboys 38-14.*

RPO (run-pass option) — A quarterback can decide whether to run with the ball himself, hand the ball off to a running back, or throw the ball (see "bootleg").

Run stuffer — Usually a reference to a defensive lineman who can stop the runner without a gain or a loss of yardage. *The Giants' porous run defense needed help, so they used a draft pick for a run stuffer.*

Run to daylight — Suggests a wide-open hole has enabled a runner to gain considerable yardage, or a "run to daylight."

Sack — (n., v.) When the quarterback is tackled behind the line of scrimmage (v.) he is sacked by the defense, or the defense records a sack (n.).

Safety — (n.) 1) A position in the defensive backfield; 2) when two points are scored when an offensive player with the ball is tackled in his own end zone. Note: Unlike a touchdown or field goal where the scoring team kicks off, the team that suffers the safety kicks off.

Safety valve — A short pass from the quarterback to a receiver when all other passing options are covered downfield. A tailback typically serves as the receiver in this situation (see "check down").

Slippery — Describes a characteristic of a running back able to escape—or slip away from—tacklers.

Scramble — (v.) When a quarterback, under pressure from the defense, runs around the offensive backfield, behind the line of scrimmage, looking downfield for an open receiver, or he may decide to keep it and run. *Modern quarterbacks must be able to scramble as well as pass.*

Screen pass — A play often used against aggressive defenses. The quarterback fakes a handoff or long pass and pretends to throw long, but instead tosses a short pass to a running back in the flat (an area behind the line of scrimmage) who has positioned himself behind a group (called a wall) of blockers.

Shank—Describes a ball that accidentally is kicked off the side of the punter's foot.

Shoot the gap — When a defensive lineman or linebacker finds open space between offensive players to rush through untouched and tackles (sacks) the quarterback or the runner for a loss of yardage.

Shotgun formation — Mainly used for pass plays, the quarterback lines up seven yards back of the center. The advantage is that it gives him a broader view of the playing field and time to spot an open receiver.

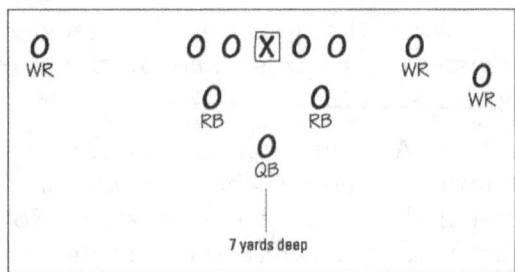

Shovel pass — A short toss of the ball underhand.

Shootout — A high-scoring game normally where the lead exchanges hands many times.

Shut-out (also: blank). (v.) When one team doesn't allow its opponent to score points. *The Vikings shut-out (or blanked) the Lions 10-0.*

Slugfest (also see "barnyard brawl") — A game in which two teams play each other strongly.

Smash mouth — Describes a style of football; hard, physical.

Special teams — Units that are used on "special occasions" like field-goal attempts and kickoffs (see "suicide squad").

Spike — (v.) Inside two minutes in the half or the game, the quarterback immediately throws the ball to the ground to stop the clock.

Square off — When two teams play each other. *The Broncos and Chiefs square off next Thursday night.*

Squeak by — Used to describe the outcome of a game when a team wins by no more than a few points (see "edge").

Stalemate — A 0-0 score (can be the final score or at any point in the game when the score is scoreless.

Stats — (n.) Statistics. The team led in stats but still lost the game.

Streak — (v.) To run fast. (n.) An unbroken skein or unbroken slate of games won or lost.

Stuff — To stop the runner at the line of scrimmage for no gain or behind the line of scrimmage for a loss of yards. *Sam Darnold stuffed the Indianapolis runner in his tracks.*

Stunt — A defensive maneuver that positions defensive linemen at an angle to confuse the offensive linemen. Properly executed, it opens a lane to the quarterback or the ball carrier.

Suicide squad — A special teams unit that is used on kickoffs. Called such because, although kickoffs can be one of the most exciting plays in a game, it's when players are most vulnerable to injuries. Players run at full speed and (to put it mildly) with reckless abandon. Rules on kickoffs have been modified over the years to minimize injuries.

Sweep — When the guard drops back (see "pulling guard") and moves to the left or right along the line of scrimmage to lead the interference, or blocking, for the ball carrier.

Tackle box — The area between where the two offensive tackles line up. This is important in determining possible infractions, or fouls, such as intentional grounding (offense) or roughing the passer (defense).

Take a knee (see victory formation) — When the quarterback drops his knee to the ground to run out time on the game clock at the end of the half or game.

Tampa 2 — Popularized by the Tampa Bay Buccaneers, this refers to a defensive alignment, typically 4-3—four linemen, three linebackers, two cornerbacks, and two safeties.

Tee-off (figurative; separable verb) — To cause anger. *The coach is teed-off by players who miss practice. A good way to tee someone off is to stick out your tongue at him.*

Tee up — 1. (literal) To put the ball on the tee (high school and college) ready for kickoff; 2. (figurative) To be prepared. *Mr. Tovar has the PowerPoint teed up for the presentation to start promptly.* (sep) *Will you tee the presentation up?*

The trenches (in) — The area at the line of scrimmage where the big guys on the defensive and offensive lines go at it.

Three and out — The term used to describe a drive in which a team gets no first down and must punt, or if close enough, try a field goal.

Tipped pass — When a thrown ball is touched by a defensive player and diverted from its trajectory.

Touchback —(n.) When the ball goes into the end zone on a kickoff or a punt and the receiver elects not to run it out.

Therefore, the ball is placed on the 25-yard line. This can also occur when the ball is kicked out of the end of the end zone.

Touchdown — (colloquially called "pay dirt") When a team scores six points by crossing the other team's goal line. This can be done by running the ball (rushing) or passing. Occasionally, touchdowns are scored by interception, fumble, punt, or kickoff return.

Trail — To not lead in the game. *The Broncos, who trailed by 3 points, 27-24, lined up to kick a field goal to tie the game.*

Trap — A running play where a defender is not initially blocked but can penetrate the offensive backfield, where he is then blocked. The design is meant to surprise the defense by allowing the defender past where the ball carrier is, leaving one less tackler to contend with as he heads downfield.

Trick play (aka "gadget play") — Designed to deceive the opponent. Effective ones can even fool the fans and the TV cameras. (YouTube: search trick play NFL)

Turnover — Examples: A fumble recovered by the opposing team or an interception.

Turnover on downs — When a team fails to convert a 4th down so the ball goes over to the opponent.

Two-minute offense (aka "hurry-up offense") — A time in the game after the two-minute warning in which the team trailing hurries its plays and tries to use the clock expeditiously to go down the field with the desired result of scoring the go-ahead points. Often two plays are called in the huddle, and sometimes there is no huddle.

Under center — The quarterback's position right behind the center, ready to take the snap.

Up the middle — A term used to describe a running back taking a handoff and going between the center and guard. Usually used in short-yardage situations.

Vanilla offense/defense— A unit with very few plays and formations. Typically used in the preseason to conceal possible plays and schemes from opposing coaches for when the game is for real; also used when an inexperienced quarterback is pressed into service.

Victory formation (see "kneel down" and "take a knee") — When the offensive team is bunched together at the line of scrimmage to protect the ball. The quarterback takes the snap and puts a knee on the turn to run time off the clock. The opposing team is out of timeouts and thus cannot stop the clock.

West Coast Offense — An offensive strategy using short, high-percentage passes as the core of a ball-control offense.

Wide — (right or left) On a field goal attempt, the ball has the distance but travels to either side of the goalposts, or uprights.

Wildcat offense — A strategy in which either the quarterback or a running back can receive a direct snap from the center, or snapper.

Zebras (aka "men in stripes") — (n.) An informal term for the officials.

Zone coverage (zone defense) — When defenders are assigned an area, or space, to cover (as opposed to man-to-man)

List of References

10 Football Passing Routes Explained. (2015, November 10). Retrieved June 22, 2017 from https://mentalfloss.com/article/70831/10-football-passing-routes-explained

1967 NFL Championship Game. (2019, May 13). Retrieved from https://en.wikipedia.org/wiki/1967_NFL_Championship_Game#cite_note-38

1980–81 NFL playoffs. (2019, January 21). Retrieved from https://en.wikipedia.org/wiki/1980–81_NFL_playoffs

2016 Official Playing Rules of the National Football League. (n.d.). Retrieved September 12 , 2016, from https://operations.nfl.com/media/2224/2016-nfl-rulebook.pdf Roger Goodell, Commissioner

"49er Fan Pastor Tim's 1-Minute Worship Service (Jan. 12, 2014)." *YouTube*, YouTube, 12 Jan. 2014, youtu.be/EbqVPt8zzWQ.

805Bruin. (2012, November 19). Retrieved April 24, 2019, from https://www.youtube.com/watch?v=VoNIK0gZ1dY

A-Z Stadium Information. (n.d.). Retrieved May 1, 2019 from https://www.lincolnfinancialfield.com/a-z-stadium-information/

About Friends of the IFL. (n.d.). Retrieved from https://iflfriends.com/about/

A Brief History of the Game. (n.d.). Retrieved November 21, 2016, from http://www.hornetfootball.org/documents/football-history.htm

Achtzener, Kevin, K., et al. (2014, November 13). Do You Still Call People Sir or Ma'am? Stop it! Retrieved 07-18-2018 from https://visualproductivity.net/do-you-still-call-people-sir-or-maam-stop-it/

Advancing a fumble. (n.d.). Retrieved September 14, 2018, from https://forum.officiating.com/football/11003-advancing-fumble.html

Alder, J. (n.d.). How Many Ways Can a Football Team Score Points? Retrieved August 09, 2017 from https://www.thoughtco.com/methods-of-scoring-in-football-1335401

Alder, J. (n.d.). Football 101: How a Football Game Begins. Retrieved June 21, 2018 from https://www.thoughtco.com/football-101-basics-beginning-football-game-1335399

Alder, J., New York Times, ESPN Radio Network, & BBC Radio. (n.d.). What Do Football Officials Do. Retrieved December 28, 2018 from https://www.thoughtco.com/football-officials-and-their-duties-1333786

American Football Lingo Glossary - Terminology & Slang. (n.d.). Retrieved from https://www.sportslingo.com/football-lingo-glossary/

Andreozzi, J. (2016, September 13). Top 15 NFL Players Who Overcame Physical or Mental Disabilities. Retrieved July 3, 2018, from https://www.thesportster.com/football/top-15-nfl-players-who-overcame-physical-or-mental-disabilities/

Antoniacci, M. (2016, September 08). 28 of the Greatest Quotes from NFL Legends. Retrieved from https://www.inc.com/mandy-antoniacci/28-of-the-greatest-quotes-from-nfl-legends.html

Associated Press. (n.d.). Retrieved from https://collegefootball.ap.org/

ATC Spotters: Another Set of Eyes for Injuries. (n.d.). Retrieved October 24, 2018, from https://operations.nfl.com/the-game/gameday-behind-the-scenes/atc-spotters/

Ballard, C., Kaplan, E., Lawrence, A., Cohen, R., & Nashawaty, C. (n.d.). When Super Bowl champs played college all-stars. Retrieved from https://www.si.com/nfl/2015/12/09/college-all-star-football-classic-jackie-slater-joe-greene

Ballet in the NFL. Retrieved January 19, 2018, from https://dancemydance.wordpress.com/2015/01/17/ballet-in-the-nfl/

Baltimore Colts relocation to Indianapolis. (2018, September 30). Retrieved 21 October 2018 from https://en.wikipedia.org/wiki/Baltimore_Colts_relocation_to_Indianapolis

Bears beat Redskins 73-0 in NFL Championship game. (2009, November 16). Retrieved from https://www.history.com/this-day-in-history/bears-beat-redskins-73-0-in-nfl-championship-game

Berkman, J. (n.d.). What Are NCAA Divisions? Division 1 vs. 2 vs. 3. Retrieved from https://blog.prepscholar.com/what-are-ncaa-divisions-1-vs-2-vs-3

Bender, B. (2018, July 09). Top 16 college football programs since 2000: Alabama, Ohio State fight for No. 1. Retrieved August 6, 2018, from http://www.sportingnews.com/us/ncaa-football/list/top-college-football-programs-since-2000-usc-ohio-state-alabama-usc-lsu-oklahoma-fsu-florida-texas/bpakpul856761v4xn7bn8zshw# Blue chip recruits; pipeline to NFL: championships

Bonagura, K. (2017, September 03). USC's Jake Olson snaps for PAT: 'Something I'll remember forever'. Retrieved 0701-2018 from http://www.espn.com/college-football/story/_/id/20553215/jake-olson-usc-snaps-successful-extra-point-western-michigan

Brief History of Football/Soccer. (n.d.). Retrieved from https://footballgenuine.blogspot.com/2015/11/brief-history-of-footballsoccer.html

British vs. American English. (n.d.). Retrieved from http://www.studyenglishtoday.net/british-american-spelling.html

Buck540, Brainyblonde, and Chippy. "Who was the last NFL player to play both offense and defense?" *FunTrivia*. N.p., 26 Sept. 2004. Web. 12 Jan. 2017.

Buffalo Bills pull off greatest comeback in NFL history. (2009, November 16). Retrieved from https://www.history.com/this-day-in-history/buffalo-bills-pull-off-greatest-comeback-in-nfl-history

Büren, J. V. (2017, April 20). Deaf NFL players. Retrieved June 25, 2018 from https://www.hearinglikeme.com/4-deaf-nfl-players-you-probably-didnt-know-about/

Byron White. (2019, March 16). Retrieved 6 Apr 2019 from https://en.wikipedia.org/wiki/Byron_White

Carnegie, Dale, 1888-1955. (2009). *How to win friends and influence people*. New York :Simon & Schuster.

Charles Woodson. (n.d.). Retrieved from https://www.heisman.com/heisman-winners/charles-woodson/

Chase Stuart. (2013, April 21). What did the media say about Tom Brady in 2000? Retrieved from http://www.footballperspective.com/what-did-the-media-say-about-tom-brady-in-2000/

Checkdown Definition - Sporting Charts. (n.d.). Retrieved June 22,2017 from https://www.sportingcharts.com/dictionary/nfl/checkdown.aspx

Cheerleaders. (n.d.). Retrieved December 29, 2017, from http://www.titansonline.com/cheerleaders/cheerleader-apperances.html

Chicago College All-Star Game. (2019, January 12). Retrieved from https://en.wikipedia.org/wiki/Chicago_College_All-Star_Game

China Arena Football League. (2017, August 04). Retrieved August 12, 2017, from https://en.wikipedia.org/wiki/China_Arena_Football_League

Chronic traumatic encephalopathy. (n.d.) *The American Heritage® Medical Dictionary*. (2007). Retrieved November 25 2018 from https://medical-dictionary.thefreedictionary.com/chronic+traumatic+encephalopathy

Coleman, D., Jr., & Brotherton, M. (2015). *No Excuses: Growing up Deaf and Achieving my Super Bowl Dreams*. New York, NY: Gallery Books/Jeter Publishing.

College Football Scholarships. (n.d.). Retrieved August 7, 2018, from http://www.collegescholarships.org/scholarships/sports/football.htm

Cortez, V., (2018, December 12). Our Three Divisions. Retrieved from http://www.ncaa.org/about/resources/media-center/ncaa-101/our-three-divisions

Crupi, A., & Crupi, A. (2018, January 02). Despite Another Ratings Slump, the NFL Remains TV's Top Dog. Retrieved June 11, 2018 from http://adage.com/article/media/ratings-slum/311777/

Davidson, J. (n.d.). NFL Experience a showcase of events – and fun – for fans soaking up Super Bowl week. Retrieved March 29, 2018, from https://www.sacbee.com/sports/nfl/super-bowl/article57663088.html

DenverSportsNut, T. (2017, October 03). Tim Tebow by the Numbers: Breaking Passing Records vs. the Pittsburgh Steelers. Retrieved from https://bleacherreport.com/articles/1021135-tim-tebow-by-the-numbers-breaking-passing-records-vs-the-pittsburgh-steelers

Designthemes. (2016, February 24). American Football League of China (AFLC) Championship a Historic Success. Retrieved from http://chinagridiron.org/american-football-league-of-china-aflc-championship-a-historic-success/

Dick Lane Biography. (n.d.). Retrieved April 2 10, 2017, from http://www.notablebiographies.com/supp/Supplement-Ka-M/Lane-Dick.html

Doctors. (n.d.). Retrieved June 28, 2018 from http://ultimatecheerleaders.com/lists/drs/ A listing of NFL cheerleaders past and present who have professions in medicine.

Dodds, E. (2015, February 15). The 'Death Penalty' and How the College Sports Conversation Has Changed. *Time*. How NCAA sanctions pummeled the SMU Mustangs--AKA "The Pony Express," from the penthouse to the doghouse

(The) Drive. (n.d.). Retrieved from https://www.profootballhof.com/news/the-drive/

Dr. Regina Bailey, MD, JD. (2018, April 05). Retrieved December 20, 2017, from https://www.drreginamdjd.com/ This site expresses the current activity of Dr. Bailey, which includes scholarly publications, physical fitness and her practice of medicine.

Dwyre, B. (2015, January 05). Green Bay's memories of 1967's Ice Bowl with Dallas are frozen in time. Retrieved from https://www.latimes.com/sports/la-sp-ice-bowl-dwyre-20150106-column.html

Edward G. Hochuli - Arizona Lawyers - Zebra Lawyer. (n.d.). Retrieved from https://www.superlawyers.com/arizona/article/zebra-lawyer/2f31606d-4d77-44b0-8175-3731aab43974.htm

Fair catch kick. (2017, December 08). Retrieved December 21, 2017, from https://en.wikipedia.org/wiki/Fair_catch_kick

Famous College Football Coaches. (n.d.). Retrieved from http://www.lootmeister.com/cfb/famous-coaches.php

Fantasy football (American). (2019, March 24). Retrieved from https://en.wikipedia.org/wiki/Fantasy_football_(American)

FAQS. (n.d.). Retrieved from https://collegefootballplayoff.com/sports/2016/10/11/_131504729625539914.aspx

Farmer, S. (2018, October 7). Ask Sam Farmer. *Los Angeles Times*, p. D3.

Félix, A. (2016, February 04). Never Forget the Time a Mexican College Football Team Beat Cam Newton. Retrieved from https://remezcla.com/sports/cam-newton-mexican-university-football/

Ferentz, B. (2019, May 29). For Book [E-mail to the author]. Reply from offensive line coach Univ. of Iowa to question about what makes offensive lineman

Fetter, H. D. (2017, January 10). How the Super Bowl Got Its Name: The Real Story. Retrieved from https://www.theatlantic.com/entertainment/archive/2011/01/how-the-super-bowl-got-its-name-the-real-story/70287/

Flutie converts first drop kick since 1941 championship. (2006, January 02). Retrieved December 21, 2017, from http://www.espn.com/nfl/news/story?id=2277308

Football Quotes: Famous, Funny and Otherwise [Web log post]. (n.d.). Retrieved December 25, 2018, from https://runningredskins.blogspot.com/2006/09/football-quotes-famous-funny-and.html

Football U. Archives. (n.d.). Retrieved from https://thefootballgirl.com/football-u/

Forgotten Teams of the NFL, AFL, AAFC: 1920-1998. (2008, November 09). Retrieved from https://foreshock.wordpress.com/origin-of-nfl-teams-1922-present/forgotten-teams-of-the-nfl-1920-1998/

Franchise nicknames. (2005, January 01). Retrieved from https://www.profootballhof.com/news/franchise-nicknames/

Gaines, C. (2015, September 13). NFL lineman weren't always so enormous - see how much they've grown over the years. Retrieved from https://www.businessinsider.com/nfl-offensive-lineman-are-big-2011-10

Gallaudet football players communicate with sign language [Television news episode]. (2017, November 16). In *CBS This Morning*. New York, NY: CBS.

Gallaudet University (n.d.). Retrieved June 25, 2018, from https://www.gallaudetathletics.com/sports/fball/index

Gaughan, M. (2014, May 18). It's Fandemonium as Miller earns Bills Wall of Fame spot. Retrieved Dec. 16, 2015, from http://buffalonews.com/2014/05/18/its-fandemonium-as-miller-earns-bills-wall-of-fame-spot/

Gesicki, J. (n.d.). Most Common NFL Injuries. Retrieved from https://blog.muellersportsmed.com/most-common-national-football-league-injuries-infographic.

Goldstein, C. (2019, May 22). Question for Book [E-mail to the author].

Gordon, A., & Gordon, A. (2014, January 22). Did Football Cause 20 Deaths In 1905? Re-Investigating A Serial Killer. Retrieved from https://deadspin.com/did-football-cause-20-deaths-in-1905-re-investigating-1506758181

Grantland Rice. (2019, March 13). Retrieved from https://en.wikipedia.org/wiki/Grantland_Rice

Hail Flutie, 30 Years Later: Looking Back on A Classic Moment in College Football. (6077, June 15). Retrieved from http://www.thepostgame.com/blog/throwback/201411/hail-flutie-30-years-later-looking-back-classic-moment-college-football

Hard Count Definition, et al. - Sporting Charts. (n.d.). Retrieved from https://www.sportingcharts.com/dictionary/nfl/hard-count.aspx

Harpaston. (n.d.). Retrieved from https://historyofsportsss.weebly.com/harpaston.html

Harpastum. (n.d.). Retrieved from https://www.topendsports.com/sport/extinct/harpastum.htm

Harwell, D. (2014, September 13). Women Are Pro Football's Most Important Demographic. Will They Forgive the NFL? *The Washington Post*

The Heidi Bowl. (2009, November 16). Retrieved January 4, 2017, from https://www.history.com/this-day-in-history/the-heidi-bowl

Immaculate Reception. (2019, June 02). Retrieved from https://en.wikipedia.org/wiki/Immaculate_Reception

Inflation Rate between 1890-2017 | Inflation Calculator. (n.d.). Retrieved from https://www.in2013dollars.com/1890-dollars-in-2017?amount=500

Interactive: NFL Officials' Roles and Responsibilities | NFL Football Operations. (n.d.). Retrieved 23 June 2018 from https://operations.nfl.com/the-officials/these-officials-are-really-good/officials-responsibilities-positions/

International Player Pathway Program (The): What it is, and why it will change the NFL. (2017, June 26). Retrieved 12 April 2019 from https://theinsidezone.com/international-player-pathway-program-will-change-nf

In the Beginning, there was Harpaston. (2013, May 09). Retrieved August 04, 2017, from http://footballfornormalgirls.com/history-2/history-lessons-in-the-beginning-there-was-harpaston/

Is China About to Fall in Love with American Football? (n.d.). Retrieved October 16, 2016, from http://time.com/4512741/nfl-cafl-american-football-china-arena-football-sports-peyton-manning/

Jaye, Donyal 2015. Ballet Slippers and Football Pads Make Better NFL Players · Guardian Liberty Voice. Retrieved January 20, 2018, from http://guardianlv.com/2015/06/ballet-slippers-and-football-pads-make-better-nfl-players/

Josh Katzowitz Jul 31, 2013 • 2 min read. (2015, June 02). Steve McLendon: Ballet is 'harder than anything else I do'. Retrieved January 19, 2016, from https://www.cbssports.com/nfl/news/steve-mclendon-ballet-is-harder-than-anything-else-i-do/

Julita. (2010, December 25). Difference Between. Retrieved from http://www.differencebetween.net/miscellaneous/difference-between-fbs-and-fcs/

Kalinauskas, N. (2014, January 14). One-minute sermon? Pastor keeps things short to catch 49ers game. Retrieved from https://ca.news.yahoo.com/blogs/good-news/one-minute-sermon-pastor-keeps-things-short-catch-162142219.html

Kiger, P. J. (2011, May 02). How the American Dream Works. Retrieved from https://people.howstuffworks.com/american-dream.htm

Kirk, K. (2011, March 11). The Role of an NFL Quality Control Coach. Retrieved July 24, 2017, from https://www.milehighreport.com/2011/3/11/2043379/the-role-of-an-nfl-quality-control-coach-denver-broncos-football-scouting

Kirshner, A. (2019, January 30). How rare it is to be a 2-, 3-, 4-, or 5-star recruit. Retrieved 31 Jan 2019 from https://www.sbnation.com/college-football-recruiting/2019/1/30/18202661/recruiting-stars-rankings-high-school-football

Klein, C. (2014, September 04). The Birth of the National Football League. Retrieved November 21, 2016, from http://www.history.com/news/the-birth-of-the-national-football-league

Kroll, J. (2012, September 14). When Art Modell moved his Cleveland Browns team to Baltimore: How the Plain Dealer reported it. Retrieved from https://www.cleveland.com/browns/index.ssf/2012/09/when_art_modell_moved_his_clev.html

Learn ESL Vocabulary and Expressions with Lessons and Worksheets. (n.d.). Retrieved 12 Dec 2015 from http://drewseslfluencylessons.com/2-advanced/football/

Leccesi, J. (2018, March 08). The 5 most commonly asked questions about being a college walk-on. Retrieved March 10 March 2018 from https://usatodayhss.com/2017/the-5-most-commonly-asked-questions-about-being-a-college-walk-on

"Lineman (gridiron football)." *Wikipedia*. Wikimedia Foundation, 20 July 2017. Web. 03 Aug. 2017.

Loews, B. (2016). *What is the history of the play calling wristbands that many college and NFL quarterbacks wear today?* [online] Available at: https://www.quora.com/What-is-the-history-of-the-play-calling-wristbands-that-many-college-and-NFL-quarterbacks-wear-today [Accessed 23 Oct. 2017].

Long, H., & Czarnecki, J. (2015). *Football for dummies*. Hoboken, NJ: Wiley.

Male cheerleaders will take the field for the first time in NFL history. (2018, August 07). Retrieved September 17, 2018, from http://sandrarose.com/2018/08/male-cheerleaders-will-take-the-field-for-the-first-time-in-nfl-history/

Miracle at the Meadowlands. (2019, April 10). Retrieved from https://en.wikipedia.org/wiki/Miracle_at_the_Meadowlands

Morrison, J. (2010, December 28). The Early History of Football's Forward Pass. Retrieved from https://www.smithsonianmag.com/history/the-early-history-of-footballs-forward-pass-78015237/

National Football League Cheerleading. (2017, December 16). Retrieved December 17, 2017, from https://en.wikipedia.org/wiki/National_Football_League_Cheerleading

NCAA. (2018, April 23). Estimated probability of competing in professional athletics. Retrieved August 8, 2018, from https://www.ncaa.org/about/resources/research/estimated-probability-competing-professional-athletics (n.d.). Retrieved May 16, 2017, from http://sportscliche.com/football.html Common clichés used by announcers

NCAA. (2013, November 27). Enforcement Process: Penalties. Retrieved August 7, 2018, from https://www.ncaa.org/enforcement/enforcement-process-penalties

Nelson, Ken. (2018). Football: Referee Signals. *Ducksters*. Retrieved from https://www.ducksters.com/sports/football/referee_signals.php

NESN Staff on Sun. (2016, December 05). Eric Berry Seals Chiefs Win with Late 2-Point Conversion Interception Score. Retrieved from https://nesn.com/2016/12/eric-berry-seals-chiefs-win-with-late-2-point-conversion-interception-score/

News Hub: NFL Games Lack Real Action. (2010, January 05). New York, New York: Wall Street Journal Video.

NFL Beginner's Guide to Football. N.p., n.d. Web. 01 Aug. 2017.

NFL Champs Vs. College All-Stars 1934-1976. (n.d.). Retrieved from https://www.yourememberthat.com/media/14404/NFL_Champs_Vs._College_All-Stars_1934-1976/

NFL Code of Conduct. (n.d.). Retrieved December 26, 2018 from https://operations.nfl.com/football-ops/nfl-rules-enforcement/

NFL Football Operations. (n.d.). Retrieved from https://operations.nfl.com/ rules & penalties, officials, formations, dress/equipment codes, history, behind-the-scenes, et al.

NFL History. (n.d.). Retrieved from http://www.nfl.com/history

NFL Kickoff Game. (2018, March 26). Retrieved March 26, 2018, from https://en.wikipedia.org/wiki/NFL_Kickoff_Game

NPR Staff. (2012, November 17). Heidi: The Little Girl Who Changed Football Forever. Retrieved from https://www.npr.org/2012/11/17/165359212/heidi-the-little-girl-who-changed-football-forever

Nunn, V. (n.d.). American Football Is Chess on A Playing Field. Retrieved from https://www.streetdirectory.com/travel_guide/46340/recreation_and_sports/american_football_is_chess_on_a_playing_field.html

Okrent, A. (2014, February 02). The true origin story of the football huddle. Retrieved from https://theweek.com/articles/451763/true-origin-story-football-huddle

Olsen, H. B. (2015, November 23). For Female Football Players, It's Pay to Play (and Pray Someone Sees). Retrieved from https://www.thenation.com/article/for-female-football-players-its-pay-to-play-and-pray-someone-sees/

Otto, J., & Newhouse, D. (2000). *Jim Otto: The pain of glory*. Champaign, IL: Sports Pub.

Origin of NFL Teams: 1922-Present. (2017, August 21). Retrieved from https://foreshock.wordpress.com/origin-of-nfl-teams-1922-present/

Paxton, K. (2016, September 08). Football 101: Offense Positional Breakdown. Retrieved from https://www.active.com/football/articles/football-101-offense-positional-breakdown/slide-8?clckmp=activecom_global_latestonactive_pos2

Peavler, L. (2017, January 31). Your guide to the stars: What the ratings for college football recruits really mean. Retrieved from https://www.deseretnews.com/article/865672217/Your-guide-to-the-stars-What-the-ratings-for-college-football-recruits-really-mean.html

(The) Play (American football). (2019, January 02). Retrieved from https://en.wikipedia.org/wiki/The_Play_(American_football)

Pollock, C. Olean Times Herald. Time for Van to Join Bills' Wall of Fame. (n.d.). Retrieved January 01, 2018, from http://www.chautauquasportshalloffame.org/vanmiller2014.php

Potter, C. (2019, March 03). I know Myron Cope invented the Terrible Towel. But why a towel? Retrieved from https://www.pghcitypaper.com/pittsburgh/i-know-myron-cope-invented-the-terrible-towel-but-why-a-towel/Content?oid=1334240

"Practice squad." *Wikipedia*. Wikimedia Foundation, 16 July 2017. Web. 03 Aug. 2017.

Price, G. (2015, January 30). How Many Countries Will Watch the Super Bowl? Retrieved May 2, 2017, from https://www.ibtimes.com/how-many-countries-will-watch-super-bowl-1799734

Professional football is born. (2009, November 16). Retrieved from https://www.history.com/this-day-in-history/professional-football-is-born

Pro Football Hall of Fame. (n.d.). Retrieved from https://www.profootballhof.com/football-history/oorang-indians/

Pursuit of Perfection: The History and Evolution of the NFL Official | NFL Football Operations. (n.d.). Retrieved from https://operations.nfl.com/the-officials/history-of-the-official/

Rose, M. (2019, January 10). What Are the Duties of Football Coaches? Retrieved from https://www.sportsrec.com/341347-what-are-the-duties-of-football-coaches.html

Sacca, P., & McGuire, L. (2014, January 13). Pastor Tim Christensen Gives One-Minute Worship Service to Watch 49ers. Retrieved September 19, 2016, from http://nextimpulsesports.com/2014/01/13/coolest-pastor-ever-gives-60-second-sunday-service-watch-49ers-game/

Safety Valve Definition - Sporting Charts. (n.d.). Retrieved June 24, 2018 from https://www.sportingcharts.com/dictionary/nfl/safety-valve.aspx

Schalter, T. (2017, April 12). The Evolution of the Super Bowl over 50 Years. Retrieved March 26, 2016, from http://bleacherreport.com/articles/2601298-the-evolution-of-the-super-bowl-over-50-years

Science Cheerleaders Perform at the USA Science and Engineering Festival [Video]. (2010, November 01). Science Cheerleader. https://www.youtube.com/watch?v=HtPGIzLuBVQ

Seifert, K. (2016, October 31). Do NFL Players, Coaches Face Fines for Criticizing Officials? [Web log post]. Retrieved December 25, 2018, from http://www.espn.com/blog/nflnation/post/_/id/219774/do-nfl-players-coaches-face-fines-for-criticizing-officials

Seward, Z. M. (2013, November 24). An average NFL game: More than 100 commercials and just 11 minutes of play. Retrieved from https://qz.com/150577/an-average-nfl-game-more-than-100-commercials-and-just-11-minutes-of-play/

Shaquem Griffin: UCF's unstoppable one-handed star. (n.d.). Retrieved 06-28-2018 from https://www.si.com/college-football/2017/11/16/shaquem-griffin-hand-ucf-nfl-draft

Shaver, A. (2015, November 23). You're more likely to be fatally crushed by furniture than killed by a terrorist. Retrieved from https://www.washingtonpost.com/news/monkey-cage/wp/2015/11/23/youre-more-likely-to-be-fatally-crushed-by-furniture-than-killed-by-a-terrorist/?utm_term=.41d30c72ccdd

Shorty Ray. (2018, May 25). Retrieved from https://en.wikipedia.org/wiki/Shorty_Ray

Shuck, B. (2017, October 03). NFL: How All 32 Teams Got Their Names. Retrieved from https://bleacherreport.com/articles/733872-how-all-32-nfl-teams-got-their-names#slide6

Slattery, E., & McPheters, P. (2017, October 18). Unique 1970's Crocheter: Pro Football Player Rosey Grier. Retrieved January 30, 2018, from https://www.crochetconcupiscence.com/2012/11/unique-1970s-crocheter-pro-football-player-rosey-grier/

Smiley, B. (2014, August 13). Craziest moments in NFL history: The Heidi Game. Retrieved from https://www.foxsports.com/buzzer/story/craziest-moments-in-nfl-history-the-heidi-game-081314. Includes quotes from Delbert Mann, director of Heidi

Smith, B. T. (2012, May 13). Impolite 'Please'. Retrieved July 22, 2018, from http://dialectblog.com/2012/05/13/impolite-please/

Sportingcharts.com. (2017). *Visualizing Statistics for the NFL | SportingCharts*. [online] Available at: https://www.sportingcharts.com/nfl/ [Accessed 23 Oct. 2017].

Spotlight: Super Bowl Halftime Producer Ricky Kirshner on Assembling the Year's Biggest Concert. (n.d.). Retrieved March 30, 2018, from https://www.billboard.com/articles/business/8097678/super-bowl-halftime-producer-ricky-kirshner-spotlight-interview

Stamp, J. (2012, October 05). How Did the Pigskin Get Its Shape? Retrieved December 18, 2016, from http://www.smithsonianmag.com/arts-culture/how-did-the-pigskin-get-its-shape-63180450/

Star-Ledger, M. F. (2014, January 30). Why is the NFL football called The Duke? Retrieved August 09, 2015, from https://www.nj.com/super-bowl/index.ssf/2014/01/why_is_the_nfl_football_called_the_duke.html

Stats (abbreviations) (n.d.). Retrieved from http://stats.washingtonpost.com/fb/glossary.asp

Steinberg, L. (2014, September 04). Why the NFL Is America's Passion. Retrieved from https://www.forbes.com/sites/leighsteinberg/2014/09/04/why-the-nfl-is-americas-passion/#2b8e60d83dda

Stites, A. (2018, February 05). How does the NFL's concussion protocol work? Retrieved May 07, 2018 from https://www.sbnation.com/nfl/2016/9/18/12940926/nfl-concussion-protocol-explained

Sunday Night Football [Network television broadcast]. (2018, December 2). *Los Angeles Chargers vs. Pittsburgh Steelers*. New York, NY: NBC. Commenting on release time.

Tait, M., & Krug, P. B. (2011, April 13). Former Jayhawk Mike Rivera volunteers time to teach crochet to city youths. Retrieved January 30, 2018, from http://www2.kusports.com/news/2011/apr/14/ex-jayhawk-mike-rivera-volunteers-time-teach-croch/

The Forgotten History of Women's Football. (2016, February 05). Retrieved from https://www.smithsonianmag.com/history/forgotten-history-womens-football-180958042/

These Officials Are Really Good. (n.d.). Retrieved from https://operations.nfl.com/the-officials/these-officials-are-really-good/

Transcript: Bill Belichick's 2019 Pre-Draft Press Conference. (n.d.). Retrieved from https://www.patriots.com/news/transcript-bill-belichick-s-2019-pre-draft-press-conference

Tribune, Chicago. "Ask Jerry Markbreit." *Chicagotribune.com*. N.p., 03 Sept. 2008. Retrieved Web. 30 June. 2016. Mr. Markbreit talks about the end of an era, replacing the starter's pistol with a whistle to end quarters.

Trickett, R. (2012). *Complete offensive line*. Champaign, IL: Human Kinetics.

Unmatched Greatness. (2000, July 24). *Daily News (Los Angeles, CA)*. Retrieved July 21, 2018, from http://www.highbeam.com/doc/1G1-83390721.html?refid=easy_hf

US Department of Commerce, & NOAA. (2017, December 20). December 31, 1967: Weather During the Ice Bowl. Retrieved from https://www.weather.gov/grb/123167_Icebowl

Visualizing Statistics for the NFL | SportingCharts. (n.d.). Retrieved July 15, 2017, from https://www.sportingcharts.com/nfl/ Statistics, rules, types of plays and formations...

Voice of America. (2018, February 08). Could Have, Would Have, and Should Have. Retrieved from https://learningenglish.voanews.com/a/everyday-grammar-could-have-should-have-would-have/3391128.html

Vooris, R. (2017, October 03). The Best NFL Defensive Unit Nicknames. Retrieved 09 June 2018 from https://bleacherreport.com/articles/431194-the-best-nfl-defensive-unit-nicknames#slide6

Vrentas, J., & Breer, A. (n.d.). How NFL and college football are not the same. Retrieved August 18, 2018, from https://www.si.com/nfl/2018/07/11/college-football-ncaa-rules-difference-pros

Wahl, T. (2017, December 13). Wristbands on Quarterbacks. Retrieved December 20, 2017, from https://www.theepochtimes.com/wristbands-on-quarterbacks_2384859.html

Walk-On Opportunities-More Chances to Play in College. (n.d.). Retrieved August 1, 2018 from https://www.collegesportsscholarships.com/2012/03/21/never-rule-out-becoming-a-walk-on.htm

Warren, M. (2018, September 02). Buffalo Bills practice squad primer: Rules, eligible players. Retrieved September 2, 2018, from https://www.buffalorumblings.com/2018/9/2/17811534/buffalo-bills-practice-squad-primer-rules-eligible-players-salary Pertains to all NFL teams, not just Bills

Webber, D. (2017, October 03). 10 Reasons Why American Football Is the Best Sport in the World. Retrieved from https://bleacherreport.com/articles/849964-top-10-reasons-why-american-football-is-the-best-sport-in-the-world#slide1

What are the Dimensions of a Football Field. (n.d.). Retrieved July 09, 2017, from http://www.dummies.com/sports/football/american-football-stadiums-and-fields/

What Ballet Does for Football. (n.d.). Retrieved January 19, 2018, from https://healthyliving.azcentral.com/ballet-football-1747.html

Why Championship Football Games are Called "Bowls". (2014, January 29). Retrieved from http://www.todayifoundout.com/index.php/2011/02/why-championship-football-games-are-called-bowls/

Why Does the NFL Have a Two-Minute Warning? (2009, November 26). Retrieved from http://mentalfloss.com/article/23359/why-does-nfl-have-two-minute-warning

Why is it Called the Gridiron? (2016, July 29). Retrieved November 18, 2018, from https://www.biggameusa.com/blog/what-does-gridiron-mean.html

Wilson, R. (2017, February 06). Super Bowl 2017: Tom Brady leads epic comeback, Patriots stun Falcons in OT. Retrieved from https://www.cbssports.com/nfl/news/super-bowl-2017-tom-brady-leads-epic-comeback-patriots-stun-falcons-in-ot/

Women's Football Alliance. (2018, October 16). Retrieved from https://en.wikipedia.org/wiki/Womens_Football_Alliance

Women's Pro Football: Not a Powder Puff League. (n.d.). Retrieved 20 October 2018 rom http://www.sportsnetworker.com/2010/03/26/women's-pro-football-not-a-powder-puff-league/comment-page-1/

Wood, R. (2008) American Football basic rules. Topend Sports. Retrieved https://www.topendsports.com/sport/gridiron/basics.htm

Zimmermann, K. A. (2017, July 13). American Culture: Traditions and Customs of the United States. Retrieved 20 August 2017 from https://www.livescience.com/28945-american-culture.html

About the Author

Timothy Wahl, who lives in Glendale, California, has taught English as a second language in adult education with the Los Angeles Unified School District and the American Language Center at UCLA Extension. An alumnus of the University of Iowa, he has also published a memoir, *Hard Times in the Country: Ramblings of a Hayseed,* about of growing up on a dairy farm in New York state. This book is the result of the author's lifelong passion for football and his skill teaching American English and culture to learners from the far reaches of the world.

Please visit *www.mrfootballogy.com*

Photo credit: Alexander Wahl

Also by ESL Publishing

These books can be ordered online with a discount for bulk orders.

www.eslpublishing.com

US Citizenship Bootcamp by Jennifer Gagliardi
When students prepare for their Citizenship interview, they usually focus on memorizing the 100 Civics and History questions. However, when they go to the interview, they are often surprised that the USCIS (United States Citizenship and Immigration Services) examiner asks 20 to 70 questions from the N-400 Application for Naturalization, and only six to 10 Civics questions, PLUS the students must read and write one sentence in English.

This book is an attempt to help students prepare for their Citizenship interview by presenting 10 interviews based on the N-400, in order of increasing vocabulary and grammatical difficulty.

Highlights:
— An overview of the Naturalization Process
— Practice N-400 Questions based on the new USCIS N-400
— Practice Civics Questions based on the new USCIS N-400
— Practice Quizzes and Answers
— Vocabulary words and definitions
— Helpful tips for comprehending and answering interview questions
— Helpful hints for the US Citizenship interview
— Easy-to-read charts to help with comprehension and learning
Internet citizenship resources and links

ESL CONVERSATION ROCKET
A Scaffolded, Grammar-based Conversation **Workbook for ESL Learners**
By Brian Branca

ESL Conversation Rocket helps students build a solid foundation for conversational English using grammar skills. This book was written by a teacher specifically for beginners and low-level learners. Throughout the book, students use an understanding of simple grammar points, as well as their personal life experiences, to have real, authentic conversations in English.

Each unit of ESL Conversation Rocket is scaffolded using a simple and easily accessible grammar skill as a starting point. From there, students utilize an understanding of this grammar skill to build competence in conversation. Each unit is equipped with six student-centered exercises which gradually build in difficulty. The units culminate in "Real Life Conversation," where students have a chance to practice real, everyday conversation.

She Built Ships During World War II by Jeane Slone

A novel for English language learners at the intermediate level. It is an excellent way for a student to learn history and English at the same time. The novel can stand alone or be used in conjunction with the companion workbook (published separately), which is designed for use along with the novel in language classes. The workbook has a rich variety of vocabulary, word-building, and comprehension exercises, as well as writing, discussion, and critical-thinking topics for use in the language classroom. Original novel by Jeane Slone. ESL revision by Michelle Deya Knoop.

With meticulous research on the WWII era, Slone weaves an intricate story of cruelty, compassion, and love, reminding us of the injustice of the internment of Japanese Americans and racial prejudice in the armed forces. The courage of women welders who built ships while their husbands were at war is depicted so *well that the characters come to life. We watch the heroine, Lolly, struggle to keep her family together while she works as a welder and her husband is away. A tender romance is threaded throughout the book, and we agonize with her as she brings it to an inevitable conclusion. Between the fascinating and sometimes little-known historical facts, and the larger-than-life sympathetic characters, the book is a page-turner to the very end.*

— Alla Crone, author of *Winds Over Manchuria*, *East Lies the Sun*, and *Russian Bride*

This workbook is designed to be used in combination with the novel, *She Built Ships During World War II*, in language classes or self-study. Intended to build vocabulary at the intermediate level, it has a variety of words, phrases, and idioms, word-building, structure, and reading comprehension exercises. In addition, it includes writing, discussion, and critical-thinking topics designed for use in the language or reading classroom. Workbook by Michelle Deya Knoop.

Highlights:

— Vocabulary and idioms are presented and practiced in the context of the novel's storyline.

— Word form and structure exercises support and develop the new vocabulary.

— Critical thinking, writing, and pair/group discussion topics inspire readers to explore the social, personal, ethical, and moral issues raised in the novel.

www.ingramcontent.com/pod-product-compliance
Lightning Source LLC
Chambersburg PA
CBHW070523010526
44118CB00012B/1059